CHICKEN SOUP FOR THE RECOVERING SOUL

CHICKEN SOUP
FOR THE
RECOVERING SOUL

Your Personal, Portable Support Group with Stories of Healing, Hope, Love and Resilience

Jack Canfield
Mark Victor Hansen
Robert J. Ackerman, Ph.D., Theresa Peluso
Gary Seidler and Peter Vegso

Health Communications, Inc.
Deerfield Beach, Florida

www.hcibooks.com
www.chickensoupforthesoul.com

We would like to acknowledge the many publishers and individuals who granted us permission to reprint the cited material. (Note: The stories that were written by Jack Canfield, Mark Victor Hansen, Robert J. Ackerman, Ph.D., Gary Seidler, Peter Vegso or Theresa Peluso are not included in this listing.)

Foreword by Robert J. Ackerman, Ph.D. Primary Source: White, W. (1998). *Slaying the Dragon: The History of Addiction Treatment and Recovery in America.* Bloomington, IL, Chestnut Health Systems.

An Angel Wore Fur. Reprinted by permission of John Crusey. ©2004 John Crusey.

"The Recovery Map." Reprinted by permission of Martin Dodd. ©2004 Martin Dodd.

The Empty Chair. Reprinted by permission of Jenni Schaefer. ©2004 Jenni Schaefer.

The Heap. Reprinted by permission of Joseph R. Cruse, M.D. ©1993 Joseph R. Cruse, M.D.

(Continued on page 352)

Library of Congress Cataloging-in-Publication Data

Chicken soup for the recovering soul : a portable support group with stories of
   healing, hope, love, and resilience / Jack Canfield . . . [et al.].
      p. cm.
   ISBN-13: 978-0-7573-0203-9
   ISBN-10: 0-7573-0203-3
      1. Recovering alcoholics—Biography.   2. Recovering addicts—Biography.
   3. Compulsive behavior.   4. Recovery movement.   I. Canfield, Jack, 1944–

   HV5275.C39 2004
   616.86'1'00922—dc22\[B]

                                                                     2004060553

©2004 John T. Canfield and Hansen and Hansen LLC

All rights reserved. Printed in the United States of America. No part of this publication may be reproduced, stored in a retrieval system or transmitted in any form or by any means, electronic, mechanical, photocopying, recording or otherwise, without the written permission of the publisher.

HCI, its Logos and Marks are trademarks of Health Communications, Inc.

Publisher: Health Communications, Inc.
             3201 S.W. 15th Street
             Deerfield Beach, FL 33442-8190

R-11-06

Cover design by Larissa Hise Henoch
Inside formatting by Theresa Peluso

We dedicate this book
to everyone who has taken
the first step toward recovery,
to those who continue
to work at it a day at a time
and especially to those willing
to help others along the way.

Contents

3. A SENSE OF SPIRITUALITY

4. FAMILIES OF ORIGIN, FAMILIES OF CHOICE

8. FULLY RECOVERING, FULLY ALIVE

Foreword

History teaches us that no society or generation has gone untouched by alcoholism and addiction. Several hundred years ago, certain Native American tribes were known to have formed sobriety circles. During colonial times in the United States, noted physician Dr. Benjamin Rush, a signer of the Declaration of Independence, began to talk about drunkenness as a disease and called for treatment.

One of the first attempts to deal with alcoholism was not on an individual basis but through mutual support. In 1840, a group of people formed the Washingtonian Society, which at the time was a new and exciting approach. It became so popular that at one point there were 600,000 members. Also around this time Dr. Magnus Huss, a Swedish physician, officially introduced the term "alcoholism." An ongoing debate about the definition of alcoholism ensued and at one time it was thought that as many as 200 different definitions were being used.

Regardless of how it was defined, many institutions were established to help alcoholics. The New York State Inebriate Asylum, the Martha Washington Home in Chicago, and the Water Street Mission in New York City are a few examples. In 1879, Dr. Leslie Keeley began to open more than 120 institutes for addiction treatment in America.

During the Civil War many wounded soldiers were treated with morphine and developed physical dependence on the drug. Their dependence became known as the "soldier's disease." Other drug problems surfaced as well, such as cocaine addiction and opiate dependence.

By the turn of the century concern over alcoholism and drug addiction was no longer limited to the addict. Responses to addiction started to develop from the government with such actions as the 1914 Harrison Tax Act to control opiates and cocaine and the involvement of the Supreme Court.

However, all of these efforts did not seem to reach the "core" of the problem for those struggling with addiction. It was obvious that addiction was not just a physical dependence on a substance and that recovery needed to be more than merely abstinence. For a brief time between 1900 and 1940, an organization known as the Oxford Group attempted to add spirituality to the concept of recovery. Abstinence from alcohol was not a mandatory requirement for this group.

It soon became clear something more was needed. Something that would help people understand they need not recover alone. Something that would help addicts experience not only loss, but also hope. Something that could replace a lifestyle of pain and addiction with one of health and healing and mend a broken spirit, not just a body, to bring peace to a troubled soul.

In the United States, that something emerged in 1935 when two alcoholics, Bill W. and Dr. Bob, found each other and realized that together they could accomplish something that neither of them could do alone. It was the beginning of Alcoholics Anonymous and the beginning of the modern recovery movement. Alcoholics Anonymous (AA) was not the first group of alcoholics to join together, but it quickly became the most explosive and universal. Unlike other groups, its members found something that helped them make sense of their lives, to support each other and to form a community that asked for nothing, but gave much, that welcomed all, judged none, and replaced despair with spirituality and acceptance.

AA offered something even more—a way of life. Based

on a program of the Twelve Steps of AA and the Twelve Traditions, this way of life was not limited to overcoming your past, but also offered guidelines for living a healthy future physically, emotionally and spiritually. The success of AA quickly spread not only throughout America, but also the world. In fact, many non-alcoholics were attracted to AA's ideas about recovery because of the Twelve Steps and their application to other life situations. Without a doubt, a community had been born and its impact had touched the world.

Other events were unfolding. Universities were beginning to take an interest in trying to better understand addiction and recovery. First among these was Yale, which developed the Center of Alcohol Studies in 1943. In 1944 Marty Mann founded what is known today as the National Council on Alcoholism and Drug Dependence. A tremendous achievement in the treatment of addiction occurred in the late 1940s when three institutions, Pioneer House, Willmar State Hospital and Hazelden developed what is known as the "Minnesota Model." Their pioneering work led to the development of 28-day programs for treatment of chemical dependency. It was also around this time that the application of AA's program to other drug addictions emerged with the founding of Narcotics Anonymous (NA).

In the 1950s, things began to expand even more. With the founding of Al-Anon Family Groups by Lois W. and Anne B., wives of the original members of AA, family members and friends of addicts were offered support and hope based on the Twelve Steps for the first time. With the addition of spouses and children of alcoholics (CoAs), the number of people involved in recovery grew tremendously.

By the 1950s, the American Medical Association and other organizations recognized alcoholism as a disease and Dr. Ruth Fox established what is known today as the American Society of Addiction Medicine.

In the next decade the American Bar Association and the American Public Health Association adopted official statements accepting alcoholism as a treatable illness. During this time other drugs were being abused as well and the level of public awareness for treatment and recovery began to grow. Drug abuse, alcoholism and chemical dependency were now mainstream in America and the country was trying to find help. Controversy ensued over social policy and the best approaches for prevention, identification and treatment. Organizations began to help and during the 1970s and 1980s hospitals developed residential treatment programs. Third-party insurance coverage now included treatment for alcohol and drug abuse and the recovery movement continued to expand.

It was also during this time that another phenomenon emerged. The children of alcoholics, CoAs, wanted to join the recovery movement. With an estimated population of more than 28 million, their inclusion further popularized recovery. Several books on the subject reached bestseller lists, conferences were widely attended and mental health professionals began to become involved in their treatment. The Children of Alcoholics Foundation (CoAF) and the National Association for Children of Alcoholics (NACoA) were founded in the early 1980s. Concepts such as dysfunctional family and codependency became everyday words. All of these changes garnered more attention for recovery and in many cases encouraged more debate. Through it all, however, one thing remained constant and that was the quest for recovery and the application of recovery programs to as many people as possible.

In the 1990s and into this new century, recovery has continued to change and grow to meet the needs of a diverse, complex society. Concepts such as co-occurring disorders, outpatient treatment and drug courts have emerged. The era of 28-day residential treatment programs has declined, due to challenges from managed care and more and more clients are treated on an outpatient basis. Gender-specific treatment and programs that are more inclusive for people of color are becoming the norm. The concept of recovery is now being applied to a variety of quality of life issues.

More than an historical accounting of dates, facts and the founding of institutions, the history of recovery is truly a story of a grassroots movement. It was not something created by professionals, social policy or directives. People coming together who shared a common history and who shared a common dream for a better life created it. Those who chose not to judge each other, but to support each other, started it. Those who struggled alone, but recovered together, continued it. It has truly become a recovering community: a community of hope, strength, acceptance, love and resiliency. Regardless of when or why it started, or who or what institutions participated, recovery is a gift that has been given to all of us.

Robert J. Ackerman, Ph.D.

Never doubt that a small group of thoughtful, committed citizens can change the world. Indeed, it's the only thing that ever has.

Margaret Mead

Acknowledgments

This book is the culmination of lessons learned and relationships restored not only by those who appear on these pages but by every member of the recovering community. Many preceded us, many walk with us today and many have yet to join us.

From family, to staff, to the writers who share a piece of themselves in order to help and inspire others along the way, we offer our heartfelt appreciation for all of the people who make a book like this possible.

Our spouses: Inga, Patty, Kimberly, Lana, Anne and Brian. Our children: Christopher, Travis, Riley, Oran, Kyle, Elisabeth, Melanie, Jason, Bobby, Katie, Mandy, Oliver, Robert, Melinda and Hayley.

The talented, enthusiastic staff, freelancers and interns who support each one of us at Chicken Soup for the Soul Enterprises, Self-Esteem Seminars, Mark Victor Hansen and Associates, Mid-Atlantic Addiction Training Institute at Indiana University of Pennsylvania, The U.S. Journal Training and Health Communications. You are the people who keep the wheels turning smoothly every day without fail, and we know it!

Thank you to our volunteers who took time from busy schedules and hectic lives to read and evaluate stories in the preliminary manuscript. Their feedback helped us select the stories you are about to enjoy and their comments assisted us in making each story the best it could be: Kimberly Ackerman, Joanie Battaglia, Drs. Gregory and Lori Boothroyd, Betty Conger, Crystal Deemer, Debbie Hill, Patricia Holdsworth, Barbara Lomonaco, Penelope Love, Betsy McDowell, Patricia O'Gorman, Kathy Lowe Peterson, Sallie Rodman, George Roth, Diane Smith, Kristin Smith, Holly Stiggleman, Holly Stiner, Carla Thurber, Lori Wilson, Madelyn Winslow and Deb Zika.

Special thanks to Julia Edelman, Earnie and Paula Larsen, Ric Pine, Steve Roman, Sis Wenger and everyone at Women for Sobriety for their enthusiasm and support in acquiring stories and spreading the word on our behalf.

Many people have helped us along the way and we are certain to have neglected to mention everyone by name, however it in no way diminishes our appreciation for their support. We received nearly two thousand stories for consideration in this book. That happened because people reached out to their communities and made them aware of the project, from individual folks speaking to each other in meeting rooms and support groups, online chats and bulletin boards, to the associations and media that serve the people in recovery so well.

And most important, thank you to everyone who submitted a story. You shared happiness, pain and cherished memories. You relived tough choices and regrets, remembered sad moments and worked through new issues. But in the end you inspired us and conveyed the hope and heart we have come to recognize as essential qualities in recovering people. We regret that everyone's story could not be represented here and we hope that the stories chosen for publication convey what was in your heart and in some way tell your story.

Introduction

You are about to become acquainted with one of the greatest communities in the world. Not one consisting of houses, buildings, streets, shopping malls and schools, but one that resides in the very hearts and souls of people who share a common bond.

Each member of the "recovering community" has successfully overcome tremendous obstacles in their lives and in doing so find themselves in a better place physically, emotionally and spiritually than they ever thought possible.

Chicken Soup for the Recovering Soul will move, inspire and entertain you with the stories from only a few of the millions of people who have become part of the recovering community. You will quickly discover that these stories are not about pain and despair, but rather about hope and resiliency. They are not stories about strategies for change, but stories about the human spirit that will not be denied. These are the stories of people who are willing to share parts of their lives in order to help others.

Most people whose lives are touched by addiction and other problems feel completely alone. They believe that no one else would understand or appreciate their situation, and, although they begin their journey in solitude, they soon find many others who share similar experiences and are willing to help them.

Often facing daunting circumstances and ever-present self-doubt, people just like you confront their fears of the future in order to change and find a better way to live. As you read, you'll understand how an individual cannot do it alone, how mentors appear at the right time and place. And you'll meet people who believed they needed no one's help but began to reach out to others and be touched in return.

Restore your faith as our writers describe the birth, growth and nurturing of spirituality that enriches the lives of people in recovery. And for so many who struggled, feeling they had no choices, new "families" are found on every page as the authors share their discovery that families of origin, friends and even our support groups can surround us with life-affirming, healthy behaviors.

You'll be filled with awe, wonder and appreciation at the resilience of people in the face of great odds to not only overcome but thrive and grow from difficult, seemingly insurmountable circumstances. Their stories are a mixture of hope, inner strength and serenity.

And, although most of the stories in *Chicken Soup for the Recovering Soul* focus on overcoming addiction to alcohol and other drugs, we've shared a selection of pieces that illustrate how the process of recovery is now applied to other quality of life issues from depression to chronic illnesses. The concepts of recovery and the use of Twelve-Step programs are applicable to many different issues with equally successful results. Supporting each other is an effective tool and consequently the recovering community is constantly growing. We should not be surprised. When something works so well, it will become part of people's lives.

Finally, one of the most cherished virtues in the life of a recovering individual is the resurrection of joy and one of the greatest indicators of recovery is a desire to share what you have found. The authors represented in *Chicken*

Soup for the Recovering Soul want to share the hope, resilience, joy and spirituality that have touched their souls. This book is about joy and life changes, a portable support group that binds millions of people together in a new community.

It is the recovering community.

Welcome.

Share with Us

We would love to hear your reactions to the stories in this book. Please let us know what your favorite stories were and how they affected you.

We also invite you to send us stories you would like to see published in future editions of *Chicken Soup for the Soul.* Please send submissions to:

Chicken Soup for the Soul
P.O. Box 30880
Santa Barbara, CA 93130
fax: 805-563-2945

You can also access e-mail or find a current list of planned books at the *Chicken Soup for the Soul* Web site at *www.chicken-soup.com.* Find out about our Internet service at *www.clubchickensoup.com.*

We hope you enjoy reading this book as much as we enjoyed compiling, editing and writing it.

1

THE RECOVERING JOURNEY

Trust is the path
   Acceptance, the direction
   Serenity, the destination
   Self-centeredness, a detour
   and
   Impatience, a rock in your shoe.

Martin Dodd

An Angel Wore Fur

God can do anything . . . the secret is in letting him.

Betty King

A bleak winter night closed over Detroit. For a lone, unsteady figure reeling along the wet pavement, the weather only seemed to punctuate how cold and dark his life had become.

Tom had bailed out without a parachute and was now plunging at top speed toward a sudden stop. He had no way of knowing that just around the corner, in a narrow, unlit alley, an angel awaited.

Tom poured himself into a business, only to see it wither and die. At thirty years of age everything was lost, including his spirit. Alone, broken, hope in the future gone, the IRS, bill collectors and his landlord were suffocating him. He escaped into alcohol and drugs. Addiction squeezed tighter and tighter.

His will gone, he staggered along the street that winter night. Drinking and drugs ruled his existence.

Tom called a cheap, fifth-floor walk-up home. But he preferred not to use the front door, as "serious" bill collectors often stalked that area. He learned to come and go on a metal fire escape hanging in an alley at the rear of the building.

Steadying himself against walls and trash cans, Tom groped along the darkened corridor. But a night spent feeding his habits was too much and with the last spark of consciousness fading, his body crumpled to the freezing asphalt.

Slowly, very slowly, a strange sensation pulled Tom back. Something wet was making quick, short, abrasive strokes over his face. As he lay on his back, another observation crept into Tom's clouded mind. There was a weight on his chest. His hand moved to investigate. Fur? "What the . . . ?" His eyes snapped open and he found himself nose to nose with a very large cat. Startled, he scrambled to his feet with all of the speed his condition would allow and, finding the fire escape, he clambered up the five floors to his apartment.

The next day found Tom a bit more in control. Descending the iron steps, he was surprised by the cat leaping from a pile of cardboard boxes to greet him. Big, black, short-haired and wearing a collar, Tom thought the cat had to belong to someone in the neighborhood, so he began walking the streets, hoping if the cat recognized his home, he would go to it. As if an invisible leash tied the two together, the cat matched Tom stride for stride. Tom and the cat were still walking when the sun slipped from the sky. Returning to his apartment, he and the cat parted company at the fire escape.

A violent winter storm gripped Detroit the following day. Tom stayed inside and gradually a tiny cry caught his attention. Opening the window, he was amazed to see the snow-covered cat looking up at him, meowing softly. It had struggled up five icy flights of steel steps and bypassed several other apartments to present himself to Tom. Looking down at the pitiful creature, he opened the window a little wider and his new friend darted in, tail fully erect.

Life hadn't yet bottomed out for the pair. In the next few months they were forced from the apartment and onto the streets. Sleeping in doorways, Salvation Army collection boxes and flophouses, Tom always felt that warm, little body next to his no matter where they passed the night.

By now Tom was so entangled in his own hopelessness, drugs and alcohol, he desperately looked for a way out. Sitting on an isolated river bank, he held a loaded revolver in his hand. Cocking and uncocking the hammer, putting the barrel in his mouth, then taking it out. He just needed a little spark or nudge and all of his troubles would be over. As he repositioned the gun's barrel in his mouth, a persistent nudge gently pushed his hand and the gun away. Tom glanced down into the golden eyes staring up from his lap. *Hey, if I do this,* he thought, *who would take care of the cat?* Putting the gun away, he lay back on the grassy river bank and slept. Each time over the next few years, when his will to hold on weakened, the cat was there, staring deep into Tom's very soul.

There was no bolt of lightning or clap of thunder, no inspiring revelation, but slowly and for reasons he still doesn't understand, Tom starting fighting for control. Eventually, he walked to the front of a room full of strangers and said, "Hello, my name is Tom and I'm an alcoholic." He found work and began putting his life together.

Eleven years had slipped by since his friend found him in that dark, cold alley. Tom came home from work one evening and after dinner sat down to watch television. As it had done for so many years, the cat snuggled down into his lap. Looking down, Tom gently stroked his friend. "You know," Tom spoke softly, "you've really been here for me when I needed you and I think I'm getting myself together. I'm gonna be okay. If you want to leave or check out, you don't have to stay on my account." Then Tom dozed off, his chin falling forward to rest on his chest.

Only a few minutes passed when Tom awoke and immediately he knew his friend was gone. Those golden eyes that spoke so clearly, for so many years, were closed forever.

John Crusey

The Empty Chair

Unless you walk out into the unknown, the odds of making a profound difference in your life are pretty low.

Tom Peters

I walked into Thom Rutledge's office with no great expectation. I had been treated by various eating disorder specialists for over six months and had not seen any improvements with my anorexia/bulimia. In fact, the bingeing, purging and starving were getting worse every day.

Almost as soon as we sat down Thom took a chair from the corner and put it directly across from me. I was certain that I had signed up for an individual therapy session. I was really not in the mood for anyone to join us.

He said, "I want you to imagine your eating disorder sitting in this chair." I looked first at the door; I might be leaving soon. Then it got stranger. Thom suggested that we name my eating disorder. That's right, he wanted to name it. He called it "Ed," which he explained is actually an acronym for eating disorder. Okay, something that made sense, but still I was wondering who was in more need of therapy—me or this so-called expert psychotherapist.

I scanned the walls of the office, looking for credentials. All of the other eating disorder professionals whom I had seen previously prominently displayed their various diplomas and certificates in their offices. Thom's credentials were nowhere to be found. Instead I saw a stuffed animal (some species I didn't recognize), an empty whiskey bottle serving as a vase for dried flowers, and an oversized deck of playing cards. Seriously, the cards were big.

Who is this guy anyway? What am I doing here? And why did he just give my eating disorder a man's name? I was confused.

After those few moments of hesitation, I remembered that I was paying this man a lot of money to help me recover from my eating disorder. So I decided to give Thom the benefit of the doubt.

I looked at the chair, completely empty and still, and imagined my eating disorder, Ed, was sitting there. Once Thom saw that I was going to play along with his little metaphor, he took it to the next level of weird: He asked me to have a conversation with Ed.

It did not take me long to realize that this chair was the most talkative piece of furniture I had ever run across in my life. This chair—Ed—actually had quite a lot to say. Thom was no longer the only strange one in the room.

Ed said, "Jenni, you are fat. Why are you listening to Thom anyway? You will never be able to get rid of me. I have been with you your entire life."

He continued, "Feel how tight your jeans fit across your waist right now. Isn't that very uncomfortable? And remember this morning you had to buckle your belt one notch larger than normal. That means you better not eat dinner tonight."

Ed went on and on throughout the session with negative comments about food, weight and more. As I sat listening to Ed, it all felt so familiar. Finally, Thom interrupted and asked, "Jenni, do you have anything that you want to say back to Ed?"

I was speechless. I had never been given the opportunity to speak back to the condemning thoughts that had ruled my life for over twenty years. I had always assumed that these thoughts were just the truth, that they were just me. I was my eating disorder. But something had shifted now. Thom was showing me that the negative thoughts that berated me day and night did not originate with me. These thoughts, these insults came from Ed, not Jenni. And now Thom was giving Jenni the chance to speak up.

I had no idea what to say. What do you say to someone who has manipulated, abused and controlled you for years? What do you say to someone who has lied to you for your entire life? What do you say to someone who ultimately wants to destroy you?

I sat in silence for what seemed liked an eternity. Finally, I asked Ed, "Why do you try to control my every move? Why won't you just leave me alone?" In the few seconds that it took me to ask those two questions, I felt just a little bit of separation from Ed. And it felt so good.

So I continued to talk to Ed: "Was it you who told me I was fat when I was only four years old in dance class? And why did you never let me eat Halloween candy as a child? One piece of candy wouldn't have hurt me. It always looked so good. And why is the size of my dress the only thing that I remember about my high school prom? You said that was all that mattered. In college it was you who convinced me to walk into my bathroom and force myself to throw up that very first time, wasn't it? Why?"

I had so many questions for Ed. Thom mentioned that I would never get the answers that I wanted from Ed but that asking the questions was an excellent place to start. Thom smiled at me. I think I smiled too.

Before I knew it, the session with Thom was over, and I was out the door walking to my car. But this time, unlike leaving therapy sessions before, I left with something new. I left with hope. In the time I spent with Thom that day, I rediscovered Jenni, the healthy part of me that wanted to live and be free of my eating disorder. I learned that she just needed lots of patience and time to grow.

I sat in my car, turned the engine over and started to drive home. I was on a new road this time; I was on the real recovery path. And now I knew I could do it.

I heard Ed chuckling in the backseat mumbling under his breath something about how he would never let me go. With all of the newfound inspiration that I had just gained from Thom's office, I imagined stopping the car and throwing Ed out. *This is definitely not going to be easy,* I thought, *but I can do it.*

Jenni Schaefer

The Heap

It is better to wear out than to rust out.

Bishop Richard Cumberland

A lot of people buy big old cars and then drive and drive them until they are much older. The definition of old begins over 120,000 miles. These cars get so old that it is difficult to tell one from another. They all begin to look alike inside and outside, but they get the job done again and again. They gain respect, a place in the family, and even acceptance and understanding of frequent breakdowns.

If you work in a drug and alcohol treatment center, the sight of an old family automobile delivering a patient is common. Once they are there, the driver hurries inside with, "I got him this far, somebody help!"

Cars rust. Rusting must start inside somewhere. Then it just pops out in spots through the paint. Once it starts, it goes fast, from a speck to many specks to a whole part. It's the same with addicts.

Rusty cars are hard to remember new. Their vexations blot out the memory of their charm, their accessories and even particular model year. It takes concentration to call up the original image. It's the same with alcoholics.

The rusting twelve-year-old auto with 180,000 miles on it brought the blond, blue-eyed young man with the effects of twelve years of drinking and drugging on his body to the door of the treatment center. (The car and the young man had started their rusting at the same time.) Dad tried to get the 210-pound body out of the backseat, but only succeeded in getting his son turned onto his stomach with his hairy legs sticking stiffly out the back door. He went inside for help.

Mom sat in the front seat staring straight ahead, but not listening to the half-anesthetized slobbering snore. There was an occasional grunt, or a moan . . . which was it? She couldn't tell. She didn't dwell on it.

She was half thinking on the sad curiosity of times and events that rust people. When did the first spots appear? When did decay set in? When did the child's acceptance turn to rebellion? When did the blue in the eyes become matched with red instead of white and perhaps next yellow? When did the tiny, soft, pink, kicking feet become rough, variegated and dirt embedded? When did this coarse, dirty black hair replace the smooth, curving, velvety, kissable skin of tummy, legs and backside? When did the smell of baby powder and baby lotion turn to the odor of an unbathed body and secondhand whiskey? When did spit-up turn to throw-up? When did wet diapers turn to wet undershorts?

Sad, so sad . . . the baby is still in there . . . with a rusting body and short-circuited brain to deal with whatever life is left. She blinked tears away and her "whens" turned to "whats."

What happened to the adventuresome youth whose methodical searching of a fascinating world became an intense panic for another fix, another drink, another free fast meal or fuzzy-memoried fornication? What happened to the athlete whose gazelle-like gait became a device to stay ahead of trouble, accountability and responsibility? What changed his innovation to deception? His persuasiveness to manipulation? An authoritative nature to bullying? What became of the energy, the schedules and numerous small jobs that were replaced by lethargy, wanderings and "big deals"? What happened to the many noisy friends whose visits to the house were replaced by whispered phone calls to just a few?

She blinked again, but her "whats" did not turn to "whys."

Spending days such as this, many days over, was not unusual in her life. Wasting time is normal, interruption is normal, angry is normal, broken promises and no plans are normal. She came from an alcoholic family. She married an alcoholic. Now her son is an alcoholic and an addict. That seems normal. She cannot question the why of normal!

Not even the why of *How come all these heaps around me are alcoholic and not me? Why am I spared? Why am I not more upset and even now myself drinking over the death and disappearance of my baby laying on the backseat?*

These things are too sad to ponder, she decides, as she shifts her own 210 pounds to reach the glove box and her stashed Twinkies behind Dad's pint. The bra strap over her giant breast prosthesis breaks again. *You are all such rusting heaps,* she reflects without emotion once again, as she bites into the spongy cake. *Oh well. . . .*

Before her teeth meet the creamy center, she already feels that familiar surge of comfort and excitement that will last but a few minutes.

Oh well.

And the gurgling, rusting baby on the backseat continued his death rattle.

> *Epilogue:*
>
> *Three hours later the young man was in severe withdrawal.*
>
> *Three days later he was successfully detoxed.*
>
> *Three weeks later he received a medallion for completing alcohol and drug rehab.*
>
> *Three months later he received a chip for attending ninety Twelve-Step meetings in ninety days.*
>
> *Three years later he was employed as a certified unit counselor in an alcohol and drug treatment center.*
>
> *He later became a Ph.D. director of such a center. . . .*
>
> *God cares.*

Joseph R. Cruse, M.D.

Touched by a Higher Power

*The mind is its own place, and in itself can
make a heaven of hell, a hell of heaven.*

John Milton, *Paradise Lost*

Dinner was at a local Greek restaurant to be followed by
dancing at one of Chilliwack's more popular nightclubs. It
was a time filled with great food, laughter, teasing and recol-
lections of the school week. Fully satisfied, some would leave
for home while the rest of us made our way to the club.
Bright, colorful lights flashed and strobes pierced the semi-
dark room filled with people having a good time listening to
a good cover of "Twilight Zone," a song originally done by
Golden Earring. The music was loud and the party was just
beginning. My hands helplessly reached for the concoction
capable of turning man to animal.

Looking to my girlfriend, I asked jokingly, "Hey, baby! Do
you mind if I get drunk tonight?" Knowing that we lived
just a couple of blocks from the club Phyllis replied, laughing, "Sure. Why not! I don't have too far to carry you home!"
Over the music I shouted, "Right on! You're my kind of girl."

The night of drinking, laughter and dancing would take its
toll. As if I didn't have enough to drink, or wasn't drunk
enough already, I always had to finish with a zombie or two,
a very potent drink of various types of alcohol and a bit of
mix. My laughter was now diminishing and the apparent
heaviness of my heart was showing on my face.

"Are you okay?" Phyllis asked.

Looking like the zombie I had just drank, I replied, "Yeah. I'm fine. And you?" Rubbing my thigh lightly as she always had, Phyllis said, "It's okay. Everything will be all right." Her eyes looked right into mine as if she could see right through me, reading my mind, seeing my soul. Feeling her love and knowing that I couldn't hide anything from her, tears began to fill my eyes.

"Had enough to drink? Want to go home?" she asked. Hesitantly I answered, motivated by the thoughts of the damage I'd now begun to do in my drunkenness, not feeling too safe inside myself, "Sure. Let's go home."

I awoke in the morning, sad, sick, sorry and extremely hungover, awaking again to the words that I dreaded hearing after a good night's drunk.

"You're not going to like yourself very much when you see what you've done." Silence filled the air. I was too ashamed to even look at Phyllis for those words only meant one thing. Defeated, I slowly made my way toward the living room, hoping in these few minutes the damage I'd done would somehow miraculously repair itself. "Oh my God! I did this?"

Phyllis scared and very concerned asked, "You don't remember?"

Fear gripped me as I envisioned the fury it must have taken to reap such destruction. "No. Why? Why did I do this?"

"We had just left Huggies. You were quite drunk and I wanted to get you home. You stopped in the parking lot across the way. I looked at you. Your eyes and your face were as if you had become a different person. I asked if you were okay. You said yes. I told you to keep on walking—we were almost home."

"Not moving you started asking, 'Why?' I asked what you were talking about, 'Why?' what? You didn't answer, you just stared. You started hollering, your fists were clenched and you ran angrily toward the house. You kicked in the door. By now you were cursing. 'Why!'"

Fearfully I asked, "Where were the kids when all this was happening?"

"I found a note on the table, they spent the night at a friend's place. There was no one home but you and me," she explained.

Not really wanting to know, I asked, "What happened next?"

"You began smashing everything, punching and kicking the walls—that's where all the holes are from. Walking over to the fireplace you knocked everything onto the floor. You flipped the couches and the armchair as if they were paperweights, smashing the coffee table, and throwing the other table around. You walked over to your weights and picked up your barbell and began repeatedly slamming it to the floor hollering and cursing."

"And where were you while this was happening?"

Phyllis replied, "Right here, next to you."

In utter dismay at the vast devastation, I asked, "Weren't you afraid?"

"No. I began to pray. You made your way into the dining room, crying, still asking 'Why?' I just watched you. I wasn't afraid."

The tone of her voice changed as she said, "I really need to talk to you about something."

My spirit, already crushed, braced itself for the worst.

"After doing all the damage, do you remember anything at all?" she asked.

Puzzled, I answered, "Nothing. Why?"

Silently she stared at me, and then continued. "From where I was sitting you were in full view—you didn't enter the kitchen, you stood in front of the doorway." Pausing again, she looked at me questionably. "You began to talk to someone . . . "

Quickly I interrupted her. "You said we were alone."

"Yes. That's true, but as I watched you were motioning with your hands, very clearly talking to someone. I couldn't understand what you were saying but I could hear you as clear as I hear you now. You spoke with this person, or whatever it was, for about ten minutes. Do you remember who, or what it was, and what it is that you talked about?"

Even more perplexed I replied, "No. Are you sure this is what really happened?"

Assertively she retorted, "Come on now. You know me. Would I make something up like this or lie to you?"

Phyllis was a woman of many years of sobriety, a woman of integrity. She'd never play such a cruel trick on me. She continued, "Whatever you two talked about, it must have been something good. Afterward you changed completely. You turned to me with an incredible look of peace back in your eyes and on your face.

"You walked toward me, and of all the damage you had done, the only thing that you picked up was the calendar with the picture of Jesus on it. You pinned it back onto the wall, then said, 'Let's go to bed sweetheart, I'm tired.'"

Powerful emotions stir as I recall that night years ago and think about the places from which I have come, worlds of seemingly unrecoverable loss and immense pain. Wondering how a hand of beauty, love and grace could reach into darkness so vile to rescue one such as I. Tears, no longer of rage and anger, roll down my face in thankfulness for the life I have now found. Sobriety; a life no longer dominated by drugs, alcohol, rage, pain. Five years, each new day bringing with it the promise of something better, this can only be so as the words he spoke still echo somewhere deeply in my soul.

Godwin H. Barton

Silent Rage

Free to seek a counselor's care
She sits in silence, unaware
That peace could ever come to reign
In triumph over wretched pain

She sits alone. Betrayed since birth
She feels no joy; she knows no worth
She trembles and cowers with deep distrust
Cursed by thoughts of her father's lust

She longs to scream to another's ear
What she knows her mother will never hear
But her cries, unanswered, have left her mute
No words to even bear dispute

Shunned and shamed her guilt grows deep
Like an ugly weed that slowly creeps
Into her soul to confuse and kill
Her sense of right . . . her dreams . . . her will

As she sits in silent rage
Entrapped within a self-made cage
Of hate that sucks away her youth
She hides her only hope—the truth.

Kay Conner Pliszka

Summer Treasures

No bird soars too high, if he soars on his own wings.

William Black

My last customer's tab had been rung up on the old cash register. I carefully placed the final dirty dish in the holding tray then shoved the tray into the gaping mouth of the huge gleaming steel dishwasher. It was finally quiet, the morning rush over. I had been working since 6 A.M. and my ten-year-old stomach had been rumbling for an hour. "Break time, Janie girl," Anna smiled over her shoulder as she finished cleaning the hot stove with oil and the big rectangle chore stone, "How 'bout I cook you some breakfast?"

I loved Anna's kind face, her sparkling blue eyes and her strong arms that would wrap around me when my mom wasn't looking. Anna had been the morning cook since my parents bought the small town café. "Auntie Anna," as I called her, was tall, big boned, thin as a rail and had huge hardworking hands. It was the custom for children raised in the 1950s to call all adults Aunt, Uncle or Mr. or Mrs., never by their first names. Anna had insisted that she was to be my "Auntie."

Just as I was about to say "I'd love some pancakes," my mother came into the kitchen with a pie in her hand and a look on her face as cold as the steel sinks. She glared at me, then Anna, put the pie in the oven and stalked out of the kitchen. She had been giving me the silent treatment for two days, ever since my father had told me that I could accept

Anna's invitation to work on her ranch in the afternoons for the summer after our work in the café was done. Of course my mother's icy silences, cold withdrawals and statements that I would never amount to anything seemed to need no reason. No matter how hard I worked or tried to seek her approval, I had grown accustomed to the cold climate of inevitable failure, just as I had grown accustomed to my father's unwelcome touches and my parents' late-night whiskey battles.

"Don't pay her any mind, Janie girl," Anna said kindly, "She just isn't in the best of moods this morning. You're a good hardworking girl, now eat some pancakes, you're going to need some energy for that work waiting for you at the ranch this afternoon." She winked at me.

I will never forget my first glimpse of the "Flying W Ranch" as we rounded the corner of the dusty dirt road in Anna's old pickup. The ancient, big, white farmhouse with a wraparound porch that seemed to radiate as much love as Anna's solid arms; the huge red barn, the corral full of beautiful horses, cattle grazing on what appeared to be endless acreage and the Australian shepherd that yipped at the tires of the truck.

After we got out of the truck, Anna introduced me to her two boys whom I'd never met, Sandy and Donny, and to her husband, Pete. Then they took me to the corral and introduced me to Fleet Foot, a beautiful black stallion. As I rubbed his silky muzzle and looked into his soft warm brown eyes, I was told that he was one of the finest cutting horses on the ranch and would be mine for the summer.

I worked on the ranch every summer until I left home at eighteen, even though my mother made it so hard for Anna that she finally quit her cooking job when I was twelve. My memories are full of summer afternoons flying through tall grass holding onto the reins while Fleet Foot did his job cutting the cattle; racing Sandy and Donny bareback across rivers and streams; kneading bread dough with Auntie Anna; sitting at the big harvest kitchen table watching her churn butter; saying grace before dinner; and hearing "Zip" lap the rich cream Uncle Pete always gave him fresh from the bucket because "He was a hardworking animal who deserved his share of the best."

I never told Auntie Anna or Uncle Pete the horrors that were going on in my childhood home; I didn't need to, although I often confided my deepest secrets to Fleet Foot and Zip. Adult children of alcoholics carry wounds from their childhood, but many, like me, also carry the treasures and gifts of people along the way who took the time to care. When my children were young they helped me make bread once a week, we shared meals around a harvest table like the one in that old farmhouse, our house was frequently full of extra children, we always had a dog, I hugged my children every day of their lives, and I still love to sit with my grandchildren on the wraparound porch of my home.

Those days on the "Flying W" were few but the work I did there was more than cutting cattle and mending fences; the lasting work was the mending of my spirit and the knowledge that like Zip, we all deserve to be treated with kindness and compassion when we give our best.

Jane Middelton-Moz

"You can live a perfectly normal life if you accept the fact that your life will never be perfectly normal."

©2002 Randy Glasbergen, www.glasbergen.com

The Skeleton in My Closet

If you have a skeleton in your closet, take it out and dance with it.

Carolyn MacKenzie

My graduation dress made a surprise appearance from the back of my closet last spring. The kids dug it out in an effort to supply vintage clothing for a fashion show the local high school was hosting.

The fabric was brittle with the accumulated filth of thirty years; the yellow chiffon muted under a layer of dust. The green velvet ribbon around the empire waist had faded to a melancholy gray, the elongated bow drooping like the ears of a well-loved stuffed toy.

My daughters covered their mouths in mock horror as the dress slid off the coat hanger and slumped to the floor. Their guffaws echoed in my head as I reached for the gown. I heard the faint rattle of bones as the skeleton I had zipped into the folds of yellow chiffon was suddenly released. The secret I had hidden behind the wedding dress, bridesmaids' gowns, outdated Christmas outfits, the "large" clothes, the winter coats and the maternity dress I couldn't bear to part with, lay blatantly at my feet.

"What's wrong, Mom?" my eldest daughter asked as I felt the color drain from my face. I held my breath, and vainly searched for words.

My youngest daughter gingerly gathered the dusty folds

of fabric in her arms, cradling them like an antique doll. "Can I try it on?" she asked.

I looked into the healthy faces of my two teenage daughters, at their cheeks faintly bronzed by sunshine, at their arms, muscled and firm, their bodies, strong and feminine, and cursed the guilty secret that was now out of the bag.

"You can try it on," I said tentatively, "but I don't think you'll be able to do it up—I was very thin in high school."

I stand five-foot-nine in my stockinged feet. The dress is a smidge smaller than a size six. Aside from a fading snapshot, safely tucked in a photo album at my father's house, there is no evidence of what I did to myself in my grade twelve year—except, of course, for the dress itself.

The dress reappeared in my doorway draped over the slim frame of my fifteen-year-old daughter. She's much shorter than I was as a teenager, more fit, more athletic . . . prettier. Billows of material mounded around her feet—but the back of the dress gaped open, the zipper strained. It was impossible to close.

We all walk with demons, of this I am fairly certain, but sitting face-to-face with one I had never acknowledged was as unnerving as anything I have ever experienced.

I had never admitted to anyone that I was bulimic. Hell, the word hadn't even been invented when I discovered what I believed to be the ultimate weight control program.

My daughters eyed me dubiously, waiting for an explanation.

"I had an eating disorder in high school," I finally whispered, surprising myself with the frankness in my voice. "My mother had to have the dress specially made for me when I graduated."

My mother. My mother had been frantic as she watched her healthy teenaged daughter melt away. She marched me into doctors' offices, pounded desks with her fist and demanded that they get to the bottom of whatever it was that was causing me to lose so much weight. They never did. I feigned innocence. My monthly cycles stopped. I exercised like a fiend, ate like a horse and quietly disappeared into the bathroom immediately following every meal. Then we couldn't find a dress to fit the skeleton I had become. I hated myself.

Twenty years later, when my mother was diagnosed with cancer, I fought with the demon again. She died never knowing my secret or the fact that her grief-stricken, painfully thin daughter was starving herself again.

The room was suddenly static with disbelief—my youngest daughter let the dress fall from her shoulders. It landed with a silent puff at her feet.

"Why did you keep the dress?" my eldest daughter asked.

I scooped the musty fabric from the floor. "As a reminder I suppose," I said, rocking it.

She sat down beside me. "Why didn't you ever tell me?" The maternal tone in her voice was laced with concern.

"It's not something I'm very proud of," I whispered. "Or something that ever goes away."

I had confessed.

The appearance of the grad dress forced me to admit that bulimia has walked with me for thirty years. That I have wrestled with its powerful grasp through every major event in my life. That even now, when the world around me spins out of control, I look inward to the thing I CAN control and fight the urge to take its hand again.

As I eyed the soft fabric in my lap I realized that eating disorders never disappear, they simply shuffle themselves to the backs of closets and lurk. Whether mine was waiting for control or acceptance, I'm not sure. But now that the skeleton is out of my closet, I hope I can learn to accept the teenager who wore that dress, and perhaps forgive her the dark secret she's been hiding.

Elva Stoelers

How Dry I Am

Rarely have we seen a person fail who has thoroughly followed our path.

Alcoholics Anonymous, Chapter V

It seems like only yesterday that I was passed out on my couch. Night after night, week after week, I'd slip into darkness, like a ship leaving the harbor at twilight. Sometimes I wasn't even particular about the couch—it didn't necessarily have to be my couch, any couch would do, or the floor. It was the escape that was important. And my Stoli.

It seems like yesterday, because I can readily recall the garbled phone conversations I had with friends where I tried so hard not to hang on to my S's, for fear that they would turn into telltale slurs. The next day the conversation would drift back to me like a fog, hazy and surreal.

But it wasn't yesterday. I know because I've been married to a man that has never seen me consume an ounce of alcohol in nine years; I was a year sober when I met him. I know because I have since borne two healthy sons, now four and six years old.

It seems like only yesterday, but it was over ten years ago.

A decade is a long time by many standards. To a worker ant, for instance, whose average life span is a couple of weeks, ten years would be the equivalent of an ice age. To a tortoise, which can live over a hundred years, a decade may be trivial. Maybe one decade is remembered as the Shark Years, another the Decade of Births.

So, I just finished my first Dry Decade. It was heavy on the major life stuff: I fell in love, got married, quit my job, moved to another state, bought a house and had two babies. How I did it all without Stolichnaya, I don't know. But I couldn't have done it with Stolichnaya, either.

"So how were the first ten years?" a friend asked as we celebrated my ten-year sobriety anniversary.

I sat mute. I could hardly remember. In some ways, the past decade has been a blur. Then again, so were the years preceding it. It was clear that I had a problem, even early on. I look at pictures my father took of me in my playpen, two years old and holding my father's Hamm's beer can, and I see an alcoholic waiting to happen.

I remember my first hangover that lasted all day when I was in fourth grade. The first time I smoked pot with my sister in sixth grade. I remember drinking like the guys, and not liking the disparity that I sensed between the sexes. Why was it socially acceptable, almost a rite of passage, for the guys to drink the way they did, but not the girls? I wanted to cross the gender line and have equal drinking rights. I wanted to ease the pain of what was becoming an increasingly violent and dysfunctional family life. I wanted to drink and laugh. It cloaked the hurt and emptiness inside.

At some point in my drinking career, I did cross the line. Not the gender line, but the line distinguishing the social drinkers from the alkies. Consciously, I didn't know I had crossed over, although people who knew me were aware of my slide. Gradually, I dropped out of contact with old friends, and became a barfly. Then I married a fellow drinker.

What would have served as wake-up calls to many—losing a job and getting a DWI—I went through in total denial. I bamboozled my way through a court-mandated responsible drinking class, and continued down the craggy path that I had chosen. Toward the end, drinking had no time limits; morning, noon and night were all perfect opportunities to imbibe. In fact, what better way to brace for the day, than with a little vodka and orange juice?

Gripped by a sudden desire for semi-honesty, I told my therapist that I was bothered by my unhealthy lifestyle. I had been hard at the bottle, any bottle, for over ten years. After my inevitable divorce at age twenty-eight, I also started smoking, and I told my therapist that it just didn't fit my self-image.

"I'm drinking martinis every now and then," I told her, throwing in, "that was my father's drink of choice, too."

"What bothers you more?" she asked, "The drinking or the smoking?"

"Oh, the smoking," I said, throwing up a smoke screen even for myself. Denial runs deep.

But I was unsettled that night. I knew on a visceral level that I was slowly killing myself. I was involved in a new relationship with another alcoholic, a new drinking and smoking buddy. We urged each other on, talking night after night about our respective divorces, drowning our sorrows in self-destructive behavior. In the mornings I went to the bathroom and retched, thinking nothing of the metaphor inherent there.

Finally, I went to an internist to see what the retching was all about. He told me I had something like Alcoholic's Syndrome, and mentioned that he had heard good things about Alcoholics Anonymous. He gave me some pills to "take the edge off" when I decided to stop the booze.

"Hello, I have a boyfriend that has a serious drinking problem," I told the voice at the other end of the line. "I thought maybe you could tell me when you have meetings around the Fitchburg area, and I'll let him know." My palms were sweaty; I was sure that they had heard this outright lie before.

That night I went to my first AA meeting. I cried. I couldn't speak when it came to be my turn, and I went home and finished off my bottle of vodka. But I went back the next day, because I knew it was a way out of the darkness that was enveloping me. I knew I wanted a better life, and I knew that I had gotten myself in so deep, that I needed help crawling back out.

It didn't happen overnight; I struggled with my sobriety for months before I finally was strong enough to just quit. First, I had to get out of the insidious relationship I was in. Then, I played some mind games with myself. Not wanting to go "cold turkey" and stop both smoking and drinking at the same time, I first tried to stop smoking while allowing myself two drinks at night. But after half of a drink, I decided that it was pointless to not smoke when I was drinking. It was all part of the same package. Maybe if I tried to smoke and not drink. But that, to me, was like a martini without gin.

So I finally just did it. All at once, just like that. On April Fool's Day 1992, I began a new way of living. Living, without the crutch of alcohol. Real living, where I felt the aches and pains of life, along with the joys and exhilaration.

So how were the first ten years?

It seemed a loaded question. How could I encapsulate all of the emotions and experiences that I have felt after belting down that last drink? To think back is at once painful and exhilarating. To see where I've been, and where I am now is both confusing and clear.

Ten years is a long time, but then not. It's ten years that I may not have lived to see, had I continued sailing into darkness.

Julia Jergensen Edelman

A Little Band of Gold

Do not look where you fell, but where you slipped.

African proverb

Ida was the cleaning lady at the medical center. I was the new admission that morning—all 88 pounds of me—trying to crawl out of an alcohol-fueled breakdown.

I got tons of visitors as soon as I arrived. My impending crash was obvious to everyone but me, apparently, and the medical center was affiliated with the university that employed me. Friends and Twelve-Step calls alike competed for my attention with doctors, bosses and my husband. I had lots of food and extra desserts to encourage me to eat and build up my strength. I had my diary to chronicle my journey back from hell as faithfully as it had chronicled my descent. I had my ever-present cigarettes and lighter.

The only thing I didn't have was my wedding band. The crises piled up from my out-of-control drinking, and my weight crashed down from my too-well-controlled lack of eating. Somehow the wedding band that my husband put on my finger just six months earlier had slid off. I remembered putting it on in the morning, but not taking it off that night. I assumed I took the ring off to wash dishes. I checked the kitchen and my clothes, tore the bedroom apart, then the bathroom, the kitchen again, and even the cat's litter box. Nothing.

With my husband on a business trip, it was the loneliest night of my life as I sat next to the kitty litter box crying my eyes out over the loss of my wedding band. When I finished crying, I went outside and sifted through two weeks of trash while the cold rain pelted me. It was no use.

I went back inside, dried myself off and tried to get rip-roaring drunk on applejack. I hated applejack, which is probably why it was the only thing left in the house to drink. I failed to even get drunk—a first!—so I kept at it for five more days, until I ended up in the medical center where I met Ida, the cleaning lady.

"The sick ones don't like to talk," she told me that first morning. "Me, I enjoy talking to people. It makes the work more interesting." She liked neatness in a patient. "You're neat, and you're not so sick you can't talk," she said.

As she cleaned the toilet, emptied the trash and dealt with my overflowing ashtray, she asked why I was admitted.

"I needed rest," I said. "And I got very upset about losing my wedding band. I'm trying to calm down."

"You need to talk to St. Anthony," Ida said. "He finds things when you ask."

Oh, how cute, I thought, and carefully wrote our conversation into my diary after she left, feeling very artistic for doing so.

The next day, Ida came back and said, "So did you find your ring?"

"No, Ida. It's still lost."

"Did you ask St. Anthony?"

Oh dear, was she serious about this Anthony stuff? "No," I admitted. She looked disappointed, so I explained as nicely as I could. "I don't know him, Ida. I can't start out by asking someone I don't know for favors."

Ida stopped wet mopping the bathroom floor to consider the issue. "I see your point," she said slowly. Then she brightened up. "Tell him I sent you. St. Anthony knows me very well. Just tell him that Ida sent you. And if I'm not on shift, leave a note at housekeeping to tell me how it turns out. Just a little note, 'Ida, St. Anthony helped.' That's so I can tell him thanks for you."

Oh, how cute. Ida left, and the place got quiet, just me, my cigarettes and my diary. Do I or don't I? I couldn't. I just couldn't. It was hokey, it was sentimental and it was hypocritical. I didn't believe in that stuff.

But Ida did, and Ida was giving me advice on the only thing that mattered to me at the moment. I had doctors giving me advice on weight gain and Twelve Steppers giving advice on AA meetings. I wanted none of it. I just wanted my ring back.

I didn't know how to pray and had never heard of praying to a saint, and didn't know if Anthony was the one in the personal ads of the newspapers or if that was the Jude guy. I was desperate. But I wasn't going to be a hypocrite. I hated hypocrites.

"I'll write a poem," I decided. Technically it wasn't a prayer, so technically I wouldn't be a hypocrite. It would still cover the bases, and it would keep me in Ida's good graces.

NOT a Prayer to Saint Anthony

Ida sent me to talk to you.
She knows you pretty well, she says.
It's about my wedding ring.
Can you help me find it?
It got lost with my sanity last week.
I'm beginning to get that back.
The ring would be nice too . . .

The skies did not open over the medical center. The heavens did not come down, and I heard no heavenly hosts singing. I closed my diary and went to bed.

The next day I was released, and my husband came to collect me and start life together anew.

While I stretched out on the living room couch, he decided to jump-start the new life by removing the six weeks' worth of empty beer bottles taking up half of our two-car garage.

Ten minutes later, he walked inside with shaking hands—and my wedding ring.

"It fell out of an empty six-pack container," he said. "I was grabbing them four at a time and throwing them into the trunk of the car. I must have tipped one just right because the ring landed at my feet."

Unaccustomed as I was to small miracles, prayers, saints or dumb luck, I knew it was going to be a different world for me from now on. I don't know if St. Anthony was impressed with my poetry. All I knew was that Ida believed and lent me both her belief and her favorite saint.

I went to the phone and dialed the medical center. "Housekeeping? I need to leave a message for Ida. It's important . . . " I didn't know how to pray or say thank you to God either, but I had the feeling that Ida wouldn't mind pitching in to help me out again.

Carol J. Bonomo

How Long Will It Last This Time?

It has been my experience that folks who have no vices have few virtues.

Abraham Lincoln

"So, it's been six weeks, Mom. How long do you suppose it's going to last this time?" Stunned, I looked deep into the eyes of my ten-year-old son. I saw skepticism, pain and disgust over my recent recovery from alcoholism. He had heard it all before when I had assured him numerous times that I would stop getting drunk.

There was the night I came home in my dented car at 3:00 A.M. with a blackened eye to find him anxiously awaiting me in the driveway. He rushed over to the crumpled fender, helped me stumble out and gasped, "I asked you not to go out! I knew something bad would happen!"

There was the night of the Cub Scout ceremony where all the other members had their merit badges appropriately sewn on their uniforms while his were shakily pinned on at the last minute by my hungover hands. He sat in his chair when his name was called, too ashamed to stand up front.

There were the many different schools where he had to make all new friends, as I outran bill collectors and drank up the rent monies. He would come home crying that the kids called him "poor boy" although his father sent child support and I earned a good wage.

Hurt by his outburst, feeling shame and guilt, I considered the toxic lifestyle I had dragged him into. I was humbled and helped as I stared back into his despondent eyes.

I had no right to be trusted this time, either. I was irresponsible. God had dealt with my wounded spirit and me six weeks earlier. I had not touched a drop of alcohol, not even mouthwash. My drunken days were over, but how could I, a loser and liar so often, convince this wonderful young boy? How could I possibly convey my rejuvenated hope to this loving, innocent child?

"Oh, it's going to last!" I emphasized. With newfound certainty I replied, "This time, it's going to last!"

He hugged me tightly and whispered, "We'll see . . ."

This year, I have the privilege of looking that same, trusting son in the eye as I have ever since that night of reckoning. I have earned credibility. I am responsible. I will reassure him and he will again hug me tightly!

This time, I will say, "It's been twenty years, Son! It's going to last!"

Janell H.

The Codependent Diet

Don't throw away the old bucket until you know whether the new one holds water.

Swedish proverb

So you eat right. Having sworn off french fries and ice cream a decade ago, it wasn't your first choice but, hey, we all learn to adapt because the other option is buying a "muu-muu" and accessorizing it with "wide load" stickers.

Okay, so how about your "taste" in relationships? Do you choose from the healthy menu . . . or do you tell the waiter, "I'll pass on dessert. Instead, I'd like a disastrous relationship with Mr. Emotionally Unavailable over at Table Five."

Admit it—you've done it! You walk into a room full of available men and, without fail, you scope out the one with the most baggage: emotionally unavailable from childhood, married but separated for the last five years, a permanent seat at the Tuesday night anger management class, or communication skills on par with your goldfish. And my personal favorite, he's divorced but still not over the fact that his first marriage was supposed to last forever and didn't, even though it's ten years later.

So why does it work that way? Why do we—normally strong women—go to so much trouble taking care of our bodies, yet remain willing, even eager, to destroy our emotional well-being with men who will never be relationship material? Although the details may differ, if this story has a familiar ring to it, chances are you have heard the word "codependent" before.

For some of us, maybe it's the challenge. I firmly believe "I can change him!" He will fall in love with me and feel something he has never felt before! I will make up for all the wrongs in his childhood! It will be incredible and magical and he will fall at my feet in gratitude and bliss! Uh huh . . . and the cow jumped over the cheesy moon shining on that oceanfront property in Arizona . . .

For others, maybe it's a comfort zone. I grew up in a house where Dad ignored Mom, or criticized her, or cheated on her—whatever it was, it now seems natural to seek out a man who does the same to me. Of course, I won't be happy and eventually might leave and go in search of . . . another man who does the same thing! It's not what I want, but I am drawn to it, because it feels like "home" to me.

Or how about this one: Psychologists claim that we all marry either our mother or our father; seeking out a personality similar to one of our parents. Perish the thought!!

And yet, it's all right there. I am guilty of all of the above. I spent years falling for guys who were still in love with their ex-wives. Occasionally I would take a break from that nightmare and find one who was totally incapable of loving anyone, including himself. Are you emotionally unavailable? You are? Cool! Let's hook up!

After roughly a hundred self-help books, a few months of therapy and several years in Twelve-Step meetings for codependent enablers like myself, what have I learned? I have come to realize that it truly is a pattern. They aren't joking when they say that insanity is doing the same thing over and over again and expecting a different result! Truer words were never spoken than "an expectation is just a premeditated resentment." I expect you to treat me nice (even though it was obvious from the first that you're a jerk) and boy, am I resentful when you don't!

And by now you are probably wondering, where is the connection between diets and relationships? Isn't it obvious?

If I go home tonight and order a large double pepperoni pizza with extra cheese and a side order of breadsticks, wash it down with a super-sized Cherry Coke, and then top the evening off with a pint of my favorite Häagen-Dazs, what do you think is going to happen in a couple of days? Most likely,

I am going to step on the scale and we are both going to burst into tears! I know it, I accept it, and I avoid letting that happen. I forgo the pizza and the Coke and the ice cream—because I would rather be able to zip my jeans without the aid of a crowbar and a crane.

So why can't we—as rational, intelligent women—do the same with relationships? If we can understand that our hips are going to spread if we eat a steady diet of french fries, why can't we get it through our heads that our hearts are going to break if we try to love someone who cannot love us back? Hello? Is anybody listening?

There are a few things you can count on in this life. Two plus two equals four regardless of whether you are speaking English or Swahili, a Big Mac has 600 calories whether or not you read the nutritional information sheet (do yourself a favor—don't). And no matter how much you believe in fairy-tale romances, that knight in tarnished armor is still going to fall off his horse!

When all is said and done, shouldn't choosing your mate be at least as important as ordering your next meal? After all, if you wanted to lose weight, you wouldn't order fried chicken, pasta with cream sauce, and salad swimming in ranch dressing . . . would you? So what do you order when you want a healthy relationship?

I, for one, would like to start with an appetizer of romance and thoughtfulness, with a dash of passion. For the main course I'll have an emotionally stable, commitment-oriented, dependable, trustworthy, considerate, all-around decent guy, please! Oh, and can I have a side order of good communication skills to go with that?

Linda S. Day

A 4C Woman

If we don't change, we don't grow. If we don't grow, we aren't really living.

Gail Sheehy

It really wasn't that long ago when I would wake up every Saturday morning on my bathroom floor, covered in sweat and vomit, crying, promising to never drink again. I'd get back in bed, sleep all day and arise about supper time. I'd have a few beers to take the edge off and the nightmare would begin again.

In September of 1999 I discovered a Women for Sobriety message board on AOL. Home from work one day, hung over and hurting, remorseful, ashamed and afraid, I turned to the Internet to help me in my search for sobriety. I literally stumbled upon the message board and was amazed at what I found. A community of women, in all different levels of sobriety. I was impressed with their knowledge, their positive attitudes, the way they looked out after and encouraged one another. They were sober and happy! I liked the humor and lightness I saw there. Could I really feel that way sober? These women showed me that recovery didn't have to be depressing and shameful, dredging up past wrongs. I wanted what these women had. Badly.

Yet, I didn't believe I could achieve it. I was different. I wasn't like them. I had too many problems. I wasn't as smart as they were. I didn't have as much money. I wasn't as educated. There was no way I'd measure up. They wouldn't accept me. I was a loser. And as long as I believed these things about myself, I would be all these things.

After lurking a few days, I couldn't resist. I posted one morning, after a few days of sobriety. I was so excited and wanted to share it with this group of women, who I'd gotten to know over the past few days. I had gone back in time and read hundreds and hundreds of old posts. I felt I knew all the gals there. Forgetting about my self-consciousness I posted a breezy hello. To my delight and amazement I received numerous responses. Oh my God! I posted again, and received more responses. It was amazing, this Internet. I was talking to strangers all over the country. Prior to this I would use e-mail occasionally, but rarely surfed. It never occurred to me cyberspace could be a tool for support.

I began to develop a rhythm to my days. I'd come home from work and go directly to the message board. It used to be the drive home from work was fraught with thoughts of to drink or not to drink. Inevitably I'd stop off for the bottle of wine and uncork it minutes after walking in the door. Now I couldn't wait to get home and fire up the computer and see what the girls were up to. I was beginning to develop friend-ships, genuinely caring about these women I might never meet. It also filled that time I would have been drinking.

I didn't realize it at the time, but I was learning so many things, on so many different levels. After isolating myself for years, drinking alone at home, I was reaching out, learning how to trust again. I was opening up and learning how to make friends and be a friend. I was learning about the WFS program and how to get and stay sober. I was starting to become aware that there was a program behind this message board: one that could help me create a new life.

I wrote to WFS and got the starter kit. I ordered tapes and books and the newsletter. I began to immerse myself in all things WFS. I used the statements as affirmations, every morning in my car, on the way to work. I'd stay on each one until I felt comfortable moving on to the next. Truth be told it felt weird, so fake to be saying these things. But I kept it up because I saw the end result. I saw these women on the board who had what I wanted. And I did want it.

It just took me awhile to get it. In retrospect I'd like to think that during those six months of fits and starts and more day ones than I care to remember, I was building a foundation. Piece by piece. Statement by statement. Some statements proved more challenging than others. Particularly "The Past Is Gone Forever," "Problems Bother Me Only to the Degree I Permit Them To" and "Negative Thoughts Destroy Only Myself." I was habitually negative. I'd get overwhelmed by my daily life and run to the bottle for solace. It was scary, this getting better. But I plugged along, slowly, surely moving forward. I was soaking up a lot of wisdom on that board, without even realizing it.

I think what had the biggest impact was how much the women on the board encouraged me. They had so much faith in me. Their belief in me carried me forward and taught me how to believe in myself. They saw something in me well before I found it. At first this attention scared me. I didn't believe them. I thought they were just saying it to be polite.

But I kept coming back, and in time I began to believe they might really mean it. I started to feel good that someone cared about me and thought I had potential. Perhaps I did.

I continued to read recovery related material and books, particularly Jean Kirkpatrick's, who founded Women for Sobriety. I was a student of sobriety, anxious to learn all that I could. I still ran to the board every day after work, but for different reasons. No longer just to avoid the drink, but to participate in this sober community. I was now a part of it! Me! I fit in! And it was finally beginning to dawn on me that maybe I was okay. Maybe I did have something to contribute. Maybe I did deserve this thing called sobriety.

Maybe these women were right.

Over three years later I'm still coming to the board daily. I've met one of the women and I've developed deep friendships and talk on the phone to many of them. I enjoy quality sobriety and can't imagine any other way to live. I am happy and healthy. I'm capable and competent, compassionate and caring. I'm a 4C woman extraordinaire.

I didn't get here overnight. And not without some heartache, much change and a fair amount of fear. That first year was tough. I felt good physically, with the alcohol no longer in my body. Mentally I was a mess. I had a lot of fear and anger. I saw the areas in my life that needed attention and felt overwhelmed by the task. So I just focused on not drinking and moving forward, day-by-day. I continued to immerse myself in recovery. I began attending WFS face-to-face meetings. And eventually, without even realizing it, I began to feel good.

I learned to take the tools I learned, in books, at meetings, from my friends on the board, and apply them to the challenges in my life. Once again, I pulled out the statements and they were powerful motivators. "I Am What I Think," "Enthusiasm Is My Daily Exercise," "All Love Given Returns" and "I Am a Competent Woman and Have Much to Give Life." These became my favorite mantras, and I repeated them daily until I believed them. And you know what? I believe them. I really believe them. I feel it in my bones. And knowing these things, feeling this sense of confidence and the power of a positive outlook has changed my life.

I've faced many challenges in sobriety. Challenges will always be there. How I react to them and what I do about them is what's different. Not drinking was just the first step. Truly learning and living the program, being the best me I can be was the next step. It's given me a rich, full life. I'm eager to see what else awaits me.

Deb Sellars Karpek

How Am I Going to Pay for All This?

The only difference between a rut and a grave is the depth.

Anonymous

Pat is cut from the same basic cloth as his brother in the fellowship, Frank. Pat had a rough start in the program, relapsing often until he finally "figured it out," as he says.

Pat was a "wrecker" when he drank. He'd tear things apart, knock down walls and leave a mess everywhere he went. This destruction was always carried out in a blackout. He says most of his sober time was spent paying for all the damage he caused while on his drinking sprees.

One night during a blacked-out relapse a tornado came through the town he was holed up in. Cars were turned over, roofs torn off houses, trees uprooted. In the morning when he staggered to the door of the motel he was in and saw the damage, he said he wailed, "Holy God! How am I going to pay for all this?"

Anonymous as told to Earnie Larsen

The Letter

Most of the shadows of life are caused by standing in our own sunshine.

Ralph Waldo Emerson

I sat down at my computer dreading this first assignment and yet knowing it was a critical step in my recovery. *"My recovery."* This was still a new concept to me with just over a week in treatment for drug and alcohol addiction. My assignment was to write a letter to someone important in my life about my addiction and to commit myself to recovery.

I knew instantly that I had to write the letter to my parents. For years I watched their confusion at the chaos in my life. Somehow I had been able to hide my drug habit so all they saw were the consequences. But now, the cat was out of the bag. They were at a loss to understand why, of their seven children, only I had invited drugs and alcohol into my life. The other members of my family led normal, happy, successful lives—lives I envied but could not seem to emulate. At the many family gatherings I felt like an outsider, living a lie, dreading the day anyone discovered my awful secret. I was the last to arrive and the first to leave, anxious to be alone with my crank pipe.

In this assignment I would meet my worst fear head-on. Finally my parents would know the awful truth about their worthless daughter. Before I could begin I actually prayed. For years I believed God would have nothing to do with me. Now in my deepest heartbreak I asked for his strength and love. Then I wrote the letter. Of course after writing it I had to give it to them.

Little did I know that on the day I chose to share my letter, my mother had prayed (yet again) for me. She gave me up to God, told God I was in his hands. Her concerns for me and for my little boy were killing her. She just could not worry about me another day.

I drove up to their lovely home. I walked in the front door and found my parents in the cozy family room with my sister Deidre. I asked them all to sit down. Then I took out my letter and read it to them.

June 1997

Dear Mom and Dad,

Hi, it's me your long-lost daughter. You know, the one with "so much potential." God, I have missed you these past fifteen years—you and Wendy, Deidre, Shari, Dean, Randy and Daren.

I suppose the best way to break this to you would be to sit quietly while I let you read the contents of this first assignment and then watch your hearts break while mine disintegrates with more guilt and shame.

You did everything right. You have six wonderful kids to prove it and yet I am such a loser. I have often wished you would discover that I was not your child after all. That would at least explain my worthlessness.

It is 3:21 in the morning and I am clean and sober—for eight days now. And I am determined to finish this letter as part of my first assignment and part of a series of steps toward my recovery. I dread telling you about me but I know it will answer so many questions for you. You always say how much you miss me. I could not figure out just what, exactly, you missed. Of your seven children, I let you down the most. "You have so much potential." Mom, you have said that more times than I can remember. I hope you are right.

I am so tired of being alienated from you all. I miss you so-so-so much. I feel as though my happiness stopped in 1977 when Dad held me so tight in my little dormitory room at Montana State University. I'll never forget the look of love and regret in your eyes, Dad, the day you left me there. And I'll never forget my own grief, how I cried at watching you leave.

I am sorry for the pain my choices have caused you. I am sorry for the agony my revelations will cause you now. You have always been there for me, when I asked and even when I couldn't. You have loved me unconditionally and that is what makes hurting you now so hard. My only prayer is that in this hurt, true healing will finally begin.

I do so want to please you again. I so much want to be part of my family again. I do not want to be an addict—on drugs—anymore, ever again. But I am so afraid of failing. You know I never tried much anymore because that way I could not fail. But this is my greatest challenge. And if I fail the only answer for me is death. So I have to succeed. I will always be an addict in recovery and I wonder, can you live with that label? Is this just too much?

I need you to know. I need to know you still love me. But I am so afraid. I suppose I am afraid of losing you. But I lost you long ago in my addiction. So maybe, I really have nothing left to lose by sharing this with you. I will do this, Mom and Dad, for my son. Yes, a drug addict has raised him—until now. And I will do this for you, and I will do this for me, in the hope that indeed I am worth it.

I love you more than life, far more than life. I even love you more than death. And, that is something because I have longed for death for so long. Yes. I love you more than death and I want "My Recovery" more than death. That statement is profound and awesomely powerful. And it means I have a chance. If I can just know you are there my recovery is only a matter of time, work, God and me.

Pray for me. And pray for all that potential. I am gonna need it. I'll keep you posted.

All my love,
Tracey

My parents moved closer and closer to me as the words spilled from the page. Deidre got up and held me. At the end we were all holding each other, crying and hurting. But through the tears we all tasted hope and I knew without a doubt that I would have all the love and support I could dream of from my parents and my brothers and sisters. I had been so afraid of their judgment and rejection.

Imagine my surprise the following Saturday when my entire family—my parents, brothers, sisters, their spouses and children and my son—showed up at my treatment center in a massive show of support and love.

That was nearly seven years ago. The love and encouragement has never wavered. Today I am fully enmeshed in my family. I belong. I have a wonderful job working for Health and Social Services. I am the Chair of RAFT (Recovering Advocates for Treatment), an organization that speaks out about the importance of treatment for drug and alcohol addiction. I am active in my church and community.

My relationship with my fourteen-year-old son is incredible. He is a 4.0 student, wise, centered and compassionate. I am there to guide him, to love him and to be a light in his world.

So, once again my mom was right . . . I do have potential. And every day in my recovery, I live it.

Tracey W. Lee-Coen

2

SHOULDERS TO LEAN ON

We are not called to go where it is easy and love already exists. We are called to go where we are sent and bring love with us.

Anonymous

Friends of Bill W., Please Come to the Gate. . .

Once you learn to walk, crawling is out of the question.

James D. Davis

Sometime in the early 1990s I was treating a woman in an intensive outpatient chemical dependency group. Let's call her "Grace." Grace was a flight attendant and had been suspended from her job with a major airline due to her untreated alcoholism. She had been stealing the little miniature liquor bottles, drinking in airport bars in uniform, and so on. Her employer, realizing she needed treatment, sent her to us.

After the eight-week program, I suggested to her it might be a good idea to solidify her foundation in recovery before returning to work as she would be working in a high-risk environment (serving alcohol, being out of town alone, etc.). Grace did, however, return to work shortly after completing outpatient treatment. One day while she was departing from a plane at the end of a long day, a major craving for alcohol overpowered her. There she was, in the Los Angeles International Airport, pulling her roller-bag behind her when this massive craving to drink came over her. She tried to just "think through it," or "just forget about it," but it was way too powerful. It was so powerful, in fact, that she was resigned to the fact that she would just go drink. Grace thought, *Oh, the heck with it, I'll get another job . . . or maybe no one will find out anyway.* But deep down inside Grace did not want to drink. She truly had wanted to stay sober, but she was in trouble.

On her way to the bar in the airport, Grace had a moment of sanity. She stopped, picked up the airport paging phone and said, "Will you please page friends of Bill W.," she paused, quickly looking around for an empty gate, "to come to Gate 12?"

Within minutes, over the paging system in the L.A. International Airport came, "Will friends of Bill W. please come to Gate 12. Will friends of Bill W. please come to Gate 12." Most people in recovery know that asking if you are a friend of Bill W. is an anonymous way to identify yourself as a member of AA.

In less than five minutes there were about fifteen people at that gate from all over the world. That brought tears of amazement, relief and joy to Grace. They had a little meeting there in that empty gate, total strangers prior to that moment. Grace discovered that two of those people had gotten out of their boarding lines and missed their flights to answer that call for help. They had remembered what they had seen on many walls of meeting rooms: "When anyone, anywhere reaches out their hand for help, I want the hand of AA to be there and for that I am responsible."

Grace did not drink that day. I would venture to guess that none of the people who came to Gate 12 drank that day either. Instead Grace had a moment of sanity, realized she could not do it on her own, took the action of asking for help and received it immediately. This help is available to all of us if we want it and sincerely ask for it. It never fails.

Jim C., Jr.

Around the Room

For the strength of the pack is the wolf, and the strength of the wolf is the pack.

Rudyard Kipling, *The Law of the Jungle*

On my way to my meeting last night I was listening to a talk show on the radio. The guest this night was a man who went through treatment some years ago but was never touched by the power there. Or maybe he was and had to find a way to justify not going forward.

At any rate, he apparently wrote a book slamming every conceivable aspect of traditional recovery. Surrender was weakness. Fellowship was a sham. Recovery was a cult. For him unmanageability was the same as opting for being a victim. He was above such "crutches" and saw himself as a hero who was willing to tell the "truth."

Anyone can make fun of anything. I felt sorry for him and wished he could come with me to the meeting I was going to. Actually, our situation isn't really a meeting. We meet at a church that has maybe eight to ten meetings going on at the same time. The meetings include AA as well as Al-Anon and Narcotics Anonymous (NA) but also Gamblers Anonymous (GA) and Sex Addicts Anonymous (SAA) and several other flavors of recovery. We all finish about ten and close together. Maybe as many as one hundred people make a circle as big as is needed to include everyone and close with the Lord's Prayer.

Wherever a person may stand in that circle most of the

faces of the others are within sight. For sure anyone can make fun of anything but I wished the man who felt he had been harmed by traditional recovery could stand where I was and see the faces I look at and marvel at every week.

Stan is young and built with the long, smooth muscles of a panther. He is a year clean of meth but the coiled strength of the drug still lives in him. It runs an inch under his skin looking for a way to break out. But there he stands, hair bleached snow white, tall and proud, a necklace tight against his neck. And with him are his two small children of five and eight.

Stan went back to court to get custody of his children from their still drug-using mother. He was never parented much so he has little experience to fall back on as to how a daddy should act. But he tries. Every week he shows up with his kids, showing them all the love he has been taught in the fellowship. No parent has ever tried harder to give his or her children a firm foundation.

Next to him, holding his hand, is older woman named Bonny. She has adopted Stan and his children. She is their grandmother. Bonny put it very simply, "We need each other. It is what God wants."

Further down the line stand two women, obviously friends, holding hands in the circle. At one time in both their lives they were exotic dancers. Who knows what else? They are both live wires—full of fun, love to joke around—and yet there is a depth and a hardness in their eyes that only comes from having seen the worst side of humanity. But there they stand, hand in hand, sober, clean, celebrating their long ride back into the light.

Texas Tom is a little further on. He has been in and out of our meeting rooms for several years. His last relapse was a bad one. He actually lived at the crack house he used for the most part of four months. It's a miracle he is still alive. But an even bigger miracle is that he has come back, again. He is so full of guilt and shame this night he can barely hold his head up. But there he is, included in a circle of love that ultimately is stronger than any addiction.

Mary and Frank stand together. They always do. She is Al-Anon and Frank is AA. Both have been in the fellowship for over twenty years. They have a hell of a story but for many years if you saw them on the street they would appear the most normal, ordinary, middle-class suburban couple. They have two biological sons and dozens of others they have adopted over the years. Not legally but in a spiritual sense. Their door is always open. Members of the fellowship who have no other place to go on holidays are always packed around their table. They are the best of good people.

I spy Art across the room. He is a giant of a man who, he says, has spent nearly all of his adult life in prison. He first got sober in prison and now three years later is still clean through the love of the fellowship and his God. He says he fears nothing on the face of this Earth. Having gone through what he has, no one doubts it. But tonight he shared that he just found out he has a twenty-one-year-old son and has decided he would try to make contact with the young man. That scares him. He says his legs feel like jelly. But there he stands in the circle—clean, sober and facing the hardest fight of his life.

On and on the circle goes—Cat who killed a man while driving under the influence and did four years in prison, now clean and giving back. John, seventeen years clean, who started a business for the sole purpose of giving work to people no one will ever trust. Bobbie and his wife, Ruth, with the old scar of a cutter crawling up her arm, who come each week with their little daughter, Charity. The young and the old, conservatives and young men with shaved heads, the tattooed and those who would never think of such a thing, the single and the married and many who once were. Some financially successful and some who steal toilet paper from McDonald's, an endless variety but with a 24-carat commonality—they are all chemical free and making something beautiful of their lives.

I remembered the man on the talk show driving home and thought, *If this is a cult, may we all be so lucky to belong.*

Earnie Larsen

A Miracle in the Making

The divine guidance often comes when the horizon is the blackest.

Mohandas Mahatma Gandhis

It's like a bad dream—a surprise party without the cake and minus the merriment.

For weeks you've been planning to save the life of someone you love. At times it feels more like plotting, sneaking out to meetings you can't talk about, reliving old hurts to get them down on paper just right, wondering how you'll ever get him there, dreading the look on his face.

You've had the same look on your face many times through the years, because you love an alcoholic who couldn't seek help.

Today, you're doing it for him.

You've held him close all night, as if to reassure him of your love and shield him from the pain. You've packed for him without his knowing, sneaking his hairbrush and his favorite slippers into a bag that is waiting in a friend's car. You've kissed him good-bye like this was any other day, wondering if he would ever again say "I love you" back.

And now—half an hour before his arrival—you sit in the intervention specialist's office with your sweetheart's two children and two colleagues who are also his good friends. His company's personnel manager is bringing him here on the pretext of some meeting important to the boss.

Your damp palms smudge the carefully edited "script"

you hold. Someone cracks a nervous little joke, and you laugh softly before returning to your silent prayers.

At last—yet too soon—you hear the familiar voice and footsteps coming down the hall. The door opens and his voice breaks off, questions in his eyes as he scans the room. Confusion and fear, the very look you dreaded, erode his half-smile and you struggle to look loving, yet firm.

The intervention has begun.

"What's going on here?" is the first of his many questions.

The intervention specialist introduces himself and explains how he helps families and industries to help other people. The suspicion and confusion grow. Alcohol is not even mentioned, until the first friend recalls a past drinking incident.

The letter from his boss—who is out of town—tells him what a valued employee he is, that he has the firm's support in getting well. He rolls his eyes and snorts.

But then the woman he loves and his children recite their rehearsed speeches about the drunkenness and the pain it has caused them. Please get help, they urge.

Today, there is no more denial. The drinker wipes away his tears.

And then your part is done. The intervention specialist takes over, negotiating him into treatment by urging him to "join your friends and family to help you get well. I know the things you've done are not the decent man you really are."

The drinker volunteers to go look at the treatment center after the specialist dispels some myths—no bars, no shock treatments, no forced illness. There's time set aside. Will he go now just to look? Perhaps check in later this week for just ten days, to decide whether or not he has a problem and could benefit from treatment?

The specialist congratulates the man for his commitment and you do, too. His embrace is half-hearted and wary, but his children are swallowed up in the big man's arms for a teary farewell.

You get the high sign to move out quickly so they can drive to the treatment center. He won't need the hidden suitcase—at least not yet.

But when the man does check-in at the end of the week, it's with a suitcase he's packed himself. Fear of the unknown fills his eyes, but this is his decision.

In the next mail, the people who cared enough to put their friendship on the line receive notes from the man who was forced to recognize that he had a disease.

And several days later when you drop by the treatment center to pick up his dirty laundry, the attached note is the best you ever receive.

"Thank you. I love you. I'm Ted—and I'm an alcoholic."
The nightmare is over.

Jann Mitchell

The 202 Club

Keep your faith in all beautiful things, in the sun when it is hidden, in the Spring when it is gone.

Roy R. Gilson

The address was 202 20th Avenue South, just off Elliston Place. I knew the neighborhood; I had partied there for years. The Gold Rush and the Exit Inn, they were the gathering places of the late seventies music scene in Nashville. That was a lot of miles ago.

Now it was June of 1997 and I sat in the parking lot outside the 202 Club, the AA house in West Nashville. I hadn't been to a meeting since leaving treatment, and I needed one. The parking lot was almost full. *Damn,* I thought, *there are a lot of people in there.* So I sat and listened to Steve Earle singing the song he wrote for the late great Townes Van Zandt. Townes drank himself to death living what should only be imagined. That's the downside of a go-to-hell-attitude; if you're not careful, you will. Over the years I had become well-acquainted with my own hell. That's why I was here. I didn't want that anymore, and I didn't have much faith that I could avoid it.

I had lived most of my adult life being what I did. From musician, to cowboy, to commodities trader—whatever it was, I was—and since my time in treatment I had realized that maybe I wasn't what I did. Maybe I was something else. Whatever that something else was, was going to have to wait a little longer. I needed to get through that door and

into the AA meeting inside. I was scared. I was self-
conscious. I felt alone.

As Earle's "Fort Worth Blues" ended, I climbed out of my
pickup and walked into the back door of the 202 Club. The
house was full of people but contrary to my fear, nobody
stopped or even paid any attention to my being there. I
immediately felt safe. I wasn't alone anymore. That's what I
needed—safety, somewhere to go when the noise in my
head was out of control, which was most of the time. The
alone was terrifying, like sitting on your surfboard a hundred yards off shore, and having a 10-foot shark swim by.

When it's just you and life and death you realize, real
quickly, how much faith you don't have. My craving to get
high was that shark, and he had been circling for two days.
I couldn't white-knuckle it anymore. So here I was, I had
made it to 202.

Looking around, I thought the scene resembled a club
house, people hanging out, talking and laughing. The meeting I was looking for was upstairs. Climbing the stairs, I
heard someone reading from *The Big Book*. Alcoholics
Anonymous was created from the shared experiences of Bill
Wilson and Dr. Bob. They put those experiences, perceptions, stories and the Twelve Steps into what is known
today as *The Big Book*.

Turning the corner upstairs, I walked into a room full of
all shapes, sizes and colors of human beings, a tribe of survivors. There was a thick blue cloud of cigarette smoke
hanging over the gathering. I sat against an outside wall as
the meeting opened. *Thank you, God,* I could breathe again. I
felt like I had just held my breath for the whole hour's drive
into Nashville.

An hour ago I could have just as easily gone to see the
dope man, or woman. In fact, I was so sure and afraid that
was where I was headed that turning left on 20th seemed
like a miracle. I was only a few blocks away from the
cocaine queen of Music Row and we had spent too many
nights together in the twisted shadows of crack and sex.

Those memories gave me a sick butterflies-in-the-stomach feeling. This time I had made another choice, those butterflies were gone and I was so grateful to be sitting in this room, full of others who were walking through their own valley of the shadow. We weren't alone; we had each other.

Sitting and listening, I flashed back on my time in treatment, when my counselor told me that getting high would never really be okay with me again. He had been right, but his being right hadn't kept me from using again. After the opening readings, the chairperson of the meeting opened the floor for a topic. The guy sitting next to me spoke softly, "My name's Lonely and I'm an addict and alcoholic."

He started talking about the last few months of his life and how he had gone back to drugging after a couple years clean. This was his first meeting since he had quit using, and he was tired and scared, and fed up with how narrow his choices seemed. I was overwhelmed, knowing he was talking to me.

Once again I flashed on memories of treatment, and how sweet the bond had been between all of us that shared that space together. This was that same feeling revisited, alive and well right here at 202. As I looked around the room I could see the compassion and understanding in the eyes of those who shared this space. Thank you, Father, I am so grateful, I don't want to be alone anymore. I wasn't.

I never spoke at that meeting. As the conversation moved around the room the stories were told of the same experiences shared by people who had never officially met, but had all lived the truth of taking refuge in a hell that seemed like the only way out. I thought to myself, *Thank you, buddy, thank you for making it here.*

I didn't need to know anything to feel gratitude for the safety of sitting in that meeting at 202. The experience was the truth. That's all I needed to know.

After the meeting I hung out and talked to a couple of

guys about the struggle of changing years of addiction. Keep coming back—that's the cliché, and the truth—keep coming back. Walking outside I was hit by the heavy humid heat of a June night in Nashville. Ninety degrees and 90 percent humidity. I realized I wasn't even conscious of the heat when I'd walked from my truck to the back door at 202 Club. That's the power of obsession, and I had been overwhelmed with it when I got there an hour ago.

It's amazing we ever get so lost and even more amazing we come back from the realms of addictions, but we do because that's the world we are born into. And we do because we are not of this world. We are that spirit that won't be trapped by definition, that light that acts for us when the shadows would have us believe only lies. It is no wonder that, with the insanity of this world, we trust so little and fear so much.

That's who I was, one who really trusted very little and feared most of all. From that point of view, all the obsessions and addictions, the guilt, shame and fear, they all made sense. I was the product of a world and a culture that had chosen knowledge over life and opinions over truth. That is who I had been, and I was realizing that was not who I had to be. I could choose again.

Making that first meeting at 202 was the second phase of a path of first experiences. The first phase had been checking myself into a treatment center. Those thirty days in treatment had broken the ice on a sea of frozen fears. The most important lesson I learned there was that I could be honest and I could change my life, and yes, it did come down to me.

Leaving that meeting at 202 had shown me that knowing what I was doing was nowhere near as important as just showing up and letting life show me. I have lived an amazing path since that June night in 1997, and I look forward to living whatever comes next, happy, joyous and free.

Lee R. McCormick

The Seat

*P*art *of recovery we can't do alone and part no one else can do for us.*

Earnie Larsen

The first time I walked into "the rooms" over seventeen years ago, I saw a group of older people sitting around laughing and drinking coffee. As I shyly looked around the room, I spied the coffee and cookies sitting on the table. A lady with a friendly enough face walked over to me and asked me if I would like to have a seat. I told her, yes, but asked her if I could buy a cup of coffee first. She told me that the coffee is always free and that it would always be brewing, five days a week, *especially* holidays, just for me.

Five years later, after interrupted attempts at staying clean and sober, despite the fact that I was singing in the choir, working, all those kind of productive-member-of-society type things, I remembered that ten o'clock meeting.

When I walked in the room, the same group of people seemed to be sitting in the exact same seats. A friendly woman walked up to me and said, "Good seeing you! We've missed you! Would you like to have a seat?" Just as if she had not noticed the "slight" weight loss I had undergone. This time, I took a seat, and then rushed to the coffee pot!

A few years later . . . hey, who's counting? But a little over seven years ago, with sunken cheeks, no teeth, and a few more battle scars, I thought about that little meeting that met every day of the week, *especially* holidays, and thought I would drop in on them again. The same people were sitting in the same seats! I walked over to the most approachable-looking older gentleman there and said, "How can I get a seat here? You have been sitting in the same seat for years."

The young lady sitting next to him said to me, "Honey, take this seat. It is now yours. I have been sitting in this seat now for almost ten years between these two gentlemen, and I have not used. They tell me that this is a good recovery seat." She then got out of her seat and offered it to me. Mr. Avery (the elderly gentleman) whispered in my ear, "Now there's another thing about maintaining your seat; you have to be the first ass in it each day!"

So, for the next two years, every day, Monday through Friday and *especially* holidays, I was the first person in my seat! I discovered the joys of "the meeting before the meeting" and learned the pleasure of "the meeting after the meeting!"

Soon, as the responsibilities on my job increased, I was not able to make the meeting every day, but would come whenever I had a day off or could take an early lunch and especially holidays. Whenever I came, I knew to come early enough to make sure that my seat was indeed, my seat!

A few weeks after my seventh year of uninterrupted recovery, a young lady walked into "the rooms" and came straight to me at the meeting and said, "I've been noticing you for a few years sitting in the same seat. How do I get a seat?" I looked in her eyes and said to her, "My sister! Welcome! You can have mine. This is a good recovery seat. The lady who sat in it before me gave it to me. It is yours now!" I smiled as I watched Mr. Avery lean over and whisper something in her ear. I knew what he was telling her!

The precious gift of recovery that they had given me had blossomed into the realization that *wherever* I sit within "the rooms," is a "good" recovery seat.

As long as I bring my ass and put it there!

Andrea W., aka Sala Dayo Nowelile

"I'll be home late. I've joined a support group for women who need a reason to stay at work until the house is picked up and dinner is on the table."

Reprinted by permission. ©2003 Randy Glasbergen, www.glasbergen.com

Serendipity or Higher Power?

Beware lest you lose the substance by grasping at the shadow.

Aesop

I spent almost ten years as a celibate seminarian preparing for the Catholic priesthood. During the last four of those years I was a closet alcoholic. After a number of drunken episodes, some bordering on public scandal, I decided to leave the security of my religious community.

I drank heavily for two years after I left and felt I had lost my faith in God (except for hoping that if there was a God, he had recorded my ten years without sex in *The Big Book of Heaven*).

When I finally hit bottom and joined a Twelve-Step group, I was very suspicious of the talk about God and a Higher Power. I went on for about five years in this state of agnostic confusion and irritation about all the God-talk in the program until an event happened that truly restored my faith in a Higher Power.

I was in Casper, Wyoming, working as a consultant for Drillco Manufacturing Oil Company. One of my bosses knew I was a recovering alcoholic. He told me that Drillco was worried about one of their brightest young geologists who was in Casper overseeing a drilling operation. He said the guy was thirty-eight years old, had three beautiful young daughters and a wife who was at the point of divorcing him. The company was seriously considering firing him if he didn't stop drinking.

I called to see if there were any Twelve-Step meetings in the area and got a recorded message saying there was a meeting on Tuesday and Thursday in some godforsaken town about fifty miles away. It was Wednesday so I could get the guy to a meeting the next day.

I called the geologist, talked to him, told him my story and offered to take him to a meeting. Being very much a control freak in sponsoring a new person, I certainly didn't talk about the spiritual part of the program or a Higher Power. He reluctantly agreed to go.

We had a hell of a time finding the meeting, which turned out to be in an old ramshackle mine shaft building. We were twenty minutes late and when I saw the motley crew in attendance I thought, *There's no way!* There was a one-armed guy talking whose voice was cracking and was somewhat incoherent, and three other people in the room: a gal who looked to be about ninety years old, a guy with palsy and another guy in his seventies who looked like a homeless bum. I knew I wouldn't come back to this meeting and I suspected my young, handsome, cowboy-type pigeon thought this was insanity.

So here I was with this bright young geologist, who was making a bucket of money in the oil field, walking into this hodgepodge of humanity. My codependent control button was ringing hysterically.

Within ten minutes, with me knowing all is doomed, the door opened and two guys walked in who were close to the age of the guy I had brought to the meeting. The first one was called on and he told a story that was almost identical to the guy I was with. He was a geologist who had sobered up two years earlier and had been on the brink of losing his job and family when he decided to quit. The other guy had six years of sobriety, was an oil field manager and was about forty-five.

Then the guy with palsy spoke. He was so profound he brought everyone to tears. When he finished, I heard it thunder outside. Suddenly I was overwhelmed with voices of people I had met earlier in the program talking about what their Higher Power had done for them. I vividly remembered the words of the second step—"We believe that a power greater than ourselves could restore us to sanity." Then I heard the words to the third step—"We turned our will and our lives over to the care of God as we understood him."

Boy, did I get it! I heard the words of the psalmist saying, "God comes when we have a wounded and contrite heart." I thought of the powerless Jesus saying, "not my will but thine be done." Grace cannot come to a closed heart and mind.

"We were powerless," the first step says. That means giving up control and being vulnerable. Then I remembered the part in *The Big Book* that has the heading "How It Works" and I remembered the answer—we needed God's help! That is how it works. My philosophical, analytical days were over. In what was, for me, a true moment of serendipitous grace I started working the steps just like they read.

By the way, the guy I took to the meeting is still sober!

John Bradshaw

The Enabling of the Disabled

At some point your heart will tell itself what to do.

Achaan Chah

Today I stand behind the fingerprinted Plexiglas at the rink, staring at my nine-year-old son on the ice. Blinking away tears, I watch Paul rush the hockey net along with his teammates and think back to a visit in a doctor's office six years ago.

Little Paul had writhed and whined inconsolably at my feet, as I was told that he had autism. Paul couldn't talk, had terrible tantrums, always kept to himself. Surely I must have known, the doctor implied with a look.

No, I didn't know. I had already had three bright, healthy, happy children. My husband and I were healthy, my parents and grandparents were healthy. My loved ones and I very rarely saw the inside of a doctor's office. We all took care of ourselves.

On that dark day in September 1998, I felt like Paul and I had been pushed off a cliff and were falling to a definite destruction. However, through much intervention, Paul was given the loan of various angels' wings to lift himself up out of his descent and take me with him. Instead of a living death we found a miracle.

The "angels" whose wings bore us up were sent to us in the forms of teachers, therapists and childcare workers. I began taking Paul to Judy Smith for speech therapy. Within a few months she was getting him to respond with basic commands such as "more" when he wanted her to blow bubbles. She forced him to look at her when he talked, although he wanted nothing more than to look away.

At Christmas, I videotaped my little boy standing straight and singing *Away in a Manger* with the rest of his Sunday school class for a concert. I brought the tape to Judy the next day to show it off and we both stared at it in tears and wonderment.

"You did that," I sobbed.

She hugged me in the emotion of the moment.

"*We* did that—Paul, you and me. We're a team," she insisted.

Through God's guidance, that team grew. When I first interviewed a worker to help Paul with his social skills, I noted she had scratches up and down her arms.

"Do you have a cat at home, Stacey?" I laughed.

"No, this is what the little guy I take care of in the after-noons did to me today. He has severe autism," she answered. Her face was tinged with sadness for the boy, as she seemed oblivious to her abused arms. She was hired on the spot. We used Catherine Maurice's excellent manual on applied behavioral analysis. Progress was slow and hard, but it was progress.

Because first impressions are not always correct, I thank God that I didn't have a say in all the angels who were brought into Paul's life. For instance, Mrs. Pora, the educational assistant placed in Paul's grade 1 class, was Polish. I have always thought accents were charming, but I did not want someone with a heavy accent trying to assist my son with his communication disability. I fought her placement in the classroom for the first month of school and could hardly sleep at night, worrying about how little she could really help Paul. I finally surrendered my fight, when after many impromptu visits to the class I saw how much his homeroom teacher, Mrs. Sinclair, had become attached to Paul. She seemed to be adequately filling in the gap he faced within the classroom.

Mrs. Sinclair did indeed work well with Paul. However, I had no idea how wrong I was about Mrs. Pora until I tagged along on an outing with Paul's class two months later. Paul had had a bad night and was having a terribly emotional morning. I was at my wit's end as to how to console him by the time we got to school. When we entered the classroom, immediately he ran into the arms of Mrs. Pora and she just held him, saying, "It's okay, Paul. It's okay." And he was fine. Fine! That was the first time in my life I was able to rely on someone else to quiet Paul down. A sensation of relief overcame me.

For Valentine's Day Paul filled out a heart that said, "I am thankful for. . . ." And he wrote "Mrs. Pora." There had been a time when this would have made me jealous, but after all Paul and I had been through, I feel nothing but intense gratitude for anyone who can endear herself to my little fella.

The next day, I dropped by to give the heart to Mrs. Pora for a keepsake. She opened her eyes wide with appreciation as she glanced over at Paul, seated in his seat. She then said, "Paul is very tired today."

I answered, "Yes, he's having trouble falling asleep at night lately."

"Well, when he came in this morning he told me he left his manners at home today. I told him to close his eyes, and picture himself going back home to get them."

What a beautiful accent Mrs. Pora has, was my first thought. Then my mind continued, *Mrs. Pora knows sometimes better than I what to say to Paul, how to say it, how to get results.*

Worried that I might startle her with the intensity of my feelings, I restrained myself from giving Mrs. Pora a big hug. Instead I just listened with a Cheshire-cat smile as she said, "So a few minutes later he came up to me and said, 'I found my manners!' and he's been fine since."

Then there was Mrs. Kalmuk, Paul's Learning Resource teacher, who had been working with him for half a period weekly. I thought she was too strict and serious, but better than nothing. Today I was walking out of the school with Paul and briefly nodded a greeting to her, but she stopped me with the biggest smile and said, "Paul's been doing so great!"

"Really?" I said, startled. I had run into Mrs. Kalmuk in the hall before and she had never bothered to talk to me.

"What did we do today, Paul?" she asked.

Paul was looking up at her, right into her eyes, and answered obediently, "We talked about our favorite things," he said.

"Right! Our favorite color, yours was orange; our favorite food, yours was hot dogs and ketchup (she actually remembered ketchup—that's very important to Paul), and what else?"

"Favorite animal," Paul answered on cue. I was astonished. Where had my uncooperative, unreachable little boy disappeared?

"Yes, yours was something big. A lion?"

"A lion and a chick," Paul said back to her. A conversation. A beautiful, intelligent conversation between two people who obviously had developed a warm relationship this past year. I couldn't believe it.

"Yes, a lion and a chick." Mrs. Kalmuk looked back to me and said, "He's come a long way this year."

A *long way* from a little lost boy who would not look at or talk to anyone just a few years before. Thanks in large part to Mrs. Kalmuk and Mrs. Pora, whom I would never have chosen to work with Paul had I done the choosing. I gladly, ecstatically, admit I was wrong. God, who knows the end from the beginning, knew what Paul needed in his particularly challenging journey and that's what Paul got.

Jayne Thurber-Smith

A Promise of Spit and Dirt

What is a friend? A single soul dwelling in two bodies.

Aristotle

We met in kindergarten, six years old, acting out Charlie's Angels on the schoolyard playground. There was an instant, lifetime connection and with spit and dirt, we made a promise of friendship.

When we were ten, we dreamed of Ireland, and walking across her with bare feet. We would dye our hair red, meet local boys on their horses and live in a castle surrounded by mist.

One of us decided not to instead.

When we were thirteen, we were going to be famous actresses going to the Oscars wearing personalized Versace, in black. A standing, enthusiastic response would be our reception, as we accepted our honor and made history, of some kind.

We watched TV instead.

When we were sixteen, we were going to be independent women. Own businesses and drive a Mercedes or two, fly first class and pay with a gold card; we were not ever going to worry about what we spent.

We got summer jobs at Movie Gallery instead.

When we were eighteen, we were going to grow our own vegetables, live in a camper and protest for animal rights. Throw away our makeup to be a pair of eco-warriors, chaining ourselves to a tree for the right causes.

We went to different colleges instead.

When we were twenty-two, I met what my life lacked and felt my future in his touch. I wanted to include my beginning with my ending, to continue the endurance of friendship.

She had things that were more important instead.

When we were twenty-five, I brought forth a new life for the world to meet. I needed her to hold my hand and lie to me about the pain. To tell me he was God's angel and perfect, to hold him for the first time, and laugh as she did when we held dolls. Only the white plague's scream was louder than my own.

Her mother came instead.

Now we are thirty-three and she cradles her head in palms stained with the night's mascara, remnants of soaring confidence. Tears recall hushed lullabies that sang true in our childhood aspirations, long before the decaying fragments of her self-esteem fell to the ground like broken wings of pride, and hope declining. In a place without sympathy, in the spit and the dirt of a far away bathroom floor, unable to stand, she calls for me instead.

I go and get her.

After all, we made a promise.

Cherie Ward

A Glimpse of Sanity

Can'st thou not minister to a mind diseased? Pluck from the memory a rooted arrow? Raze oe'r the troubled memories of the brain, and with some sweet oblivious antidote, cleanse the stuff'd bosom of that perilous stuff which weighs upon the heart.

William Shakespeare, *Macbeth*

San Francisco, 1978. I had lost one of my shoes somewhere in the city, a lens from my only pair of glasses was missing, and my wallet had been stolen a long time ago.

Compared with my fears of the coming day, these discomforts were minor. The few functioning cells in my brain struggled to focus on a solution to my immediate dilemma, the magnitude of which I dared not contemplate. There seemed to be none; those with whom I had once been friendly no longer recognized me. No more rescuers! I had been abandoned.

From my vantage point under the Harrison Street on-ramp to Highway 101 South, I watched the cars speeding toward me, their headlights long gleaming streaks on the wet street. Stopping briefly at the traffic lights as though to tempt me from my lair, they then headed southward up the ramp and over my head: crmp-crmp-crmp-crmp, like a disembodied heartbeat as their tires contacted the tarred joints in the concrete pavement.

I had lived north of the Golden Gate Bridge for the past

ten years, slowly being engulfed in the quagmire of alcoholism. My professional life eventually became pantomimic; I was the laughing stock of the waterfront. Disinclined to attend meetings of Alcoholics Anonymous because I still thought I was not one of them, I reluctantly took in one or two meetings when I realized that my drinking was out of control.

In March 1978, avoiding arrest by the county sheriff for failure to appear in court, I fled to San Francisco where I knew I would find friends to rescue me and perhaps help me start a new life. Refusing to give me any alcohol, they cruelly took me to a detox on Howard Street and asked the counselor to kindly take care of me.

I left the detox after a couple of hours and wandered the alleys off Market Street searching for a drink. Befriended by a couple of San Francisco's professional homeless, I eagerly swallowed some of their Thunderbird and followed them "home"—a collection of cardboard boxes under the freeway.

Pulling my jacket closer about me I watched the darkest, coldest hour of the morning arrive, and heard the rumble of traffic as the city began to awake. A motorcycle cop shifted the focus of my nightmare. Using his baton on the soles of my feet, he reminded me that I had no right to any space in any part of the city.

The same counselor who had tried to persuade me to stay allowed me back into the detox. Mickey told me that everything would be okay. "Stick it out," she said, "and things will get better."

Her words of encouragement fell on deaf ears as she found me a bed and thoughtfully removed my only valuable, a wrist watch.

Curled up as though in my mother's womb, I came to on the second day after numerous fitful awakenings. The atmosphere reminded me of the familiar confines of the Marin County Jail—the hideous din of men trying to reconcile their todays with their tomorrows. Dare I ask someone what would happen to me now? What was required of me? Or would I simply let authority direct me where it would?

Mickey told me that I could stay five days. "Then what?" I asked, anticipating a response that would force me back under the Harrison Street on-ramp. Embarrassed and shamed, but forced into a rare moment of honesty, I told her about my homelessness and the sheriff's arrest warrant. My counselor wrote something on a piece of paper and then looked up, smiling as though I had paid her a compliment. "You're in the right place, Peter. Welcome! Let me see what I can do." In a space of five heartbeats my spirits soared. I had been granted a reprieve, from what I knew not, but the seed of hope had been planted. A week later Mickey placed me in a twenty-eight day program in Redwood City, a mandatory requirement before admittance to a halfway house. Before I left the detox, she allowed me one telephone call to let my wife know where I was and to talk to my children.

"Hi, Dad, where are you?" A simple question, but one I didn't know how to answer.

"I'm in the city, sweetheart. I've a lot of things to do. I won't be able to see you for some time."

"How long will that be, Dad?" I could hear her talking to her four-year-old sister.

"It's Dad; he's in San Francisco. No you can't see him— not for some time."

I pictured them at home waiting for me, just as they had always waited for me—and had always been disappointed. I started to cry. I could hear her quick breathing as she waited for me to say something.

"Okay Dad, maybe you could write or something," she said. I thought I heard a dull flatness in her voice.

"Okay, Lovey," I managed to say, choking back the sobs, "I'll write soon."

She hung up leaving me fraught with anxiety and worthless with shame.

John and Kitty McD. managed the twenty-eight day program. I liked them immediately, and put my entire trust in them. "Apart from not appearing in court, what else are you hiding from us, Peter?" John's question caught me off guard and rekindled my fear of the law. I thought that if I kept quiet about it, the sheriff would eventually drop the charges.

"Nothing," I said in a humbled voice. "Do I have to do something about it?"

John looked pityingly at me just as the captain of my first ship had done when I stepped on board.

"Yep!" he said with finality. "You can't start a sober life with a record. I'll make arrangements with the court, and we'll go and take care of it."

The following week, I stood in the courtroom with a public defender and twenty or so prisoners in orange jumpsuits. I became aware of a feeling of composure—of doing something right at last, and I knew that I was in good hands.

"Three years' probation, confinement to a halfway house for two years, and weekly attendances at meetings of Alcoholics Anonymous."

With those words I began a fractious honeymoon with my newfound, sober life.

As I settled into my new life at the halfway house, my days became more peaceful, my chronic anxiety less intrusive. The children fitted into a part of my soul I had made especially for them. Not perfect, but still part of me. I still yearned to be free again, but patience had become one of the rewards of sobriety. The urge to drink no longer plagued me. The seed had been deeply sown and it was now up to me to keep it nourished. Could I do it or would I fail again like I had so many times before?

It is twenty-six years ago almost to the day that I tottered into that San Francisco detox helpless and hopeless—but all at once, no longer homeless. It was there that I came to know the real meaning of true love—one drunk looking after another drunk. It was there that I learned that if I took certain simple steps, my life would improve in ways that I could not then envisage. I visit my family in England regularly and a loving understanding is our bond, laughter our antidote to past sadness. My two American daughters live close by and we are once again a family.

These promises have become my reality.

I take note of a curious characteristic about the manner in which sobriety subtly makes itself manifest in my spirit. It is as though I have been given the chance to relive part of my life again. Only in retrospect does each year become gentler than the year before and the change is as inconspicuous as the beating of my heart.

Peter Wright

With a Little Help from My Friends

Spirituality is not about how far up the mountain we get but how many we take with us.

Earnie Larsen

When the day finally came that I realized I was truly an alcoholic I still had a home, clothes, a business, money in the bank and all the other things that at first led me to believe that I could not possibly be "one of those alcoholics." I made the phone call.

Several months earlier I had attended AA meetings for a few weeks but didn't continue. By abstaining for thirty days I felt I had proven my point to family and friends, but this time I had been drinking daily, almost around the clock, and was in bad physical, mental and spiritual shape. A local judge had even decided it was best that I not drive an automobile for six months.

I had been chased "in hot pursuit" by a deputy sheriff. When I finally stopped I was on my own property so being the sane, sober person that I was, I tried arresting him rather than he arresting me. He was, after all, trespassing on private property. I am anything but a violent person but my first few swings were good ones. He quickly called for help and when his fellow officers arrived they let me have it. I was promptly taken to jail and booked—but not held—because I was an upstanding member of the community. When the court date arrived it was arranged that I meet with the judge in his chambers. He was a fellow Kiwanian and had partied hearty with me on several occasions. At this informal meeting he laid the cards on the table.

"Bob, you have to plead guilty to at least one of these charges." When asked what each entailed he replied, "Let's overlook the chase, not stopping for a police officer and resisting arrest, but you must plead guilty to assault and battery of an officer, or the driving while intoxicated (DWI) charge."

The assault and battery charge would mean automatic jail time. The sentence for the DWI would mean six months' probation, during which my license would be suspended and I would report weekly to a probation officer. It goes without saying which I chose!

With my license suspended I immediately did what any normal person would do. I called a horse dealer and bought two horses. I had two children so it would only make sense to have two horses, even though they were too young to ride. For a time I rode the larger of the horses every night to my not-so-nice hangouts. Many mornings I woke up in my own bed, the horse out back and no recollection of how I (we) had gotten home. Many years later at a Twelve-Step Spiritual Retreat, a newcomer told us about a bar her husband had owned years earlier and this young man who would arrive drunk on a horse. During group she mused, "I wonder what ever happened to that guy? All of a sudden he stopped coming." I took the opportunity to properly introduce myself, to the amusement of the rest of the group.

I kept hearing "Get a sponsor, get a sponsor," which I finally did. He was a strong-willed individual, took no crap, would often tell me "You can't bullshit a bullshitter" when I would have excuses for this or that. Sometimes I dreaded seeing him, fearing more questions, instructions or suggestions. Annoying as he often was he kept me in line when I needed it most. My next sponsor remained my sponsor for several years. Although it was suggested we have sponsors of the same gender, I had gotten to know this lady pretty well at meetings and always liked what she had to say. When I asked her to sponsor me she agreed and we went from there. She shot straight from the hip, called a spade a spade, and said it like it was. Yet, she was one of the kindest, most empathetic individuals I had ever encountered. I knew I could tell her anything knowing it would be held in confidence. I also knew that if I didn't follow her suggestions she would respect my decision and move on. The longer I stayed sober the less I would confer with her and the less she would give advice. I guess having her shoulder to lean on helped renew my self-confidence and self-worth enough to make some decisions by myself. She never judged. Often we didn't agree, but she never judged. She was, and still is, a fine lady.

My divorce had definitely been a "booze-induced" split and as I grew in sobriety so did my relationship with my ex-wife. While my license was suspended, I sometimes relied on her for transportation to AA meetings. This time around we became friends and eventually best friends. We developed a much stronger and healthier relationship than ever before, remarrying a couple of years into my sobriety. We chose the same date as our first wedding, May 14. For our twenty-fifth anniversary our children had a surprise party for us and the invitations read "25 years with a sabbatical," which I will never forget. Now, after thirty years of sobriety I can truthfully say she is still my best friend. I am not saying stuff never comes up. It does, but now we work through it sensibly, quickly and hopefully calmly. Did I mention she holds a black belt in Al-Anon?

Sobriety is not something one attains just by putting the cork in the bottle. It is suggested that our emotional growth stopped the day we started drinking and as we acquire more and more sobriety we "catch up." I am often asked why I still attend meetings after this many years of sobriety. The answer: my presence might help the new-comer. Also I often hear opinions I hadn't thought about in a long time and they hit home with me. Meetings keep my thinking straight, and most important, keep me away from a drink. I know that I am addicted to alcohol and am just one drink away from a drunk, and drunkenness is something I never want to experience again. For me, staying sober is paramount in my life. Without my sobriety and spirituality I am nothing.

There is a bond that develops among sober alcoholics that cannot be described and I am eternally grateful for all the people who continue to help me live a happy and productive life. I am never alone and no problem is too big or too small for the loving heart and steady hand of AA.

Rev. Bob Lew

Dancing with the Elephant

We don't see things as they are; we see them as we are.

Anaïs Nin

Loud, pulsating music filled the high school gym for our last senior dance just days before graduation. The smell of perfume and hairspray mixed with sweat and cologne as my girlfriends and I waited with nervous anticipation for the cute boys from the soccer team to ask us to dance.

We had practiced the latest dance steps for so many hours that we paired off onto the dance floor like one body. As my partner spun me around I laughed, feeling silly and losing myself in the moment. It felt wonderful but uncomfortable at the same time.

Suddenly, above the noise of the band, my best friend's voice brought me back to reality. "Your father's here!" she said urgently, pointing to a large figure in the doorway silhouetted by the bright lights of the corridor. The head turned back and forth, searching.

I quickly ducked down into the crowd and made my way to a dark corner behind the stage next to the powerful speakers. My heart was pounding from anxiety and fear, not from the beat of the drummer. *If he comes in everyone will see him—they'll know.*

I frantically rubbed my lipstick off with the back of my hand and rushed toward the doorway where the imposing figure scanning the crowd still stood. As I made my

way through flailing arms and stomping feet I said good-
bye, not stopping to answer the questions that flew into
the air—"Why is he here so early?" "Do you have to leave
now?" "Where are you going? The dance isn't over 'til
eleven."

"Hi, Daddy! I'm ready to go," I said, trying to sound
nonchalant and happy to see him. I gently guided him
away from the doorway and down the corridor to avoid
the inevitable humiliation I would have felt if he had set
foot on the dance floor or spoken to someone. The smell
of his breath, his slurred words and the confusion in his
eyes would be a dead giveaway—*they'd know.*

In September I spent the ride to college remembering
the friendships that had grown over the last four years. I
always tried to focus on the good and forget the bad. I
recalled the time spent at friends' homes, watching mothers and fathers, sisters and brothers laughing and eating
together as a family. They could never understand how
lucky they were to have their father sitting at the dinner
table passing the potatoes, not beers to his buddies at the
bar. When their dads went to the store at eleven o'clock in
the morning, they didn't stagger in hours later carrying
sour milk.

Moving into the dorm went smoothly—no arguments,
no accidents. My mother, father and sister set up my
room to be comfortable, my new home. After an exhausting day of emptying suitcases and boxes, my family left
and I lay on the dumpy dorm mattress and looked around
the room. Roommate asleep, nice view of the moon from
our window—just like my room at home. It even had that
special touch—loud snoring accompanied by the smell of
stale beer and cigarettes.

This was my fresh start, a new life.

My classes went well until I found myself sitting in a
lecture hall hearing about the latest clinical techniques for
dealing with alcoholics. I already knew how to deal with
them and didn't want to spend another day, let alone the

rest of a lifetime, dealing with those people.

There's always an excuse, always a fight, always a scene. Pouring their booze down the sink doesn't help. Forget that family vacation at the beach because promises are made to be broken. And there's no point in saying a word as your mother wakes you up in the middle of the night. You don't complain while standing on the dark street corner in your pajamas and winter coat watching and waiting for your uncle's blue Chevy to come into sight. But you pray with all you're worth that no one you know will drive by and see you. You're on the run again, hiding your secret like you hide your face from the head-lights of the approaching Chevy.

The other college freshmen talked about their reasons for enrolling in the class. They wanted to understand the causes, the prevention, the treatment plans for alcoholic clients. They strived to be professionals in the substance abuse field. They wanted to learn more about AA.

Daddy, maybe you should go.

"Hey, I'd go to AA if I was an alcoholic, but you see, I'm not an alcoholic."

Okay, Daddy—whatever you say.

As the discussion continued, someone mentions "Al-Anon" and it caught my attention. That was a new one on me, a program for spouses and families of alcoholics. No harm in checking it out—for clinical research reasons. *No one will have to know what I left behind.*

Because college was three hours from home, not one face at the meeting looked familiar, but they all looked hopeful. As I looked for a seat way in the back I began having second thoughts. *Maybe this wasn't such a good idea; I can leave now with my secret still intact.*

Someone touched my arm. "Please join us."

As this woman swept her arm across the room, the faces blended into one another, looked at me and smiled. I didn't know what to do. I didn't know if I belonged there. I felt their eyes searching my face, looking for clues as to what was in my head, trying to read my mind, uncover my secrets, my memory, the essence of who I am.

In a single moment, one of true clarity, as I tried desperately to come up with an excuse for leaving, the woman simply said, "It's okay—we know."

Patricia Holdsworth

Finding the Healing Moments

*Some people come into our lives and quickly go.
Some stay for a while and leave footprints on our
heart and we are never, ever the same.*

Anonymous

One of the biggest challenges against the war on alcohol
and drug abuse is always fought on the field of prevention.
Do all of the efforts to reduce addiction and the pain for
many families really help? Year after year we continue
with prevention efforts, but there is always more to do.

Sometimes you never know if your efforts make a difference. Sometimes you wonder if anyone is listening.
However, once in a while you get a sign that someone
was listening and that your efforts are appreciated.

Many years ago as a director of an alcohol and drug
abuse treatment program for the U.S. Army, I remember
all of our efforts at prevention as well as treatment. As
part of our prevention efforts we spoke to many groups of
people and especially to students in the local schools.
Teachers would call us and ask if we had anyone who
could come to the school and present information about
alcohol and drug abuse as well as interact with the students. Rather than sending just one person to present I
would usually send a team of three or four people to not
only talk about alcohol and drug information, but also to
share their stories when appropriate.

One particular request came from a local junior high
school. For some reason I decided to go with the team

that morning and to help with the presentation. We had a group of students who were seventh- and eighth-graders for about an hour and a half. When the presentations were over, I asked the teachers if they would help to evaluate what the students got from the time we shared together. However, my request was a little different from the typical feedback. I wanted the teachers to wait for two weeks and then ask the students who attended to write on one side of a piece of paper what they liked about that morning's presentation and on the other side of the paper what they didn't like.

For a while I forgot about the students' evaluations. I was getting out of the military at the time and I was busy with out-processing, preparing the program for a new director and getting ready to move. Like many others at the time, I was also soul searching over the Vietnam War.

The day before I was discharged a package arrived from the junior high school. The students sent me their evaluations complete with a designed cover and a letter. All of their comments were on sheets of white paper except one. Their comments were overwhelmingly positive as they expressed their appreciation for answering their questions and how honest the presenters were about their lives. Most of the papers had very similar themes. However, in the middle of all of these white papers there was one blue sheet of paper. It attracted my attention not only for the color, but also because of what the student wrote and how the student wrote it. Some of it was written in print, some of it in script, and the further down the page you read the larger the size of the writing as if the author was trying to find a way to show his enthusiasm beyond using mere words.

On the following page is a copy of the actual blue sheet of paper.

Read. Read Read Read

ПOTE.

I told my mom about you speakers
I told her about the things
it could do My Mom is
an Alcoholic I convinced her
into going to the State Hospital
she is going I THANK YOU
VERY MUCH FOR COMING
TO OUR SCHOOl.

Read

This paper was sent to me in 1976. The original paper is in my office today. I do not know who sent me this paper. I do not know where this seventh- or eighth-grader is today, but I do know that I was in the right place at the right time. I know that I made the difference in the lives of two people that morning and that the healing moment was created for both of them. I know that the healing process began that morning for that student and that the healing process also began for me.

For those of you who often wonder if your efforts make a difference, I hope that you too get an old blue sheet of paper.

Robert J. Ackerman, Ph.D.

Charlie

Your friends love you anyway.

Dave Barry

Twenty-five years ago, at the age of thirty-one, I had a Ph.D. in psychology, a college teaching position in a very nice, small town in the frigid upper midwest and two daughters under the age of ten. I had been divorced for three years and had been drinking heavily on and off for fourteen years. I had grown up in an alcoholic family in the San Francisco Bay area and had learned early on to cover up the embarrassment by excelling in school and acting as if everything was just fine.

As I descended into my own personal hell of more drinking, more hiding out and more loneliness, my attempts to cover it all up with achievement became less and less effective. My shame and fear of being "found out" were so compelling that when I overheard a colleague commenting that he thought another colleague would never be able to change a bad habit that he had, I immediately applied it to myself. I was doomed to spiral down and down and down until there was nothing left of me. There was no way out.

In one desperate, last-ditch effort to break through the "shame barrier," I went to my father in the Bay Area, and with my voice shaking and tentative, said, "Dad, I think you're an alcoholic, and I think I am, too." But his shame and fear of rejection were even greater than mine. His advice, which I now know was out of misdirected love and concern, was, "I'm not an alcoholic, and neither are you. And don't go to AA. It will ruin your career."

With my tail between my legs, I returned to that small midwestern town, resigned to a life of failure and despair. I continued presenting the community seminars that I had committed to do, and during one of my presentations I asked the participants to break up into discussion groups. As I walked around the room facilitating the conversations, one person stood out among the hundred or so participants. I wasn't even sure why, except that he seemed so comfortable talking about what to me were fairly personal things. He was, paradoxically, both humble and the "star" of the breakout groups.

I caught his eye at the end of the seminar, chatted briefly, got his name and went home. Something drew me to him. I called him up and invited him to lunch. It turned out that he was not only a plumber, but also a recovering alcoholic. My head was so filled with theories and data and research and concepts from my Ph.D. training and subsequent college teaching, that I was able to think myself into one blind alley after another. Sitting across from this man and listening to his life story, his heartaches with his children and his struggles with his sobriety, cut through all those highly educated defenses.

It was like a fresh breeze blowing through an otherwise stagnating soul.

This went on for over a year, until I could endure it no longer. I knew I needed help. But the intensity of the battle between the healthy part of me that knew I needed help, and the part of me that had learned to survive for so long by hiding out, was exquisite. It was so powerful, in fact, that I was literally shaking with fear when I picked up the phone to call this man and ask him to help me. As I stared at the phone, I realized that not once in one-and-a-half years did he ever say that he suspected I had a problem, that he thought I might want to take a look at my drinking, that he thought I needed help. It was at that instant that I knew it was safe. I grabbed the phone, punched in the numbers, heard his voice at the other end, and then I said, "Charlie, I think I'm an alcoholic. I think I need to go to a meeting. But I'm so terrified of failure and rejection that the thought of going to a meeting alone is more than I can imagine. Will you take me to a meeting?"

I could feel a comforting, accepting smile beaming out of the telephone. Through the fog of my terror and shame, I heard him say, with nearly infinite warmth, "I've been waiting a year and a half for you. Of course, I'd love to take you. It would be an honor."

John C. Friel, Ph.D.

3

A SENSE OF
SPIRITUALITY

*Religion is for those individuals trying to
avoid going to hell.
Spirituality is for those of us who have been
there.*

United Methodist Church bulletin

My Little Son Showed Me the Way

Love is the only thing stronger than whatever is wrong with us.

Earnie Larsen

Like every other junkie during my many using years, I mastered the skill of killing my feelings. I didn't want them, didn't like them, didn't tolerate them and ran from them every way I could.

Twelve years of recovery has taught me another road. I have learned to recover. I must be honest with how I feel with others and myself. Like a million other folks in recovery I am a long way from perfect on this score.

Last week I was at the breakfast table with my four-year-old son, Pete. Pete trusts me and I love him with every fiber of my being. But that morning I was not on my game. He did something and I snapped at him, hard. I told him to stop being bad, sit up straight and be a good boy.

The look in his eyes about killed me. I had betrayed him in a way he never thought possible. In a second he ran from the table and hid in his room.

Guilt is one of the feelings I have always had the worst time with. I'm good at guilt. Guilt ate my lunch most of my life. But I'm learning. I'm getting better. Recovery works if you work it.

I went to Pete's room, took his hands in mine and told him how sorry I was. I told him Daddy sometimes doesn't feel just right and makes mistakes. I told him Daddy was probably going to be crying in a minute but that was okay because tears sometimes happen when you feel something as deeply as I did.

Pete turned the table on who was holding whose hands. He held mine and said, "Daddy, I'm feeling something deep." I asked him what it was. He said he didn't know the name of the feeling. But he crawled up inside my arms and put his face right up against mine. He was crying too. We stayed like that a long time.

I've met God a lot of times in recovery. I've had some pretty powerful spiritual experiences early in recovery but none more powerful than that moment with my son. Pete lives in my deepest core and God comes riding right into it through the beauty of my little boy.

Anonymous as told to Earnie Larsen

The Little Yellow Room
My Higher Power Built

It was high counsel that I once heard given to a young person, "Always do what you are afraid to do."

Ralph Waldo Emerson

For a long time, I thought the little yellow room was a recurring dream. In the dream, I entered a tunnel and scrambled forward on my hands and knees, like a child climbing up a slide. At the end of the tunnel was a small square opening, about the size of a doggie-door, big enough for only my child-sized body to fit through. Once I made it through that opening, there was always a sense of relief. I had made it, once again, to my little yellow room.

The room was the size of a small powder room, painted a pale yellow the color of cool sunlight on an early summer morning before anyone else is awake. There were no fixtures or furniture, but there was a ledge that I always climbed to sit upon. Beside the ledge, there was a window with pretty ruffled curtains blowing in the breeze.

Throughout my childhood and into my adult years, I remembered these recurring "dreams," and sometimes wondered what they meant. They seemed more real to me than any of my other dreams, and other than a few repeated "flying" dreams, which differed from one another, they were the only dreams my mind returned to time and time again. The little yellow room dreams were always the same, and the room never varied. I always sat beside the window and waited in peace.

The year my daughter turned five, I started having flashbacks about what happened on the other side of the small square door to my little yellow room. I learned that year that survivors of childhood sexual abuse often remember their abuse when their children reach the age they were when the abuse started. I also learned the reason behind my lifelong struggle with depression and compulsive eating. My mind had been at war with these memories for two decades. I learned when physical trauma is too harsh to face, the mind protects itself and finds ways to leave the body behind. I learned that the little yellow room was not a dream, and that psychologists call it "dissociation."

After three years of therapy and the support of a loving and wonderful husband and best friend, I found Overeaters Anonymous, a Twelve-Step program for compulsive overeaters that treats overeating as a physical, emotional and spiritual illness. I attended online meetings and found an e-mail sponsor who would help me work through the steps. I wrote down every bite I ate and practiced "abstinence." Twelve little steps seemed like the quick fix I needed to cure my eating problem.

The first step was easy. I had known I was powerless over food for many years. Growing up in a family of alcoholics and drug addicts, I knew to stay away from those drugs, but I had convinced myself that food was a safe way to numb the pain and stuff the memories. The second step said I had come to believe that a power higher than myself could restore me to sanity. I was less sure about this step, but I certainly hoped there was! I was thrilled. The Twelve Steps were a breeze. I'd be down from a size 18 to an 8 in no time.

Step Three, however, brought me to a sudden halt. Step Three said I was to make a decision to turn my life and my will over to God as I understood him. I couldn't do it. I couldn't even say the words. Unlike with the second step, I didn't even hope for it.

I thought about the years of Sunday school, the little girl who showed up every week but was afraid to speak. Why hadn't anyone noticed? I thought about the church I belonged to when I first remembered the abuse, the grown woman who was moved to tears nearly every week and who once even had to leave the chapel mid-sermon to compose herself. Why hadn't anyone reached out to comfort me? I thought about the horrors that went on behind that little square door. Why had God allowed that to happen to me?

I was stuck. I knew if I were to progress in the steps, I would have to examine my relationship with God. Step Three said to turn my life and will over to God as I under-stood him. I didn't know what I understood. I only knew the sense of panic I felt when I started to think about a relationship with God. My heart raced. My chest hurt. The abuse and the loneliness I felt afterward taught me not to trust anyone, not even God. How could I turn my life and will over if I couldn't trust? I turned, as I often do, to the pages of my journal.

What is my relationship with God? Guarded, like with everyone else. Stand behind the yellow line, please. Call me on the phone, don't talk to me face-to-face. Guarded. I am afraid. Afraid God will hurt me, afraid he will not love me. If I open myself to him, I am making myself vulnerable to pain again. I handled pain by eating when I was a child. Also, I hid in that little yellow room.

The next words seemed to come through me, as if someone else were guiding my hand. I wrote quickly, without questioning.

I hid in that little yellow room, and I know now that this room was built by God. So, he is a carpenter after all. God, you built me that room? Thank you. That was a safe place for me to wait.

I was stunned. For twenty years, I thought that little

yellow room was a dream. Then, for awhile, I thought it was some abstract psychological phenomenon, a defense mechanism that happened automatically to protect my psyche from the horrors of abuse. Now, I believe that room was built lovingly for me by my Higher Power, as if he had come down from heaven with his hammer, nails, some Sheetrock, and a bucket of pale yellow paint that looked and felt to me like cool, early morning sunshine on a summer morning before anyone else was awake.

Shannon

Hope

I spent each day, just searching,
For my purpose here in life,
And still I could not seem to find,
A reason to survive.
I struggled through my childhood,
Without a loyal friend,
And every single broken heart,
Just never seemed to mend.
My parents didn't have the time,
To tell me that they cared,
They never came to comfort me,
Those nights when I was scared.
They told me I should toughen up,
Don't cry, and be a man,
And when my life soon fell apart,
They couldn't understand.
I turned to anything I could,
To bury all my pain,
And when my glass fell empty,
I'd fill it up again.
And over the years I drifted through,
Many different towns,
Longing to find something,
To turn my life around.
I spent each night, alone and cold
Hungry and ashamed,
Desperate to find shelter,
From the ugly stares and names.

And as I lay on the concrete steps,
Of a church to get some sleep,
I felt the presence of someone,
Gently kicking at my feet.
And as I opened up my eyes,
A stranger stood and smiled,
I brought something for you to drink,
You've been sleeping quite awhile.
He reached a sturdy hand to me,
And helped me to my feet,
I thanked him for his kindness,
And my heart began to weep.
This stranger gave me so much more,
Than a drink to quench my thirst,
He taught me of compassion,
And the value of self worth.
From that day on, I grew to love,
These concrete steps much more
For one day as I reached the top,
I opened up the door.
I held my tattered hat in hand,
And searched to find a pew,
I heard the voice of someone say,
There's a seat right here for you.
For on that day, my life began
And I soon would understand,
That even though I made mistakes,
I was a worthy man.
This church became my loyal friend,
The home I never knew,
For in this house I found a love,
That always comforts you.

Dedicated to a homeless man who has unknowingly
made a difference.

Lisa J. Schlitt

Healing Tears

If you give what you do not need, it is not giving.

Mother Teresa

It had been almost six months since our daughter Kendall died, at the age of nine, after a five-month battle with a brain stem tumor.

It was a devastating loss, but with two other children to love and nurture there wasn't always the time to slip away and let the tears flow. Still, not being made of stone, it wasn't easy to hide when the grief rushed in and made its presence known.

It was around this time that I became aware that my youngest child, Celeste, was modeling herself after a jester to urge my husband, Paul, and me out of our intermittent times of sadness.

It was not her job to keep us smiling, and I didn't want her to take on the role of "caregiver and keeper of her parents' hearts." She knew, however, that there was a particular smile that she could flash at us, that pushed our emotions to the side and caused us to explode in an unbridled laugh.

Now, this was a welcome change at most times, but there also needs to be a time of tears to cleanse.

Rest assured, Paul and I were doing our best to keep up a good front when the family was together. Yet moments of sadness might overtake us, when it wasn't easy to retreat into the bedroom, the shower, or schedule it for a later slot. These times were relatively sporadic, but to a six-year-old child it must be painful to see your parents grieving.

Celeste came over to me as I sat pondering a memory. Apparently, sadness and loss must've been obvious across my face. "Mommy?" She said. As I looked up to answer her, she flashed that cheesy grin that usually precedes a spontaneous "crack-up." And true to form, it did.

Because I wanted her to know that it wasn't her job to keep us smiling, I asked her to sit on my lap.

I wanted to protect her heart so I guarded my words carefully. "Celeste, Mommy likes it when you make her laugh, and you have a special way of doing that, too." Celeste smiled with approval.

"You know that we all miss Kendall," I continued, "and sometimes when we think of her . . . we will be happy, and sometimes when we think of her . . . it will make us sad that she isn't here with us."

I paused to read her expression. "Sometimes when we're sad we might cry."

Celeste was gazing at me steadily and mirroring my facial gestures in an effort to empathize.

"The thing is, Celeste, that I know it makes you feel sad to see Mommy or Daddy sad, and you want to make us smile, but there is a reason for the tears." She was nodding her head to show her dislike for our tears.

"You know when you fall down and scrape your knee?"

"Yes . . ." Celeste's eyes were large and intense.

"What do we have to do before we put the Band-Aid on?"

"Wash it." She was confident in her answer.

"That's right. When Mommy and Daddy cry, it is like God washing our hearts so that he can put his bandage on us and help us to heal."

Was this really me talking? I felt as if I was receiving an example from God.

Celeste was thinking this over.

"So even though you may not like to see us crying,"

Celeste was shaking her head from side to side as I spoke, "sometimes we need to. Because the tears are actually helping us to heal." I held her face in my hands.

"And even though I love to see your beautiful smile, please don't be upset when you see us having a short moment of tears. Just know that God is helping us to wash our hearts, so that he can heal them."

We concluded our talk with a tight hug and tickle and Celeste bounded down the stairs to resume her play.

"Thank you, God," I prayed, "for not only helping me to explain to Celeste, but for explaining it to me."

Loretta McCann Bjorvik

Free Flight

We must face what we fear; that is the case of the core of the restoration of health.

Max Lerner

For two days now, I had been sharing my work space with a small hawk. He would fly within ten feet of me and rest even closer, watching as I performed my duties.

Somehow, he had become trapped in this large one-story warehouse. My heart ached, because I knew that he would inevitably die if he did not leave the building.

He did not attack me, nor was he afraid of me. He simply could not trust me to help him.

Upon my arrival at work the second day, I continued where I had finished the day before. There I was again, working up in the truss area of the building.

I didn't see the hawk flying around, but my thoughts were on him. Did he get out? Was he lying dead on the floor somewhere?

I continued to work, occasionally looking around for the shadows of wings, as he would swoop near the lighting fixtures.

At first, there was no sight of him. Then I noticed something there, resting on a sprinkler pipe. It was the hawk. He seemed to be sleeping, his head tucked under his wing, not moving a feather.

I wondered if he would still be there when I finished the task at hand. I told myself that I would grab him. Yeah, like I could catch a hawk with my bare hands.

I finished my job, and maneuvered my drivable man-lift under the sleeping bird. Slowly I raised the lift.

Mind you, this is not a quiet machine, with hydraulic pumps operating, ungreased metal joints squeaking, and my heart pounding. Finally, I was at a point where I could reach him.

There was still no movement from the hawk. He must have expended all his energy, and was growing weaker.

Was I close enough not to miss? I was not sure, so I moved even closer to him.

If he started to fly, could I hold on?

Then it happened. I encircled the bird of prey in my hand, and I removed him from the pipe.

As I held the bird gently but firmly in my grasp, fully expecting to be bitten, he awoke, and looked directly in my eyes in disbelief. It was the same look that my co-workers had when they saw me with the bird, for they had also seen his flight skills, the way that he would twist and turn, flying unharmed, missing all the obstacles that a large building had to offer.

As I walked across the building, the bird did nothing more than stare at me in silence. There was no struggle, no clawing, nor pecking from a beak designed to tear flesh, nor the typical high-pitched cry of a hawk.

I exited the door and walked out into the parking lot fearing that if I released him too quickly, the bird might return to where he was once trapped. I removed my one hand, and allowed him to rest in the other.

The bird remained perched on my hand.

I wondered why he had not immediately taken flight. Surely, he had never been held before. The restriction of my grasp must have seemed uncomfortable in comparison to free flight.

Then, with a final twist of his head, I saw in his eyes my own life.

I was like the bird who had known freedom, and then

READER/CUSTOMER CARE SURVEY

REFG

We care about your opinions! Please take a moment to fill out our online Reader Survey at **http://survey.hcibooks.com**.
As a **"THANK YOU"** you will receive a **VALUABLE INSTANT COUPON** towards future book purchases
as well as a **SPECIAL GIFT** available only online! Or, you may mail this card back to us.

(PLEASE PRINT IN ALL CAPS)

First Name _____ MI. _____ Last Name _____

Address _____

State _____ Zip _____ Email _____ City _____

1. Gender
☐ Female   ☐ Male

2. Age
☐ 8 or younger
☐ 9-12   ☐ 13-16
☐ 17-20   ☐ 21-30
☐ 31+

3. Did you receive this book as a gift?
☐ Yes   ☐ No

4. Annual Household Income
☐ under $25,000
☐ $25,000 - $34,999
☐ $35,000 - $49,999
☐ $50,000 - $74,999
☐ over $75,000

5. What are the ages of the children living in your house?
☐ 0 - 14   ☐ 15+

6. Marital Status
☐ Single
☐ Married
☐ Divorced
☐ Widowed

7. How did you find out about the book?
(please choose one)
☐ Recommendation
☐ Store Display
☐ Online
☐ Catalog/Mailing
☐ Interview/Review

8. Where do you usually buy books?
(please choose one)
☐ Bookstore
☐ Online
☐ Book Club/Mail Order
☐ Price Club (Sam's Club, Costco's, etc.)
☐ Retail Store (Target, Wal-Mart, etc.)

9. What subject do you enjoy reading about the most?
(please choose one)
☐ Parenting/Family
☐ Relationships
☐ Recovery/Addictions
☐ Health/Nutrition

☐ Christianity
☐ Spirituality/Inspiration
☐ Business Self-help
☐ Women's Issues
☐ Sports

10. What attracts you most to a book?
(please choose one)
☐ Title
☐ Cover Design
☐ Author
☐ Content

TAPE IN MIDDLE; DO NOT STAPLE

**NO POSTAGE
NECESSARY
IF MAILED
IN THE
UNITED STATES**

BUSINESS REPLY MAIL
FIRST-CLASS MAIL   PERMIT NO 45   DEERFIELD BEACH, FL

POSTAGE WILL BE PAID BY ADDRESSEE

Chicken Soup for the Soul®
3201 SW 15th Street
Deerfield Beach FL 33442-9875

FOLD HERE

Comments

Do you have your own Chicken Soup story
that you would like to send us?
Please submit at: **www.chickensoup.com**

became isolated by his own mistakes.

The bird, and I, were able to negotiate the immediate dangers—for awhile. But did he know that death was in his future? Was he so trapped that he almost welcomed it? Did he, too, know each and every one of the scars from his misadventures?

Did he know that help was so close to him? Maybe he sensed it, but he did not have the faith, or trust, to accept it. Only after depleting his resources, only after he had collapsed with exhaustion, could he find a way out—not on his own, but with the help of a stranger's gentle hands.

I would have helped him days earlier, if he had only trusted me.

The bird and I were able to find our way back to freedom, which God had intended for both of us.

When you find yourself trapped, there is only one way out. That way is your trust in a Higher Power. You do not have to wear yourself out until you are near death. Look around. He may reveal himself to you also, just as he revealed himself to me, when I became willing to be carried in loving hands.

David Mead

Whispers of an Angel

Character, the willingness to accept responsibility for one's own life, is the source from which self-respect springs.

Joan Didion

It was with unshakeable confidence that I began a reconciliation with myself, only to come home and quickly begin drinking again. I was in full-blown relapse, broken, hating myself and what I had become. I hated that I was smart, intelligent, had good sense and was educated about the disease, yet no knowledge was enough, no friend supportive enough, no husband patient enough, no children scared enough to make me stop.

From my very first drink at seventeen I couldn't handle it well, but I did it anyway. I went on to get married, have children and a job, all the while I drank socially. Usually too many and usually wishing I had stopped at two. That was never an option for me; once I started, I always craved more and after the first couple, who cares if it's two or twenty. I still managed to moderate, after all I was a mom, a wife, active in my church, and taught Continuing Christian Development (CCD) to the high school kids. I drank for the same reasons anyone would: to relax, have fun, to take the edge off my nerves. Never did I want to be addicted and have a problem with it. I did quit teaching CCD and lectoring at Masses. I had become a hypocrite, preaching one thing and living another. Telling kids to turn to God, when I would turn to wine—I couldn't live with that anymore. So instead of quitting the wine, I quit my service work.

It took a night in hell for myself and everyone else at a party to end the years of drinking. This time I entered treatment able to hold my head up and say I was an alcoholic. I went to group meetings and shared my story. I was asked to write my Step One of the Twelve-Step recovery program. It took me five days and was eight pages long. I could look you straight in the eye and tell you all about my drinking and history, but I couldn't tell you about Julianna. That is what cracked the case. It became obvious to everyone where my pain lay and the price I paid for grieving.

On December 18, 1995, I gave birth to my fourth child, Julianna Maria. She started life at less than four pounds, with three holes in her heart. Within a few weeks she had gained enough weight to allow her to come home, but she didn't thrive. She outgrew two of her heart defects, but developed hearing loss, multiple seizure disorders and acute respiratory distress syndrome. As Julianna celebrated her first birthday she was diagnosed with Lennox-Gaustaut Syndrome, a form of epilepsy and chromosomes deletion. A chromosomes deletion is just what it sounds like, part of a chromosome(s) has been deleted. Julianna's was chromosome #1. A deletion can occur on any chromosome, at any band, and can be large or small. What a deletion causes depends on how big a piece is missing and what genes are missing in the section where the deletion occurred. Prognosis: not very good.

Julianna had early intervention services in place at six weeks old. She had an infant teacher, physical, occupational and speech therapy once a week. We had an audiologist to check her hearing aids periodically and she rode around in a fancy light pink wheelchair. Through all of this, she was a peaceful and content child, aware of us, and who we were to her. She had started to smile and make the sound, "Ma." I remember little chuckles from time to time. Those were precious moments. She was more accepting of her little life than I was and she taught our family to take each day at a time.

The night before she died we had been told that she was a very sick little girl and they didn't expect her to make it. I knew every inch of her body, every hair on her head and every little grunt or hum she made. And I knew that the doctor was right and that the ventilator was not God. We went to a room nearby and I was terrified, not sure how I would ever live without her or what would happen to us without her. When the time was right I held her wrapped in a pink blanket and they took the vent out. She took two tiny breaths and was gone, dying peacefully and with dignity in my arms on February 18, 1999.

I said good-bye my way: I planned the funeral my way and I wrote the eulogy and read it my way—in the first person—from my heart. And then came the debilitating despair and depression and I began a downward spiral into numbness. The sweet release of alcohol never lasted long because drinking gave me an avenue to grieve and my grieving gave me an avenue to drink, the perfect cycle for doom.

I journaled every morning and the entries screamed out in agony, always seeking forgiveness for my lack of faith, for my selfish desire to make the pain go away, for my weakness when I knew I was hurting my family, for my cowardice at not trying faith on for size. My hangovers were equal to how bad my heart was hurting. No way was faith, hope and love going to make this broken heart go away and God didn't seem to be in a hurry to rescue me. And I needed Him to rescue me—before five o'clock or I would be pouring that glass of wine.

Every day for almost eighteen months I drank and grieved and slept, rarely eating a bite, withering away to 92 pounds with not a lot of hope that I would ever get well, physically, emotionally or spiritually. My husband, Don, threw himself into his job and acted like this wasn't happening. He ignored my pitiful cries and angry outbursts at his lack of sympathy and understanding. He had a new job that consoled him and he left me at home to raise three kids, salvage my marriage without his help and find a way to maintain my alcohol dependency. Little did I know under these circumstances, that he was doing exactly the right thing. He wasn't buying into my self-pity or my drinking and he would wait me out. Wait me out for a day that I would give up the good fight, the fight to maintain my comfort zone of depression and numbness.

My alcohol abuse had catapulted me into the later stages of alcoholism and Julianna's death broke my heart, leaving me little desire to remain in this world. I could say, "I am an alcoholic," but if anyone asked me about depression or grief, I couldn't talk about it. I returned to my first step and I was zinging right along until on the fifth day I got to the question: How has your drinking affected your relationships with your immediate family? The same gut-wrenching pain of Julianna's passing came over me like an earthquake. I didn't know the answer! I couldn't answer it! I didn't remember anything. I wouldn't know the answer until I returned home to face whatever damage I had inflicted on my husband and my children.

How did I affect my children? I wasn't there for them in their grief. What if they are hurt emotionally from the stress? What's left? Is it too late? What will I do? How can I repair the damage? It was in this moment of recognition and acceptance that my recovery truly began. It meant going home and facing the very people I hurt and finding a way to forgive myself and to ask for forgiveness. I also had to find a way to turn my back on alcohol and never again see it as an escape, a friend, a reward, a celebration, a vacation. I had to fight for my own life, the life that I counted as unworthy. All the unconditional love that I had given to Julianna I now had to give to me. It is hard to love difficult people; how much harder it is when we become the most difficult of all.

And then, surrender. This was the moment I had always dreaded, the minute that I knew I could never drink again and nothing would bring Julianna back. I was going to have to find a new way to live, to survive my despair, to regain my soul and I had to find a way to be happy or at least content in this world. I had to find a way to talk to God. I had to find a way to believe that there was still something worth living for in this world, something maybe not equal to loving Julianna, but at least good and rich with purpose.

One of my most profound memories of my early recovery are words I spoke out loud, hoping God would hear.

"God do you know how hard it is for me to love you now? Do you know how hurt I am? Do you know that even though I don't understand why me—why I am an alcoholic, why on earth I had to lose my child, why?— why?—why?—I don't need to know the answers to those questions anymore. In spite of every trial and cross that I carried, either by my own free will or by your command, even though my soul cries constantly for release, even though I will always feel this way—I still love you, God. Even though I wanted to blame you and hate you, I love you anyway."

I cried and cried, praying for God to be there, for relief from my hopelessness and despair. This time it came. A small flicker of faith, a bit of courage and tons of honesty, acceptance and surrender became the foundation of my recovery. With my heart open and my tiny angel tugging on his sleeve whispering, "Hey, can you help my mommy? I think she's lost." I had just enough courage to trust him for one day.

Julie Orlando

Looking for a Sign

I experienced an overwhelming passion to become an American Sign Language interpreter long before laws were passed to assure communication access to deaf people. In other words, I volunteered my interpreting services often. Sometimes, I'd work for a hug or a home-cooked dinner.

It took me nearly ten years to develop fluency and skill as an interpreter. The work was mentally and physically challenging. It was also incredibly rewarding when the thoughts and feelings of a hearing person went through my hands and actually registered understanding in the eyes of a deaf consumer. It was equally exciting to be the channel through which hearing people discovered the intelligence, talents, humor and value of individuals within the deaf community. It was truly fulfilling work.

Then it happened.

It started out like any normal Saturday morning. We were driving to a downtown restaurant to treat ourselves to brunch. My husband, Loui, was driving and I was window-shopping from the passenger seat. "Mountain of Love" was playing loudly on the radio and I was dancing in my seat as I celebrated the meaning of this song as it applied to our wonderful relationship.

Then BAM! I felt a force that thrust my head away from my body. I thought in that second, something really terrible is happening to us. I wasn't sure what. I fought the force to reclaim my head and turn to see Loui, perhaps for the last time. He did the same. As our car continued to spin in what seemed like slow motion, we locked eyes and without a word said it all—including good-bye.

When the car finally came to a stop, a crowd of people peered into our car window. We ignored them and embraced each other in a hug that I was determined to last forever. When we finally got out of the car, I realized what had happened. A young man had been on his cell phone and had forgotten he was driving. He sped through a red light and smashed right into our lives.

I felt pain in my neck and back immediately, but felt sure I was fine. When I was not able to fill out the police report, I just assumed it was a result of the shock from the accident. However, as time went on, I realized I had difficulty remembering things. I was scheduled to interpret a very simple assignment at a television station and found I could not get the ideas from my head to my hands. I could not find the signs.

The doctor said my brain had been bruised in the accident. This could be temporary, but may be permanent. Only time would tell. I stopped interpreting and waited for time to give me the answer.

I was a person who was defined by what I did. My work was my reason for being. I was faced with the question— If you take away what I do ... who am I? It was a long and trying time searching for the answer, looking for a sign.

Every day, I would secretly attempt to interpret to see if the spell was broken. I'd listen to the radio, or watch a few minutes of television and try to find my hard-earned skills—and the meaning of my existence. Each time, I was unable to retrieve the ideas from my brain, to express through the signs that now seemed forever lost to me.

I was also struggling with simple life tasks. I would begin to express an idea only to come to mid-sentence and lose the end of the thought. I would enter a room and not remember why I was there.

While it was one of the most difficult times in my life, it

was the impetus for me to discover I am much more than what I do. I began attending a church for spiritual support. I went to a church that provided an interpreter. There were several deaf friends who attended so I enjoyed the social contact as well as the spiritual inspiration.

One Sunday, there were about eight deaf people in attendance. The church service began with an upbeat song. However, the chair where the interpreter usually sat on stage was empty. My legs kept urging me to run up there and fill the space. My heart argued with my "bruised brain." Would I be able to do it? As I saw the deaf people's disappointment, I knew I had to try. I walked up the stairs to the stage following the rhythm, not of the music, but of my rapidly beating of my heart.

On stage, the music flooded into my ears. The words came at me like a challenge. I looked out into the large congregation and drew a terrifying and now familiar blank. I was beginning to panic. But as I looked into the receptive eyes of the deaf congregants, I raised my arms and, to my amazement, my hands took flight. It was as if they had a life, or perhaps a voice of their own.

As the sermon began, the words and their beautiful meaning came to and through me. Articulately expressed with the voice in my hands, it all landed lovingly in the hearts and minds of my deaf friends through expectant eyes. In the service of others, I had found and reclaimed my self.

After church, a large burly man approached me. "I'm not overly religious," he said shyly, "but I need to tell you . . . I saw something around you when you were signing. Others saw it too. We don't know what it was, but it was something to behold."

I don't know if a miracle happened that day. I only know that it is through reaching out in service to others that we most often discover the path to our own healing.

Jenna Cassell

Recovery: A Reason as Well as a Road

A man's greatest strength develops at the point where he overcomes his greatest weakness.

Elmer G. Letterman

The huge silver and black bus rolled out of the Los Angeles County Jail and made its way down the 110 Freeway to the courthouse in nearby San Pedro. The chained and shackled inmates used the opportunity to fill their eyes with scenes more interesting than a jail cell and to chat with the person on the other side of their handcuffs.

At 5'3" and fifty-two, I made an unlikely inmate. I was the only former jockey, Eclipse Award winning journalist and successful TV production studio owner aboard this bus. Yet, I belonged. After deciding to stop my psychotropic medication, drinking heavily and undergoing a manic state that had kept me awake for nearly fifty hours, I had hit my girlfriend. Both the state of California and I thought the act inexcusable. It was the sixth day of my incarceration and I was recovering from cold-turkey detox and strep throat. To pass the time, I struck up a conversation with the young man who shared my chains and we talked about the events that had put us there.

My childhood had been as black as the bus. My most vivid memory was of sitting on the steps in our little country house in southwest Virginia listening to my mother scream as she waited for a visiting nurse to come and give her another shot of morphine for the pain from stomach cancer. When she finally died, her mother raised me until her own sudden death six years later. When my father remarried I lived with him where a relative sexually abused me for more than two years.

I graduated from high school at only sixteen. Two months later my father gave me $40 and put me on a train bound for Lexington, Kentucky, where I had found a job at a thoroughbred breeding farm. Within three years I was a successful jockey, living in a downtown Baltimore high-rise. In my first year of racing, I made more money than my father had made in a dozen years working as a rail-road conductor. The rage that boiled inside my heart because of abandonment issues and the sexual abuse fit well on a thoroughbred racing in a pack at 40 mph. Nineteen years, thirteen broken bones and about 1,200 victories later, I retired as a jockey.

During my riding career I nurtured my love of writing and had been published in virtually every major newspa-per east of the Mississippi including the *New York Times* and their *Sunday Magazine*. Retirement led to writing one column a week for the *Dallas Morning News*. When I resigned eight years later, I left with an Eclipse Award for newspaper writing. Next, I convinced a self-made million-aire to invest in a small television production company and signed a personal services contract that allowed me to own 20 percent of the company. Here, my rage manifested itself as ambition and I became a workaholic, writing a documentary that won a second Eclipse Award for televi-sion production. I was nothing if not an over-achiever.

Casualties of my success were a marriage of fourteen years and my sanity. A friend found me unconscious from a suicide attempt after which I was diagnosed as bipolar and made the first of my two stays on a psychiatric ward.

Thoughts of my wife with another man brought back the long-suppressed memories of my sexual abuse. For reasons even two years of weekly sessions with a psychi-atrist never fully revealed, I became determined to live the life of a bisexual. Because of a strong religious background it was a life I couldn't accept, yet it was one I couldn't leave.

Even with medication the bipolar episodes continued. No amount of success mattered, I was miserable. Excited to the point of ecstasy over heading up a successful company one minute, I would walk into my office and burst into tears the next.

I soon found myself in a second mental hospital and the woman I married ten days after my divorce—who looked much like and had the same first name as my first wife—divorced me after six years. Having few alternatives, my partners bought me out and I lived in ritzy Laguna Beach for two years, largely wasting my life. A brief stint back in Texas producing my own television show on horse racing failed, as did an affair with an exotic dancer which I had hoped would return me to heterosexuality.

I came back to California and began living with a woman while still riding a roller coaster of frustration, depression and rage. I decided that seven years of lithium and three years of Paxil was enough. They weren't helping anyway. After a long bout with mania, my rage turned toward my girlfriend, which landed me in the Los Angeles County Jail and a free bus ride.

We reached the San Pedro Court where we were kept in several large holding cells, barren except for a cement seating shelf lining three walls. An older inmate related how he was a teaching elder in his church and was only in jail because he had been fishing with his son and a check of his fishing license by a game warden revealed a twelve-year-old warrant. As soon as he saw a judge he could be released.

Prisoners were escorted to the courtrooms for appearances and one man, in his early thirties, returned to sit on the floor. He began crying. My bus friend talked with the man who said he had just received twenty-five years to life for a third strike petty theft. He would not be allowed conjugal visits from his young wife and he would not see his two young children grow up. My friend began praying with him. The church elder began to preach and my bus friend stood up and started talking about God. Then I did the same. One of our other cellmates, a hefty man, told us how God had kept him alive when a rival drug dealer put a gun in his face and pulled the trigger only to have it misfire.

I pulled the New Testament from my back pocket and handed it to him. He opened it and read from the first chapter of James beginning with, "Count it all joy ..." As I listened, I saw the cell fill up with a blue metallic haze. I looked around and everywhere prisoners were on their knees, using the shelf as an altar or prostrate on the barren floor. All were praying or crying.

I cried as well, first in sorrow for what my life had become, then in shame for all the things I had done and the people I had hurt. Then realizing I had been forgiven, I cried for joy. What felt like a beam of light flowed through me as if I had stuck my finger in a light socket. I was filled with light. Every one in that room, about a dozen, stood, held hands and prayed that Christ would change our lives.

I often wonder if that moment on December 16, 1996, had a similar effect on the rest of my cellmates. I am forever different. In the eight years since, I have not touched alcohol, drugs or psychotropic medication. I found a good church, began holding tent crusades in notorious South Los Angeles and raising funds for an orphanage in Mexico. I quickly found a marketing job then left it for ministry. I traded a San Pedro apartment overlooking the bay to move into a single room at the Los Angeles Dream Center, a former 1,400-room hospital near downtown Los Angeles that had been turned into an outpost of hope.

Sober, celibate and focused, I led a midnight Hollywood outreach to transsexual prostitutes and homeless youth. Many returned to the Dream Center to live and resurrect their lives. While taking Bible courses to become a minister, I met Sandi. Seven months later we were married in the Dream Center's chapel. Today, I am an associate pastor in a small church near Santa Anita Racetrack. I work full-time as the Development Director of the Race Track Chaplaincy of America, which sanctions and oversees forty-eight track chaplains who serve at nearly eighty tracks and training centers.

That day in the holding cell, I received the power to forgive my abusers. My rage was gone, along with any issues regarding gender and abandonment. Was it a miracle? Yes. Did I still have to strive to live a disciplined life? Yes. Am I beyond temptation? No.

Despite the miracle in my life, recovery remains a day-to-day process. It began with the supernatural power to forgive and it continues with a grateful and ever repentant heart. Miracles do happen. Seekers do get healed. Lives can be forever changed. Recovery is not just a road, it is also a reason.

Rev. Ed Donnally

The Richest Man in the World

*The greatest of faults, I should say, is to be con-
scious of none.*

Thomas Carlyle

All meetings begin with songs at the Mission, especially the alumni meetings. At first thought putting
"alumni" and "Mission" in the same sentence seems
weird. What kind of alumni might the Mission have? The
answer is good ones. Blessed ones. Amazing ones.

Last week a family of several generations came back to
the alumni meeting. They filed in right in front of me.
There were several very senior citizens who no doubt
were at least grandparents. Several middle-aged men and
women and four children. One of the children, a lovely
young girl, appeared to be maybe ten or so. A big man of
maybe thirty sat right in front of me. Tattoos crawled
down his arm beneath his rolled-up sleeves. He wore
glasses and a black mustache. He looked like a guy who
had quite a story. A guy it would be good not to mess
with.

During one of the songs the young girl came and sat on
his lap. She snuggled up like a kitten that had finished a
bowl of milk. I happened to hear her half whisper in her
dad's ear, "I love you, Daddy."

I don't think he noticed but a lot of the men still in
treatment were watching him and his daughter. Or
maybe he did know it? Maybe that was why he came

back. To show his brothers what was possible.

I leaned up and whispered in his ear, "You are the richest man in the world." As he glanced back over his shoulder to catch a glimpse of me, his face was an incredible mixture of gratitude and the kind of amazed wonder of someone who just won the lottery against millions to one odds. He said, "I know it. I don't know how it happened but I know it."

Earnie Larsen

A Birthday to Remember

*If you find it in your heart to care for somebody
else, you will have succeeded.*

Maya Angelou

Every year our family looks forward to the annual
"Superweek" retreat sponsored by our church. The days
are filled with children of all ages gathered outside of our
lodge for fellowship. They play 4-Square, Double Dutch
jump rope, and whatever can be done when friends and
imagination pair up. Beautiful Lake Geneva in Wisconsin
was the site of the reunion scheduled for the week of June
10th, 2000.

In our family, I pack for vacations for each member
while my husband, Paul, gets the children out of the
house, to a fast food joint, the mall, or an arcade so I can
accomplish things with a minimum of distraction (i.e.
stress!).

The plan was coming along splendidly, until I realized
that the big suitcases were still stored in the ladder-
accessible-only attic. The suitcases within reach were the
smaller, children's size suitcases . . . the same suitcases I
packed and unpacked over the last three months for our
daughter Kendall's hospital stays.

As if a wet cold sheet had been suddenly tossed over
my head, a surging wave of emotion enveloped me the
instant I grasped the suitcase's gray handle to pull it from
beneath my bed. Just a few weeks ago, on May 21st, our

beautiful little girl lost her valiant five-month battle with a brain stem tumor.

We had considered forgoing the retreat this year, coming so soon after our loss. When we thought of how much we had always enjoyed the week as a family, we realized we needed to do this as part of our healing process. When someone anonymously sponsored our family's expenses, it only confirmed the feeling in our hearts that it was the right thing to do. Knowing the week would be strewn with memories of Superweeks past, I was more than grateful to have so many loving hearts around us as we forged through the week.

The packing got completed later that evening, once the family was home, and the next morning, after a ninety-minute car ride, Lake Geneva was a welcome sight in spite of the steadily falling rain. After a quick trip into town for a couple of rain ponchos and a hot pink umbrella, we were as comfortable as ducks in water. So far, so good.

On Wednesday, the sun came out after lunch and I watched from the porch as the kids played. These children had been "crib pals" with my children in the church nursery. I knew them when they could only scoot on their butts to cross a room. Paul or I had changed many of their diapers. Watching the children play was a sight to behold—except for the feeling that I was looking at a jigsaw puzzle with a single, solitary piece missing—Kendall.

The realization became more than I could manage. I went into the back room of the cabin and secluded myself within the lower bunk. The tears flowed. The questions flowed. The answers didn't.

"I don't know if I even want to be comforted!" I blurted to the God who knows my heart. "I don't know if I want to be hugged . . . or held . . . or ignored! I just don't know what to do, or how to act, or how to move on!

"I can't do this anymore!"

The next day was Kendall's birthday and in years past the congregation would gather after lunch for the birthday cake and candles. I just couldn't bear to face tomorrow.

Suddenly, the room brightened with an illumination, causing me to open my eyes. I wondered if an angel, or Jesus, or Kendall might be sitting beside me, but the light was only the sun peeking from behind thick cloud cover to set beautifully over the western lake. The brilliant rays streamed through the window, lighting up the bottom bunk where I lay.

Sniffling at the awareness that instead of an angel it was "only the sun setting," I went back to my hankie. Within a minute, Paul came in and excitedly asked: "Do you want to come with me for a minute?"

"Why?" I managed weakly.

"To see a pretty rainbow."

He didn't have to ask me twice! Rainbows had held a special place in my heart during Kendall's battle.

I have seen rainbows before. They rarely look like the kind you see in pictures or movies. But this one was truly spectacular! It contained all the spectrum colors and seemed wider than any I ever remembered—maybe three times as wide as any before.

At first, the rainbow appeared as a single column rising into the clouds. But as the sun shone brighter behind us, the light turned the colorful volume up.

I nuzzled into Paul's shoulder and cried, thinking about Kendall and our "rainbow connection" that repeatedly surfaced throughout her trial—the rainbows always reminding us of God's never-ending love for her . . . for us.

I hurried toward the peninsula to gain a better view of the sight. Was it a column, or a full bow? I had to know. I don't know why, I just had to see it all!

I finally came to the porch at Sunrise Cottage, where I could see the entire bay.

The rainbow was still shining brightly, and stretched from coast to coast, forming a perfect arch! The rainbow stayed brilliant and perfect for at least ten more minutes.

While we watched the spectacular light show sent from

heaven, a little bird began doing aerial tricks over our heads; real daredevil stuff.

I noticed the dark-eyed junco's nest was built into one of the porch rafters, and that the brown and black bird must be flying in "protect mode." As the mother bird made its third descent, thinking to comfort it, I said aloud, "Don't worry Mama Bird, your babies are safe."

Those words echoed in my heart as if God had spoken them.

"Don't worry, Mama Bird, your babies are safe," I repeated as the rainbow began to dim.

I cried. Only this time, the tears were a different type; they were tears of joy.

Kendall made it to Superweek for her birthday after all.

In memory of Kendall Christine Bjorvik
June 15, 1990–May 21, 2000
Loretta McCann Bjorvik

Angels Dancing

There are very few monsters that warrant the fear we have of them.

                                    Andre Gide

As I approached my thirty-first birthday, though parts of my life had never been better, in other ways it seemed as if my life might be in a free fall. One of the most serious problems was that, at the rate I was spending money, if something didn't change I, and my family, would be destitute within a few years. I made what most people would consider a lot of money, but I was spending three times the amount I could afford each month. A group of caring friends helped me see the truth about my out-of-control financial behavior. As I looked back, I realized that the overspending had seldom been self-indulgent, but had been motivated by helping others.

My acceptance of the problem led me to a therapeutic workshop where my wife and I began to address our spending behaviors. We learned that there were not only the typical external factors in our relationship with money such as income, spending plans and cost cutting, there were also internal factors—mostly unconscious feelings, dreams, beliefs and goals that were just as important. One thing we realized was that I had been trying to make up for a lack of family in my childhood by trying to "buy" one. In my attempt to take care of others I had, for years, ignored my own family and myself.

At one point in the workshop, one of the topics being discussed was that of ways to cut expenses, both personally and professionally. I had been in show business for more than a decade and I have always performed with a wonderful, talented group of musicians who I think of and treat as family. As I sat there that afternoon, for the first time I seriously contemplated what it might be like to appear on stage with just one or two musicians. The thought frightened me terribly. I wasn't sure that I would ever be able to do that. Though I had been performing for years, all over the world, before millions of people, I had been told more than once that I had no talent and that whatever success I had been able to achieve had to do with luck and the people around me rather than any talent I might have. Though I wanted to believe they were wrong, I carried the secret fear that perhaps they were right.

As fate would have it, a few months later I was appearing on a TV special and was challenged by the producers to perform without my usual entourage. From somewhere inside a voice said, "Sure," sounding much more convincing than I felt. I chose a song with a meaningful message, one that has been a theme for my life, of wanting to love and be loved. As I stood and approached the microphone the faces, voices and messages of those people over the years who had shared their doubts about my abilities suddenly came rushing back at me like a tidal wave.

I decided there was no time or place like the present to go toe-to-toe with this nemesis that had shadowed me all my life. I found it ironic that it just happened to be in one of the most visible public settings imaginable, with millions of people watching, rather than the small concert or club setting I had envisioned.

As I stood up to sing, instead of fear and doubt, I felt a sense of incredible peace. It felt as if God's spirit somehow washed over me, moved through and blessed me. I don't believe that I ever sang better. By the last note, everyone— the audience, my wife and family and even the host of the show—was moved to tears by what they had experienced. People who knew nothing of what a challenge my performing alone meant have since told me that even watching from thousands of miles away, they felt like they were witnessing a miracle. As has often happened in my life, I had done my job of showing up and God had used me in a very special way. Little did I know just how special.

Two of the people watching that show were a mom and her daughter. While I was singing the song, the little girl exclaimed to her mom, "Look, Mommy, I see angels dancing all around him." Though her mom was not able to see what her daughter was seeing, she was stunned by her daughter's comment.

Incredibly, a few weeks later this girl's mother learned that I was performing near their hometown and brought her daughter to the concert. During the show, the mother sent a note to me explaining that her daughter had seen angels dancing all around me during the TV special. I recalled how I had felt God's blessing and energy bathe me during that performance and what a powerful moment it had been for me. I wanted to meet this special little girl and I invited them to join me backstage after the show. As she was sitting beside me, she could hardly sit still.

"You seem scared and nervous," I told her. "I am," she replied, letting a moment of silence linger between us before she began talking a mile a minute. At one point in the conversation she said, "You know, I saw angels all around you the day you sang on TV." I was awestruck. There was no doubt in her mind what she saw, and there was no doubt in my mind that she was telling me her truth. I remembered my own sense of being touched by God as I performed that day, and this little girl said she saw it happening. Profoundly moved, I thanked her for sharing what she had seen and told her of my belief in God and angels and their power in my life.

As they were leaving, the little girl's mom leaned over to me and whispered in my ear: "You know, my daughter is autistic. The first words she has spoken in her life were 'Look, Mommy, I see angels,' the day you appeared on TV. The second time was when she was sitting next to you tonight. This is truly a miracle for us."

I sat there stunned, speechless and in awe. We hugged as I choked back my tears, and as they left I once again felt fully blessed.

How am I doing with the money issues? Well, we have been able to reduce our monthly expenditures by 40 percent, but I am far from finished. I have a long way to go—I have learned this is a process, not an event.

What was a far more powerful lesson for me was that in having the courage to do the work necessary to get our lives in order, God used us to perform his miracles in ways we could never have imagined.

Anonymous

4

FAMILIES OF ORIGIN, FAMILIES OF CHOICE

Children are like wet cement. What gets imprinted there hardens and becomes who we are.

Earnie Larsen

Panning for Gold

Never put a period where God has placed a comma.

Anonymous

With my head bowed, through my tears and grief, in a barely audible choking voice, I was finally talking with my dad. After decades of mundane conversations about sports, the weather and gossip about relatives, I was rehearsing all of the things I wanted to say to my dad but never could. Things like, "Thank you for staying with Mom when I know you wanted to leave," and "Thank you for playing with me that one day when I was a kid." At the same time I was unconsciously hoping that he would tell me all the things that I had waited forever to hear from him. Simple things like, "I love you," and "I am proud of who you have become."

In what was one of those sacred moments in group therapy that I have since come to treasure, all of my fellow group members were crying, my therapist was crying, I was crying, we were all crying, or so I thought. When I looked up at the man seated across from me, the man I had chosen to play the role of my father, he sat with a totally stoic unaffected look on his face. He noticed that I had stopped talking, and looked down at his watch as if to say, "Are you finished yet?"

I silently shook my head and thought, *That's exactly what my dad would do if he were here.* At that moment, a level of grief like none I had ever known came over me. I literally collapsed onto the floor as convulsive sobs shook my body. I lay there for a long time during which I fleetingly wondered if I would be the first person to literally cry to death during group therapy.

Later, as the group was giving me feedback, the man who had played my father asked, "I wonder if I did something wrong? It looked for a while like you weren't going to make it."

"No, you did nothing wrong," I replied. "In fact, what you did may have been the best gift I was ever given." In this man's moment of being totally detached and unaffected by my tenderness and longing, I realized that my parents, my father in particular, could never be there for me in ways I had always wanted, certainly deserved, and still longed for.

I understood that no matter what I did or said they could not parent any better than they had. It became crystal clear that it was beyond my parents' ability and more important, was nothing personal. I was thirty-eight years old.

My life changed with that experience and though it is difficult for me to determine exactly when my recovery started, I grew up that day. In terms of my relationship with my parents, in some kind of spiritual way I was able to release my mom and dad from their roles as my mom and dad.

A few weeks later my dad was scheduled to undergo his third hip replacement surgery. Now, my father did not have three legs, but he had been among the first to ever have that surgery, and at the time, the process often needed to be repeated.

The call from my mother relaying the details made me realize that my father and I had never expressed our love for each other in words. A voice inside said, *You need to tell him you love him before you lose the chance.* By this time in my recovery, I had begun to know and trust that voice so I decided to drive the 300 miles to see him and tell him that I loved him.

For moral support I took my wife and two young

children with me. We arrived at the hospital the day
before the surgery was to take place. My mom, sister and
brother were in the room when we arrived. Though I
entered the room with great resolve, and I had shared
with my wife and children what I intended to do, when I
opened my mouth I couldn't get the words out. My throat
literally closed around the words. My family lived in great
denial about most things and the possibility of my sixty-
eighty-year-old father dying as a result of this surgery
was never considered. After twenty minutes of small talk
and my repeated attempts to say those three little words
with no success, I felt an overwhelming need to get out of
the room.

I said my good-byes and good lucks and left the room
with my father's parting words ringing in my ears: "It was
stupid of you to drag those kids all this way just to see me
in the hospital."

As I walked down the corridor feeling like a complete
failure, to this day I swear that I heard a voice come over
the hospital's intercom saying, "Just go tell him." I
stopped right there in the middle of the hallway and said
out loud, "I'm just going to go say it." My wife and kids
said in what seemed to be unison, "We'll wait here."

I turned around and walked back to my dad's room and
said, "Dad, the reason I came was to make sure you knew
that I love you."

Now, I don't know what kind of response you might
predict I would have gotten, but I doubt that it would be
what happened next. My dad reared up in his hospital
bed and began having an uncontrollable coughing fit. My
mother launched herself across the bed to comfort him
and screamed, "Oh, no!" while my brother stood up and
gave me a look that said, *Why do you always cause trouble?*
My sister began quietly sobbing in the corner.

As I turned around and walked out the door I felt victorious. I had verbalized the words "I love you" to my
father, words that had never been spoken between us. I

also thought, *That's $2,000 I won't have to spend in therapy because I had that piece of unfinished business with my dad to deal with.*

I now look back at that moment as the first time in my life that I had ever acted as an adult with my father.

Six months later on my next visit as we were saying good-bye, I had the spontaneous urge to give my dad a hug. The last time my father and I had touched in any way was thirty-three years earlier on my fifth birthday. He had carried me from the car where I had pretended to fall asleep and put me to bed. It was a game my brother and I had perfected, our childish way to get the touch from our dad that we craved. During all the subsequent years, through all of life's adventures, celebrations, trials and tribulations we never shook hands, slapped each other on the back or touched in any way. If I followed through on this urge to hug him it would represent a significant shift in our relationship. It was time for the second adult act of a lifetime with my dad.

As I stepped up to him I said, for the second time in my life, "Dad, I love you."

I put my arms around him and gave him a hug. He suddenly got very rigid and actually began trembling. When I stepped back from him, I felt this surge of pride, knowing that in initiating this physical contact I reclaimed a part of what I had always wanted from my dad and perhaps saved another $2,000 in therapy.

If my dad would have said, "I don't ever want you to touch me again" or "I don't ever want you to say you love me again," I would have honored that, but he didn't. I took his silence on the matter as permission to continue what was considered, at least for my family, this brazen behavior.

A few months later at the end of another visit as I stepped up to hug him, his arms involuntarily opened about four inches as I moved to give him a hug. That time as I stepped back, I choked up realizing that I was teaching my father how to touch his son. Those four inches of movement represented all he had to offer at the time.

Over the following months and years I continued to express my love to my mother and father and to hug them. Before I realized it, they actually began hugging back. In fact, one time when I was leaving and walking towards the car my dad yelled, "You forgot to give me a hug." Slowly the expressions of love that had started out as unilateral behaviors on my part became mutual. I was something of a prospector panning for little nuggets of gold.

After my mother's death, my dad became more and more curious, asking questions about my work. By that time my wife and I were owners of Onsite Workshops, a recovery business created by codependency pioneers Sharon and Joe Cruse. When he was seventy-two years old, my father began attending programs—"seminars" he called them.

At the closing ceremony of what was to be his last workshop four years later, I watched with my now adult-aged son as my dad stood in front of all the participants and staff and said, "I have come to believe that if Ted's mom and I would have known what I have been able to learn doing these seminars, Ted and his children's lives would have been very different."

Shortly after that, my father was diagnosed with brain cancer. After his first surgery, I accompanied him to physical therapy where we put rings on posts and threw balls in baskets. Laughing and joking, for a moment I was transported back to that day decades ago when we had played together when I was twelve.

That night as I stood before the mirror brushing my teeth, I was overcome with a sense of gratitude and full-ness. This confused me because I had come home with the clarity that my dad would never walk again and that he was dying. Then the words "unconditional love" came to me and I understood that this is what I had experi-enced with my dad that day. I had no expectations of him or him of me, we just were together and that alone made the day very special.

One of the most precious gifts of my recovery was accepting that my parents just didn't possess boundless love, endless nurturing, playfulness, tenderness or fun to give. However, I was lucky enough and had the courage to find a way to let go of my idealized vision of what my parents' love should look like.

On the day of my father's last surgery I was aware of my pride in him and how he had lived his life. He was teaching me by example that it is never too late to learn, that it is never too late to start "recovery" and now, at this point in our relationship, how to die with grace and dignity.

In the last few moments before he was taken to the operating room, I blurted out, "Dad, you know I love you, and I am so proud of you." Giving us a minute, the attendant stopped wheeling the gurney. With tears in his eyes, reaching for my hand, my father turned toward me and said what I had waited a lifetime to hear, "Ted, I don't think I have ever told you how proud I am of you, and the life you have made for yourself. And I know I didn't tell you often enough of my love for you."

Those were the last words my father ever spoke. He passed away several months later.

Ted Klontz

Out of the Blue

You can't shake hands with a clenched fist.

Indira Gandhi

"I'm sorry, who's calling?" I asked into the phone as I struggled to compose myself.

"This is Doris," she repeated. "Doris, in Michigan, your sister." Doris!

She was the first daughter of my dad, but we had different mothers. We never knew each other or had a relationship as sisters. Why is Doris calling me out of the blue? Is she going to cause problems? I don't need more family problems!

Doris persisted. "I'm calling about Dad," she continued. "Your mom wrote me, saying he's in the hospital. How is he doing?" My heart sank.

"I didn't know Dad is in the hospital," I replied as I felt the knots tighten in my stomach. "Although my parents live six miles away they haven't communicated with me in years." There was silence. Then I heard crying in Michigan.

"Oh, I'm so sorry, I had no idea," Doris sniffled. "All these years I envied you. He was never a dad to me, but I thought you were his special princess. I imagined how you were enjoying everything I always wanted. I'm just shocked to learn that you don't have any more of a relationship with him than I do!" Doris gave a long sigh and continued.

"Since Dad's in poor health, I need to come to Florida. It

could be the last time I see him. Will your mother allow that?"

Years ago when my father taught school he fell in love with one of his students, a girl fifteen years his junior. He left his wife and young daughter and married the student, who became my mother. She made sure Doris wouldn't be a part of her father's life.

During my childhood I heard brief mentions of Doris when she sent gifts to my dad. I saw her only once, at her wedding, when her father gave her away. My mother was always a controlling woman. When I married and had a family of my own, she lost some of her control. To retaliate, she shunned my husband, my children and me. I was abandoned as an adult.

"Are you still on the phone?" Doris asked softly.

"I'm still here," I assured her. "I can't speak for my mother regarding your visiting Dad, but if you decide to come, you are welcome to stay with me."

After Doris called my parents and they authorized her visit, she and her husband bought tickets to fly to Florida. She suggested that we all meet for a barbecue at my home. I was terrified of facing my parents again after they ignored me for so many years, and I felt anxious about meeting the sister I never knew.

"I hear you've joined the enemy camp," my mother snapped into the phone, before Doris arrived. "I can't believe you've invited that horrible woman to stay in your home!"

I fought the urge to hang up. Instead I endured another one of her tirades.

When Doris and I spent time together I was impressed with her courage and her talents. I learned she was a professional soprano, a gourmet cook and an accomplished seamstress. She was a daughter who should make her father feel proud. I admired her forgiving spirit toward a dad who had abandoned her. She was here to say a final good-bye to her father, my father.

When my parents joined Doris, her husband and my

family for a reunion dinner, there was tension in the air from the unresolved agendas. My mother wore a forced smile as she sat coiled near my dad. We knew she could strike with a venomous attack at any moment. The camera captured pictures of smiling family faces. It didn't reveal the aching hearts inside.

"Come visit me in Michigan," Doris urged, as she embraced me before boarding the plane. A year later I accepted her invitation. As we sat cross-legged, munching sugar cookies fresh from her oven, we looked at pictures from the past. Then Doris lifted an old snapshot from a cluttered shoebox. I stared as I studied the smiling young man who stood on a rural porch and held his little girl's hand. This was a picture of Doris with her father before he married his young student, before he became my father.

Then a thought struck me. Doris and I feel pain because our parents abandoned us. Is it possible we could heal by becoming sisters?

On the fiftieth anniversary of the wedding where I first met Doris, I flew to Michigan with my daughter Betsy to attend the commemorative ceremony in a little country church. Doris would perform a solo, and I would hear her sing for the first time. I felt chills as her powerful voice resonated across the pews of the sun-drenched chapel. My throat tightened and I choked back tears.

That evening, as the guests and our blended families celebrated together, Doris and I slipped away from the crowd and took a short walk.

"The Lord has blessed us with good husbands and great kids," Doris commented as we watched the orange sunset dazzle the horizon.

"We have strong relationships with our families, and each other, because we refused to repeat the mistakes of our parents," I responded.

As we walked hand in hand in the deepening shadows, I was grateful that the sister I never knew called me out of the blue.

Miriam Hill

Perfect Grief

Wisdom is knowing what to do next, virtue is doing it.

David Starr Jordan

Like many adult children of addicted parents, I was taught to be a perfectionist. As a kid I tried to be a perfect student, have the perfect science fair project and be the perfect Little League baseball player. Errors would haunt me for weeks. This need for perfection continued into my adult life and into my career as a social worker and professional speaker.

May 29, 1986, I was giving a speech and was interrupted five minutes into the talk and told that I had an urgent phone call in the room next door. It was my mother; my dad had just died in a closet at work, smoking his drug of choice, cocaine. The autopsy revealed that the cause of death was a drug-induced heart attack.

After he died, I even approached my grief in a perfect manner. Raised as a traditional male, out of the mold of John Wayne, I had learned, by age nine, that men do not cry. In fact, men do not show any emotion. I never saw my father or grandfather cry, and I hugged my father three times in my life—when I graduated from undergraduate school, graduate school and in his casket. Being the perfect social worker also affected my grief reaction. Instead of feeling my own pain, I was thinking as a social worker, "What do I need to do for my younger brothers and sisters?" In short, I barely grieved at all.

In 1995, nine years after the death of my father, my wife and I had our first child, a five-pound, five-ounce boy we named Joseph Sanders. In true ACoA fashion, I searched north, south, east and west for the perfect name and decided to name him after Joseph in the Old Testament, the young man who maintained perfect obedience to God after being abused by his half-brothers and imprisoned by Pharaoh. Joseph gave me the greatest gift one can receive: unconditional love. He was my greatest joy.

As a speaker, my greatest challenges are the days I am on the road and away from my son. On May 13, 2001, I was traveling to the U.S. Virgin Islands to speak to a group of youth workers on drug abuse prevention among teens. My son was asleep, so I left him a note next to my picture, which said, "Joseph, Daddy will see you in three days." I delivered the speech on May 15th and was then invited on a cruise on the Atlantic Ocean. The U.S. Virgin Islands are so beautiful, particularly from the ocean, that I asked God, if I don't get to heaven, to please send me to the U.S. Virgin Islands, because they look the way I envision heaven. When I arrived back at the hotel, the red light on my phone was blinking. I called the hotel lobby, and the attendant told me to call my wife, that there was an emergency at home. I did so, and my wife told me that our son Joseph had just died. I went from heaven to hell in just one moment.

I started questioning God. How could you let this happen to me? I've spent my entire life helping others, trying to do the right thing. My heart was broken. I thought that I would never be able to do my work again.

My flight home was about to be the longest ordeal of my life. I boarded a 45-minute commuter flight from the Virgin Islands to San Juan, Puerto Rico. I arrived at San Juan at 11:00 A.M., and my plane to Chicago was not scheduled to depart until 1:00 P.M. I had always wanted to visit Puerto Rico, but under such painful circumstances, it was lost. While sitting at the airport at San Juan, I spotted a man who looked familiar. I recognized him as a former high school classmate. I approached him and told him my story, and he sat with me for two hours. I spent most of my adult life helping others; for one of the few times in my life, I allowed someone to help me. When I returned home, another former high school classmate who'd lost her husband nine years earlier told me that people will probably want to help me with my grief, and that I should allow them to do so. I did. I called everyone I knew—friends, relatives, colleagues, and hundreds of people attended my son's funeral. My wife and I stood in line as they viewed my son in his casket, and we hugged each of them—hundreds of hugs, and I remember each one. I did this for myself; having spent so many years giving to others, I allowed myself to receive what I needed. Still, I was unable to cry the day of my son's funeral. After years of not crying, I had many frozen tears, tears that held me hostage.

A week after the funeral, I met with my insurance broker, a man whose daughter had committed suicide a year earlier. Suffering from postpartum psychosis, she threw herself from the twelfth floor of a hotel room to her death. "Love is eternal," he said as we talked about our losses. Then he told me how much he had cried over the death of his daughter. As I got into my car, thirty years of frozen tears came flowing. This older, distinguished gentleman gave me permission to do what no other man had given me—permission to cry. Even in the midst of my tears, I wondered how I looked crying: Did I look perfect? The question soon dissipated; it felt good to cry. I received my tears back.

In the midst of grieving the death of my son, I have also been able to more fully grieve the death of my father. I have been able to accept all of him, the hardworking man, the drug-addicted man, and the drug-selling man. In accepting all of my father, I have also been able to accept more of my own imperfections. On April 25, 2003, my wife and I had another son. We named him after my father, Elton Sanders.

Mark Sanders

"You're spending the best years of your life doing a job that you hate so you can buy stuff you don't need to support a lifestyle you don't enjoy. Sounds crazy to me!"

©2002 Randy Glasbergen, www.glasbergen.com

To Do the Work of Angels

Good people are good because they've come to wisdom through failure.

William Saroyan

The fear of death is considered by many folks to be the worst fear of all. Second to love, the topic of death has made for the most profound subject matter in classic plays, operas, poems, songs and books. For many of us, this is as close as we want to get to death. Simply put, death is much too stressful to face head-on, whether it's our own mortality or that of someone close to us. Avoidance is a common coping technique, albeit an ineffective one. Death cannot be avoided.

American culture has a way of shielding the process of dying from our collective consciousness. As if the consequences might prove to be too painful, the topic of death and dying, not to mention exposure to it, are often sanitized to become more palatable. It is quite possible today to go through life and never see a dying loved one or a deceased relative, while in other cultures, and even in this country a century ago, to be in the presence of a dying person was not an uncommon occurrence at all.

The works of people like Elisabeth Kübler-Ross, M.D., and Steven Levine have brought dignity to the topic of death and dying, and have helped minimize the element of fear involved with this stressful event. In Kübler-Ross's words, "No one should ever have to die alone." The hospice movement, which she helped pioneer several decades ago, has been remarkable in its efforts to maintain the dignity of chronically ill and dying patients. My first exposure to the mission of hospice work came in the last few days as my aunt was dying of stomach cancer. It was then I knew, unequivocally, that no one should ever die alone.

A year later I was to face death again, this time with more direct contact and closer heartstrings. Although I was not afraid of death, in hindsight I realized that this time, I had a special role to play.

Some people call alcoholism a form of death and dying. Some even call it a slow form of suicide. My mother died of alcoholism at a young age. Ulcerations in several internal organs eventually led to blood clots in her lungs. My father, convinced she would recover, persuaded me not to fly across the country to see her until she got better. She never did. She slipped into a coma and, ironically, died on New Year's Eve. For reasons too difficult to explain, neither my sisters, nor myself could attend her funeral. Yet, perhaps in a way of balancing karma, the story would be different for my father's death.

He too, was an alcoholic. The devastation of chronic alcohol to the body comes in many ways, not the least of which is a compromised immune system, and the shadow of death loomed close by his side with several compromising health issues.

A project engineer for a large aerospace company, in 1978 my father was transferred to Florida, where he worked for several years before he retired in the hopes of playing endless games of golf and taking countless deep-sea fishing trips. In the spring of 1993, I was making a career transition from Washington, D.C. to Boulder, Colorado. It was at this time, a year after his sister's death from cancer, that I learned that, he too, had been diagnosed with cancer—again. "Not to worry," he assured me. "It's nothing. It will be gone in no time." I took his comment at face value. I'm sure there was an element of denial on my part, and perhaps his as well. Indeed, this time would be different.

By the end of August I had a strong premonition that all was not well, despite my father's assurances to the contrary. I cancelled several speaking engagements and quickly made plans to visit him at the end of September. Three days before my scheduled departure, I received a phone call from my sister, who lived nearby, telling me that indeed, Dad was deathly ill. "Get here as soon as you can. He's on his last leg and asking for you," she cried.

Greeted at the airport by his wife, I was quickly briefed on my father's condition. He had over sixteen tumors and his condition was well beyond the effective range of chemotherapy and radiation treatment. He had a week at the most, she explained, perhaps only a few days. Through her tears, she tried to warn me about how bad he looked. When I walked into his bedroom, the man I knew as my childhood hero was nothing more than a frail, emaciated skeleton. It was quite shocking and, despite his wife's warning, I was still caught off-guard. Dad offered a weak smile, raised his arm to shake hands and then closed his eyes in fatigue.

That first night, lying in bed, I reflected on the man I knew as my father. Baseball was his passion. He had even been recruited by the Red Sox before WWII, but decided, like so many men, to enlist in the Navy instead. He valued a good education; he was a Yale graduate, yet advocated travel as life's "real school." He secretly admired Vince Lombardi and always rooted for the Green Bay Packers. I remembered his taste for fine restaurants, excellent wines and liquors (obviously, too much of these), the stock market and Ian Fleming novels. As an aircraft engineer, he somehow made planes fly, but his work with the government never allowed him to talk about his job. Perhaps this added to the pressures of drinking. I will never know.

He married young. His first wife, a nurse, caught tuberculosis and died. He never talked about her. At the age of twenty-three, he contracted tuberculosis himself and nearly died as well. Three years later, he married my mother. She died in 1981.

As are many men of his generation, he was quite stoic, yet at times displayed a good sense of humor. During my short visit, there was plenty of time to talk, joke around, smile, reminisce and forgive. Forgiveness is also the work of angels and I, too, needed to resolve many issues that I had tucked away regarding his alcoholic tendencies. Forgiveness is a means of simply letting go. As the expression goes, "If you expect an apology, you'll be waiting a long time."

Being more of a right-brain person (in contrast to his left-brain personality) I never really knew what my dad thought of my work and interest in matters of stress and human spirituality—that is, until this visit. Each day he beckoned me to his side and with a spiritual hunger, he inquired about many things regarding the mysteries of life. All of this made for a remarkable healing.

On what was scheduled to be my last day, my father took a serious turn for the worse. My sister and stepmother were absent (in their grief, they explained, they could just not be with him), so I sat alone by his side, holding his hand, whispering loving words of kindness and veiled glimpses into his future.

Early that morning a knock at the door informed me the hospice nurse arrived for what was to be her final visit. Because of a hectic schedule she couldn't stay long, she explained, as she made her way to her next appointment. I sat in silence and prayed. As my father's breaths grew extremely shallow, drawing down to his final respiration, I held his hand tightly and offered my love, and congratulations on his transition.

I would like to say the room grew bright at his passing, but if it did, I didn't notice. There was certainly an air of calmness and a feeling of what I could only call "grace." Within moments of his passing, I was moved to open the windows, perhaps as a symbolic gesture of his soul's freedom. Then I left the room to tell his wife that my dad had died, and I offered her a warm embrace.

Elisabeth Kübler-Ross expressed it so well when she wrote, "I want to assure you that it is a blessing to sit at the bedside of a dying patient. What you learn from dying patients you can pass on to your children and to your neighbors, and maybe our world would become a paradise again. I believe the time to start is now."

The last few days spent at my father's side provided moments I will hold close to my heart forever. They not only served to assure me that there is nothing to fear in death but that to be called to help in this transition is to do the work of angels.

Brian Luke Seaward, Ph.D.

Memory of Two Friends

You cannot run away from a weakness; you must sometimes fight it out or perish. And if that be so, why not now, and where you stand?

Robert Louis Stevenson

Hidden in an attic, or buried at the back of a closet, or tucked away in a cluttered corner of a garage . . . somewhere, we all have a box of mementos—pieces of memories saved to preserve time gone by. Mine is a small varnished pine box with brass hinges that I made in my seventh-grade wood shop class. I have a lifetime of childhood memories carefully stored there: my first-aid merit badge from Scouts, a brightly colored miniature abacus that was a stocking stuffer from my ninth Christmas, a ticket to a Giants game, and the two photos.

I've had many friends so far in my busy life. Calvin and Allen were two good friends from long ago, but they play an important part in my life now, even more than in those distant times. Every few years, I drag the step stool to the highest shelf in the garage and rummage for the pine box. There, between my second-grade report card and a poem written by a high school girlfriend, are the two photos of Calvin and Allen.

They both had so much in common, even though they lived on opposite sides of town. Both came from loving families, with parents proud of their accomplishments. Their every day was filled with the challenges of school, but both were excellent students. They each shared a love for sports, too. In the photo of Allen, he's standing barefoot on the sidewalk in front of my house, with bat poised, waiting for my sister to pitch the ball. It's easy to see his total concentration, even though his face is contorted in attempts to see into the bright July sun. Calvin's game was tennis. I shared many school evenings with him on the courts, with me receiving a thrashing. Although we were both on the school's junior varsity team, he was a much better player than I could ever hope to be. They were both friends, and (in a way) they were my heroes.

The last similarity between the two had the greatest impact on their lives and the lives of their families: both became entangled in the terror of drug addiction. They must have shared a common fear, a common pain, a common feeling of hopelessness and helplessness—not just them, but their families, because the families shared the pain of their sons' deaths. My friend Allen died of a heroin overdose at twelve years old. Calvin never saw his twentieth birthday.

Neither would ever experience the satisfaction of looking into the eyes of their new bride . . . or the nervousness of holding the first baby in the delivery room . . . or their son's game-winning double, their daughter's practiced role in the dance recital.

So periodically I bring out the box, dust off the two photos and hope. I hope that somehow I've learned the magic formula needed to prevent history from repeating itself with the two children that mean everything to me. I know it takes more than love, but I'm not sure I know the answer. But then, Calvin and Allen's parents have asked the same question many times. For those of us left, we can only hope that we can make a difference.

David R. Wilkins

The Grace of God Shows

He that will not apply new remedies must expect new evils, for time is the greatest innovator.

Francis Bacon

Let me start out by saying that I am a thirty-nine-year-old husband and father. My wife and I have been married for almost twelve years and I have always been considered strange or outrageous. My sense of humor is different and my reactions to life events tend toward the extremes. Most who know me consider me loyal and very protective of my family.

Two years ago we went through a very hard time as a family. I provoked it. Things were going too well for me. It was time to self-destruct again.

I grew up in a very violent home where a tyrant imprisoned us. He was hard to predict and you learned to read him quickly in order to keep yourself out of harm's way. I never considered myself an abused child until much later in my life. Then, it was simply what happened in life. I figured everyone else had the same problems. I was wrong.

I had an anger problem in my teen years. My parents divorced when I was twelve and all hell broke loose for me when I was fifteen. My mother pushed me into therapy and she got me a "Big Brother" from the Big Brothers, Big Sisters organization. She put her all into saving me from myself. I dropped out of high school in the tenth grade. I got my GED and went to work. It was understood that if you were not in school, you worked.

When I was sixteen, I told my therapist that the only good

man was one with a "dagger stuck in his head and one in his chest." I told her, "You couldn't trust one that breathes." At that time, I would consider it no great loss to watch a man die in pain. Remember the "strange or outrageous" part?

One day when I was seventeen years old, I was sitting in our dining room, by the kitchen. I was smoking a cigarette and holding a butcher knife. I was pondering ending it right there. Suddenly the phone rang. I picked it up and my sister said, "Put it down!" I said, "What are you talking about?" She said, "Don't give me that s--t. You have a knife in your hand and I know you want to kill yourself. Put it down and let's talk."

I quickly put it away and we talked. She came down from Philadelphia with my new niece to see me shortly after that. The only explanation for her knowing what I was doing at that table was God!

That was the last time I really considered suicide.

I went to college with what would have been my class and went on to graduate school as well.

Finally two close friends and my wife urged me to go over the "Incest Survivors Checklist." For years I had been urging clients to use this during their assessment for treatment. They pushed me to take it, so I did—to prove them wrong. As I went through the list I was answering most of the questions affirmatively. I sat at our computer and cried. I didn't want this to be true.

It was time.

A friend who practices hypnotherapy had been trying to get me to come see her professionally for a long time. I called her and she told me to come over immediately.

I feared I would be hurting my family. I was afraid of who I might see in my mind. Over the next four hours we proceeded to break the dam of memories. I saw people I had not thought of in years and described places in vivid detail.

The sexual abuse had begun when I was almost three years old. Under hypnosis I described the bedroom and house of my babysitter in detail. She, her husband and one daughter had all been involved in sexually abusing children.

As I continued the process of acknowledging my past, I would confirm places and people with my sister, who is older by almost four years. She identified people I could not remember names for.

A significant breakthrough came when I recalled telling my father about the abuse. Predictably, that only made the situation worse and my life from the age of seven until my parents divorced became a series of sexual liaisons with women and men involving my father and members of his church. Many of them I did not know, but others I did.

One memory that resurfaced was helping my stepsister survive our being raped once. I whispered for her to look at me and not to focus on the pain. She looked at me and we both survived it. I was eight at the time, she was six.

As my past began to unravel, there were times I wanted to deny it, but everywhere I turned my memories were being confirmed for me. The history filled in missing pieces from my life. I was remembering things in detail. I truly was a survivor of child prostitution and pornography.

My sexual molestation explained so much. My extreme reactions to "threats" toward my family or me and my tendency to sexualize everything. It explains why I think the way I do and why I struggle so with my relationships with men.

I am not alone as a male survivor, but I am finding that I might be one of very few men who have kept their faith in God and are still led by this grounding. If it were not for the faith that my mother gave us, I would have given up.

Even with my background as a professional I was as unprepared for these revelations as any other survivor is. But my life has started to make sense. Throughout this journey, my wife has been instrumental in my being able to overcome the episodes of self-destruction. She refuses to let me go. She refuses to let me ruin our marriage. She has been my biggest advocate and I watch her in amazement. She has shown me grace and mercy in a time when those attributes are in very short supply. In a time of disposable marriages and people, my wife has gone against the mainstream. She is truly an angel from God.

Stuart Brantley

A Light at the End of the Tunnel

In spite of warnings, nothing much happens until the status quo becomes more painful than change.

Laurence J. Peter

April is always a hopeful month, and that's how I was feeling as the windshield wipers kept time with the miles. A gentle rain was falling on Sunday morning as I drove through the rolling hills outside of Richmond, Virginia, on my way to the intervention of a beloved seventy-three-year-old mother and grandmother. Her binge drinking had been tolerated for decades, but lately things had gotten much worse.

My work brings me in close contact with many families in crisis, but I was especially moved by the story of Ruth. I hadn't met Ruth yet, but she had to be something special. Her family not only loved her, they revered her. They told me I, too, would fall in love with her as soon as I met her. She exudes a love, they said, that makes you feel all good and warm inside. At just under five feet tall, they continued, she had more capacity to give than anyone they knew. She volunteered at a hospital, food pantry, literacy program and church. She made beautiful wreaths to give to the men and women living in nursing homes so they would have something pretty to put on their doors. She was renowned for her talents in the kitchen and always had a full house of happy, well-fed friends and family. Ruth had a way of making people forget their

troubles when they were in her company. She was everyone's ray of sunshine. It was hard to believe she was also
an alcoholic.

Her son and two daughters were grown now, and they
were reluctant to talk to their mom about her drinking.
Confronting her seemed disrespectful. After all, she drank
infrequently, and the binges were easily pushed to the
back of their minds during her periods of abstinence. But
after their father had a heart attack, their mom's binges
became more frequent and more dangerous.

Ruth began disappearing for days. She'd start drinking
secretly at home, but after a few glasses, she'd get behind
the wheel and drive to another town. She'd check into a
motel room and begin drinking uninterrupted. Her
family, thrown into a panic, would call motels, hospitals
and police stations. Her son would drive to the places
they discovered her in the past. Everyone feared the
worse until she was found.

A week ago, Ruth disappeared for two days. She was
rescued only after teenagers working at a fast-food chain
called the police to report a woman passed out on the
floor of the restaurant. Her son decided the family could
wait no longer. They must help her before she had a terrible accident or died alone at a motel. He called me and
asked about intervention.

I explained how we would harness the power of love to
intervene on Ruth's alcoholism, and, by doing so, preserve her dignity. We chose an older adult treatment center for Ruth so she'd be among people her age rather than
younger adults addicted to street drugs. Over the next
several days, the family team—Ruth's two daughters,
son, daughter-in-law, husband and granddaughter—
worked together to thoroughly choreograph and rehearse
the intervention.

The day of the intervention, Ruth was invited to her
son's house after church to celebrate her granddaughter's
twentieth birthday. The cake was out, the coffee made,

and the doorbell rang. It was Ruth and her husband. I greeted her and began the intervention by saying:

"Mrs. Williams, your family asked me to be here today because they love you very much and have something important they'd like to share with you."

I told her that everyone had written her a letter. She agreed to listen as her son began to read.

Letters were read with many tears, each person detailing what they loved most about Ruth and recounting the ways she'd helped them throughout the years. The letters also tackled the job of showing Ruth how alcohol was failing her. Each letter ended with a straightforward request, "Will you accept the help we're offering you today?"

As Ruth listened, she alternately wept in gratitude and choked with pain. All the letters had a profound effect on her, but none more so than the one read by her twenty-year-old-granddaughter, Miranda:

Dear Granny,

You and I have always had a special bond. We like to sit and talk about life and philosophy, and it always seems we end up solving the problems of the world. I can always count on you for anything and everything. I think you know you are like a second mother to me. I told you just the other day how much Christmas time means to me, and I thanked you for providing me with so many warm memories. As far back as I can remember, every stay at your house was a joy for me. I know you always go out of your way to make things special for me.

I love you so much—it's more than love, even—you're just more important to me than you could possibly imagine. You and Granddad keep this family together; you make us whole. I am here for you today, because I want you to be healthy. While I may speak of the past, this is about the here and now—today, and our future together as a family. So, please know this is not meant to hurt you, but about bringing our family together with love.

Granny, when you are sober, you are as reliable as a clock.

Since you have long periods when you do not drink, I can let myself ignore the fact that you suffer from this disease and just concentrate on the good times. I always think, "Maybe she won't drink again. Maybe that last time was her last."

Last spring, when a binge landed you in the hospital, Mom, Dad, Janie and I decided for about the third time that we were going to do something to get you help. But then you got pneumonia, and that allowed me to forget about the drinking and concentrate on other things. It is easy for me to pretend nothing is wrong—especially a week or so after a drinking binge. It is more comfortable for me to concentrate on the good stuff.

Last April, after I got back from visiting you and Granddad, my mom told me you drank again. I was so surprised and all those old feelings I push out of my mind came rushing back. They always come back when I hear about a binge. Questions run through my mind. "What made her do it this time?" "How bad was it?" "How long did it last?" "How far and where did she drive?" "Did she hurt herself?" "Is she at home or in the hospital?" "Is Granddad okay?"

You may not know this, but I usually find out when you've gone on a binge, even a small one. Mom might say, "We think Granny's drinking." It isn't a secret. Everyone knows, everyone hurts; it's on everyone's mind.

The Thursday you started drinking this last time, I remember coming home and finding you sitting in the kitchen. Granddad was doing the dishes, and you and I had a great conversation for about five minutes before I realized your laugh was a little too hearty, you were talking a little too much. The realization came upon me like a slap in the face. I actually backed away from you physically and could only respond in one-word sentences. I just wanted to get out of there and forget what I was seeing. When Mom told me you had drank, it felt like a punch in the stomach.

I don't have many memories of witnessing your binges. Instead, what I have is a feeling that is always with me. It is a fear that nags at me, "Someday Granny is going to die from alcohol." *A lot of the time, I rely on my denial so I can go on without going crazy from that thought. A picture that stays in my head is you lying dead in a snowdrift, having passed out after a binge. I read about a woman in her forties dying that way a few years ago. The image stays with me. Granny, I don't want to have those kinds of thoughts about you.*

A few days ago, I started thinking about the fact that despite this devastating, debilitating disease you've been suffering with for nearly half a century, you've accomplished so much and deserve the love and respect of so many. You're really quite amazing. It takes a strong woman to do what you have done for so long in the face of a disease that kills so many. I know you can beat this disease, but that is not accomplished alone. If it could be done alone, you would have done it by now. But, no one recovers alone. It requires reaching out to others.

So, will you please accept the help we are offering? The help I am asking you to take? We are together as a family, and I promise I will do my part. Please take the first step toward recovery with us today.

Love,
Miranda

Ruth looked up at Miranda and, through tears, with a small smile said, "Yes, my dear, I'll accept your help today."

Everyone jumped up and hugged Ruth and each other. After all the tears dried, they celebrated Miranda's birthday with a piece of cake and a cup of coffee. Then everyone got ready to go with Ruth to the treatment center.

Before walking out the door, this little wisp of a woman turned to me and said, "When I get the urge to drink, it's like a locomotive is coming right at me and I can't stop it."

I smiled and said, "But today you've made the decision to get off the tracks."

Debra Jay

Time and Recovery

In this age, which believes that there is a short cut to everything, the greatest lesson to be learned is that the most difficult way is, in the long run, the easiest.

Henry Miller

Sometimes it takes a long time for things to heal. Recovery comes when we are ready, and preparing yourself for the next step often means letting go of the pain inside.

When I was growing up, one of the first things that I learned from my father was never to talk about his dad—my grandfather—who died when I was two. I never met my grandfather, however I did know his son and I knew that my father had very bitter feelings toward his father. According to the stories that I heard, my grandfather drank himself to death at the age of fifty-two. He was very tough on his family physically and verbally, especially on my father.

Once in a great while my father made remarks about his dad, but they were always full of anger, hurt and rage. He simply had nothing good to say about the man. In an argument between my father and my mother I once heard my mother, out of exasperation, tell my father, "You are just like your father." I swore I saw steam coming out of the man.

Many years later I was in a restaurant having breakfast with my dad and my five-year-old son. You know what five-year-olds are like in a restaurant. They are good for about six seconds before they get fidgety. I was concerned about how much patience my father would have with his grandson. When I was growing up you just sat there with my dad and hoped that you did not annoy him. But, here was my father and his grandson having a great time together. They were laughing, sliding things back and forth across the table and just enjoying each other.

As I watched the two of them, I recalled something Bill Cosby said: "This is not the same man that raised me! This is an old person trying to get into heaven." I looked at my father and said, "Hey, this is not the same man that raised me." My father smiled, paused and said, "You're right, I'm not."

A little later during our breakfast my father looked at me and said, "Your grandfather sure wasn't much of a father and sure wasn't much of a business man." At that moment I remembered everything I had been taught about counseling and recalled that "when someone finally shares something very important don't fall out of the booth." After a pause he let out a sigh and then said, "But I guess the man did the best he could."

I studied my father's face and for the first time in my life I saw something new in the story it told. Eight years into my father's own recovery and thirty-one years after the death of my grandfather, my dad had started to make peace with his father.

Robert J. Ackerman, Ph.D.

What Was Left Unspoken

The longer you carry a grudge the heavier it gets.

Anonymous

My earliest memories while still in my playpen are the clink of ice in a highball glass and the taste of green olives. My mother was a beautiful, vivacious woman but by the time I was a toddler, a dozen years into their marriage, my father left, defeated and dispirited.

When I was old enough to use the phone, I would call him for reassurance, frightened by my mother's drinking. We experimented with spending a couple of weeks together each summer and on one memorable trip he spent so much money trying to win me a giant stuffed panda bear the carneys felt sorry for him and gave it to us.

By the time I turned ten, we had given up our feeble attempts at trying to have a relationship. No matter how hard I tried, I was never able to say good-bye without a flood of tears, leaving both of us feeling emotionally raw. I blamed myself for chasing him away.

As I entered my teens, my mother married a violent alcoholic who used his fists freely and often. There were no child welfare agencies or domestic abuse hotlines in those days. What went on between a husband and wife was no one's business and the kids were collateral damage. My mother was beaten often, once badly enough to be hospitalized. I came home from school to discover the aftermath. I cleaned up the blood, threw away the broken pieces of a life lived badly, did my homework and went to bed.

My stepfather spent a few days in jail and went through the motions in rehab after which they reunited and we moved. I suppose we were all so desperate to feel *something*, pain was acceptable. Consequently nothing changed.

One late summer evening, another argument ensued. I listened from my room for the signs that would tell me where on the Richter scale this one would fall. The sound of crashing glass and a blood-curdling scream brought me into the living room where my stepfather began coming toward me. Something had snapped and when our eyes made contact I knew I was next. I turned, opened the front door and ran. A police car was heading toward the apartment; lights flashing and sirens wailing. I went the other way.

I would be fourteen in a couple of months, we had just moved to another state and I had no idea where I was. I wasn't enrolled in school yet, had no friends, no money, only the clothes I was wearing. But I knew one thing with every fiber of my body: that I wasn't going to live like that any longer. If my mother had chosen that for her life, it was her life and she could live it.

I stopped running as I came to the busy main highway. I stuck out my thumb and started walking. Within a few yards I came to a phone booth and it occurred to me I should let someone know what had happened. I stepped inside and placed a collect call to a number I hadn't dialed in a long time. As I heard my father's voice say "Hello," it was all I could do not to hang up. Already in a hyper state of anxiety, hearing his voice overwhelmed me. In a matter of seconds I was fighting back feelings I had suppressed for years. *Why couldn't he have saved me from all this?*

My dad was hard of hearing so I had to shout. "Dad, it's me. I need your help, I don't know what to do." I began to explain what had just taken place and rushed to finish before I completely lost it. I would not cry; that had driven him away once and I would never do it again. I could feel my heart pounding. I heard each beat inside my head. My hands were shaking and clammy and my knees were barely holding me up. I was hyperventilating and felt nauseous.

All I wanted to hear was, "Okay, it'll be all right," but from the other end of the phone, what he said was, "Theresa, I can't help you . . ." and that was all I heard. I hung up the phone with so much force I thought I broke it, slammed the phone booth door open and started walking. I don't know how far I went before I spent all the emotion—miles and years, it turned out.

When I was finally numb I knew I had to think. It was then I remembered we had ended up moving to that area because a close friend of my mother's lived nearby. She was listed in the phone book and I placed another collect call.

A few days and phone calls later my father knew I had found a place to stay and the friend interceded on my behalf to convince my mother I was better off not living with her any longer. There turned out to be a few strings attached with the new living arrangement but nothing I wasn't prepared to live with. I started my sophomore year of high school the week before Thanksgiving, found a job and stayed out of trouble.

For almost thirty years I put that part of my life behind me, having virtually no contact with anyone in my family until one day, the phone rang. Someone had tracked me down through an old friend who knew where I worked. My dad was dying.

From then on I spent as much time with my father as thousands of miles would allow. One afternoon as we sat quietly in the small living room of the rowhouse where he was born and raised, I told him that I was sorry for all the time we had lost. I explained that there was very little in my life I would change, even the worst parts that broke my spirit and my heart.

I could tell from the look in his eyes there were many regrets, more than we had time to make up for, and that he didn't have the energy to do this now. We sat silently and let the moment pass.

After a rest he reached for my hands, holding them in both of his, and closed his eyes. "You were my little girl and I didn't help you," he began softly. "I knew things were bad for you, but in those days kids stayed with their mothers." He opened his eyes and breathed deeply before continuing.

"But look how you turned out. You took care of yourself. You have people in your life who love you and protect you." Tears traced their way down his cheeks to be lost in the stubble of his chin.

"That night you called, I felt so helpless. I was hours away and I couldn't help you. I was going to try to calm you down and figure out what to do until I could get there, but. . . ."

I don't know what more he said. I was suddenly a terrified little girl again, trying to be brave in a phone booth hearing him say, ". . . I can't help you . . ."

An overwhelming sense of grief washed over me as I realized that my rashness in hanging up that phone had sentenced my father and me to a lifetime of estrangement.

I buried my face in his lap and cried like the baby he had left so many years ago. He stroked my hair and patted my back. He became my father that day, and I, his little girl. I can't say how long we stayed that way, but it felt like a lifetime—at the very least, a childhood.

He died a few weeks later, but during the time we had left together it was never difficult to say the few words that could have made such a difference so many years ago, "I love you." "I forgive you." "It'll be all right."

Theresa Peluso

Tears

I struggle with myself to keep them inside
The feelings that I have tried to deny.

I tell everyone that I am okay
When I battle to make it through each day.

In my world of illusions where everything was right
I cried myself to sleep each night.

You notice the tears filling my eyes
As I begin to shed my shallow disguise.

My pain, confusion and a few of my fears
Drop to the ground in the form of my tears.

It feels good to release the emotions built up
To say what I feel instead of bottling them up.

As I cry a weight seems to lift from me
I feel so much better now that you can see.

And now that you know what it is that I feel
Will you fight the battle with me and
help my wounds heal?

This poem is dedicated to my loving mom,
Jennifer Sumner.

Arianna Johnson

5

THE RESILIENT SOUL

No one can tell what goes on between the person you were and the person you become. No one charts that blue and lonely section of hell. There are no maps of the change. You just come out on the other side . . . or you don't.

Stephen King, The Stand

Christmas Hope

Do what you can, with what you have, where you are.

Theodore Roosevelt

The clink of shattering glass against the hardwood floor echoed in my ears like an old record stuck on a scratch. The china dinner plates? A crystal vase? Curiosity willed me to sneak downstairs. I cracked the creaky wooden door just enough for one wide eye to peak through.

My life was no Brady Bunch movie, not even on Christmas Eve. Other families sang carols at midnight Mass or sat around the tree reading *'Twas the Night Before Christmas*, but not mine. My heart wrenched at the sight of the once lovingly decorated tree sprawled across the living room surrounded by fragments of glass and plastic. My parents stomped angrily over the ornaments, crunching them like potato chips.

My surge of anger was quickly overpowered by fear as I retreated to the safety of my bedroom. I sat stiffly on the edge of my bed, staring into space and listening, willing my heart to go numb. Somewhere amidst the yelling and slamming doors, I heard a faint tapping. Just as I was about to dismiss the sound as squirrels running on the roof, a small head popped into my room.

Paul would turn nine next week, but as he shyly shuffled across my room, he looked much younger. Holding an old teddy bear in one hand and trying unsuccessfully to hide his tears with the other, Paul crawled onto the foot of my bed. As he curled himself into a tiny heap, I put my arms around him and held him as a mother would a child. His heavy cries came out in gasps, each new breath forcing his small body to rock so the large buttons on his shirt scraped against my chest.

One of Paul's hands remained clenched. I pried his fingers away from his palm to reveal the remains of a delicate glass bulb. Paul had witnessed the terrible scene, too. The angry shouts still drifted up from downstairs as I took the glass from my brother. Drops of blood speckled his hand from squeezing the rough edges. I quickly found a scarf from my closet and used it to bandage Paul's hand. The cuts weren't serious. I wish I could say the same about the tears.

We talked. What else was there to do? I made up silly stories about mischievous elves and cracked a lame joke or two. Paul gave me a sad, little smile, and together we did our best to salvage Christmas. We laughed. We cried. We prayed.

Sometime after midnight, when the yelling finally faded but sleep was still nowhere in sight, Paul shot out of bed like a rocket. He placed a finger to his lips and stood completely still, stiff as a board. Taking in a sharp breath, he turned to me. "Listen, reindeer!"

I started to laugh but quickly bit my tongue at Paul's disapproving stare. So I listened silently to the scraping on the roof, reminding me of squirrels once again. Staring at my brother, I saw something amazing—a smile. The Christmas tree was destroyed; presents were smashed; our father was drunk; and for a moment, one moment, none of it mattered. Belief and awe sparkled in Paul's aqua eyes and, for one amazing moment in time, I, too, believed in the miracle of Christmas.

Years have passed and those heart-wrenching holidays are little more than a distant nightmare, but I will always remember the gift I received that Christmas—a gift of hope.

Raquel M. Strand

Amanda Stays Safe

If they drop the atom bomb, if I want to have half a chance of survival, I want to be with a bunch of ACoAs.

Cathleen Brooks

Unquestionably a diminutive eight-year-old dynamo, in many other respects Amanda was well beyond her years. Framed by blonde curls and green, almond-shaped eyes, her smile welcomed the world. Everyone wanted to be Amanda's friend. Giggles and muffled laughter accompanied her wherever she went. But this warm, carefree façade barely concealed a little girl challenged by her confusion, hurt and fear: Amanda adored her mom more than anyone in the world, yet suffered and struggled with her mother's steady descent into the abyss of alcoholism.

Her parents were separated and Amanda lived with her father the majority of the time. He was an awesome parent, but despite his best efforts to shield Amanda, his youngest, from the chaos and insanity of her mom's illness, she and everyone else were entangled in it. Despite his concern, her dad accepted the deep bond Amanda had for her mother. Weekly, for almost six years, he drove her over an hour each way to participate in a children's program so she could better understand and successfully cope with the family's circumstances. A loving act. In exploring this extraordinary commitment he once remarked, "What I would have given had there been a program like this for me when I was a kid."

His eyes filled with tears and he gave me a long heartfelt hug as he whispered, "Thanks for helping my daughter." He was giving his little one the gift he had been denied as a child—a safe place to grow, learn and heal.

Amanda made great strides in the program. She quickly saw that she was not alone, that millions of other children love parents challenged by alcoholism and other drug addictions. She was relieved to understand that children don't make their parents drink and can't make them stop. These thoughts had really troubled her, often causing stomachaches and nightmares. Mom's drinking was not her fault. She became steadfast in her adherence to the basic program tenet—people with addictions are not bad people though sometimes they do bad things. "My mom is full of goodness," she would share. "That Mom plays with me, tucks me in bed at night, teaches me stuff and tells me how special I am. I really love her." After a long sigh she continues, "I hate the mom who drinks. I would give anything to have my real mom back." Many heads nodded affirmatively. Her sentiments echoed with all.

One night after an emotionally laden group session, Amanda hung around until we were all alone. "I must tell you something now. I can't hold it in any longer." We sat across from one another separated by a long awkward silence. Finally she found courage to explain what happened every other Saturday when she visited her mother. In the morning they would drive to her mom's favorite bar where Amanda sat alone in the car waiting for Mom to return. As tears flowed she blurted out, "Sometimes Mom comes out in twenty minutes, sometimes longer." Then, sobbing, she declared, "Jerry, sometimes I wait 'til it gets dark outside. I pray for Mommy to come back and I get so scared." I held this brave girl as she released emotions she'd buried deep inside for too long. Finally she continued, "Please don't take me away from my mom. I've never told anyone 'cause I'm scared I won't get to see her anymore. I love my mom."

In the Children's Program, youngsters learn the

importance of staying safe. They identify individuals, their "safe people," whom they can trust and call upon whenever they feel threatened or scared. Week after week we focused on these concepts. When Dad became aware of the circumstances he took many steps to protect his daughter but legal proceedings often take lots of time. I made sure Amanda always carried a small plastic container that fit easily in her pocket with the names and phone numbers of her safe people, along with fifty cents. Both her dad and I reviewed various scenarios where it would be necessary for her to call a safe person.

Many weeks later on a Saturday morning Amanda waited in the car again for her mother to come out of the bar. "I started to panic but then I remembered it's important to stay safe," she would later tell her group. She crossed a busy intersection at the crosswalk and found a pay phone.

There was no answer at her dad's and she couldn't get through to her grandma. Finally, she heard her big brother's strong reassuring voice, "I'll be there in ten minutes." Amanda re-crossed the street and walked into the bar to search for the mom she adored.

Finding her at last, Amanda crawled into her mom's lap and hugged her ever so tightly. Amanda kissed her and said, "Billy is coming to get me right now. I love you but I can't stay with you today. I just want to be a kid." Then, hopping to the floor she said, "I love you, Mommy. See you in two weeks." She navigated her way through the dimly lit bar and headed outside to find her big brother waiting.

Jerry Moe

"Of course I can accept you for who you are.
You are someone I need to change."

©2002 Randy Glasbergen, www.glasbergen.com

We Can Still Sing

Those who wish to sing, always find a song.

Swedish proverb

Every month it is my job to read the stories of children and their families who have been ravaged by tragedy and abuse. I am supposed to decide who can benefit from the particular services that my agency provides for children with psychiatric and behavioral problems as a result. The power of that statement is a bit heady even as I go back and read it. My employer is well-known in the United States and I am proud to say that I work there with an amazing team of professionals. I am but a small cog in the wheel.

I read an average of fifty to seventy "stories" or packets of clinical information every month. They just keep coming—it does not stop. We don't come to the end of the line and get to say "Okay! Let's close up shop! There are no more abused children left this year . . . no more parents who abandoned their kids today . . . no more teens who turned to drugs or ran away . . . no more parents who exploited their child or beat their spouse. . . ."

Quite often I answer the phone and the person says simply, "I need help with my son and was told you'd know what to do." Once in a while a desperate parent shows up at the door asking to drop off their child because they "just can't take it anymore." It can be overwhelming and depressing and sometimes I ride the freeway home and cry the whole way over the injustices of the world. It is hardest when the kids are so young, especially as a mother of a five-year-old. Most days I am simply amazed and proud of these kids and that despite their acting out and "behavior problems" they have simply survived.

But this is not my story . . . it is theirs.

I remember lots of kids in particular but one stands out that I thought could "speak for the group" if you will. Seven-year-old Marissa had been found by authorities at the age of six months, home alone with her four-year-old sibling who had been trying to diaper and feed her. The continuous crying finally alerted a neighbor. No one knows who her dad is and her mom left one day to score drugs, never to return. Marissa has spent the last six years of her short, short life moving from foster home to foster home, unable to emotionally attach to the adults who have come to care for her and separated from any biological family she may have known. In one of the foster homes, she was subjected to molestation by a caregiver for several months on a nightly basis.

Now she sits with me in my office, staring with huge doe eyes, swinging her legs back and forth. She's had her hair braided this morning and is holding a brown, stuffed dog. This is a big day. She has been told she is coming to stay for several months to work on her "anger" and "aggressive behaviors." I look at her and remember all of the cold clinical facts of her case. Now that she is right here in front of me I'd love to say "Hey, I'd hit and bite some folks too if I had been through what you have!" but instead I begin my talk with her, keeping her particular issues in mind so as to make her feel as safe as possible. I want her to feel comfortable to ask any questions she'd like.

The first thing she wants to know is what kind of "field trips" we'll go on. As I am explaining what I think is pretty serious stuff about these "field trips," her behaviors, the program expectations . . . blah, blah, blah . . . she stops me and simply says in a loud, clear voice, "Wanna hear me sing a song?" She caught me so off guard—I mean, what a perfectly wonderful seven-year-old thing to say! I nodded my head and she stood and sang, standing proud with her chin in the air and her eyes shining. She sang to a stranger with her stuffed dog in hand and all she owned in suitcases by the door.

I was treated to the best rendition of "Itsy Bitsy Spider" that I have ever heard to this date. Her ability to do that reminded me that despite the awful things I read and see every day, mine is a great reward to meet each and every one of these kids. I should drive home every day on that freeway with a grin on my face for that gift. Most important, Marissa reminds us that no matter what happens in our lives . . . we can still sing.

Jennifer M. Reinsch

Could You Be the One?

No one can make you feel inferior without your consent.

Eleanor Roosevelt

From the age of ten I had been involved with a street gang, rising to the rank of leader where part of my job was to disseminate gang literature to young recruits. A series of drug and gang-related crimes quite predictably led to prison where I finally confronted my addictions and took an honest look at the choices I had made in my life. Even in the early stages of my recovery I knew that I wanted to go to college to learn to counsel drug addicts. The only problem was I had completed only three months of my freshman year of high school and I was functionally illiterate.

Toward the end of my prison term I was moved to solitary confinement where the former inmate had left behind a copy of *The Autobiography of Malcolm X*. When I arrived I promptly picked it up and threw it in the corner of the cell, where the book sat for two months, until one day, out of boredom, I picked it up again. Being unfamiliar with books I figured the "juicy" part had to be in the middle, so I opened it to the middle—to a page where Malcolm X describes being in prison and unable to read. That got my attention. As I read more I learned that we were arrested at approximately the same age and that he, too, was a dropout. Malcolm X learned to read in prison by reading the dictionary from cover to cover. I decided I would do the same. As I read his autobiography and came across a word I didn't understand, I worked through the frustration and looked it up in the dictionary.

I left solitary confinement a different person. While I couldn't deny I was still an inmate, I no longer felt like a prisoner. Once I learned to read, I was free. Inmates in the general population were required to lock themselves in their own cells each evening, and I found the act of doing so impossible. My cellmates did it for me.

I re-entered society through a prison-based, long-term, residential drug treatment program, where I also began working on my GED. I'd spent most of my life as a hustler, gang member, drug addict and convict. But there, in that class, I studied hard, even though I felt inferior. I re-read some of the gang material with new understanding and saw the hypocrisy between the message and the real lifestyle of a gang member. From that point on my heart and my mind left the life of crime and drugs behind. I knew I needed a high school diploma in order to get a job, and there was a part of me that felt a diploma would compensate a bit for my criminal past. I took the GED test with my inner voice saying, *You'll fail; you're a convict* and I failed. But I had come so close to passing, I knew I would pass the second time—and did.

I was thirty-one years old when I got a Social Security card, a state I.D., and registered to vote for the first time in my life. I found temporary work in construction and a full-time job in a factory, but what I still wanted to do was help others—drug addicts and gang members, people who had gone through experiences similar to mine. I enrolled in a training program for addiction counselors at a community college, and when a job opening as an assistant counselor at a drug rehab program became available, I figured it was now or never and scheduled an interview.

As I got off the train on my way to the interview, my feelings of inferiority kicked in and my confidence started to erode. I felt that I had an invisible sign in the middle of my forehead that read, "Ex-convict, dope fiend—don't hire me." And I was paranoid; the program was in a rich suburb where I was sure the police would be ready to arrest me as soon as I got off the train. Fortunately, my determination overshadowed my self-talk and I was hired.

For months I sat in staff meetings completely quiet, thinking that if I opened my mouth, my colleagues would know that I was a high school dropout with a GED. One day a psychiatrist made a statement, which my street knowledge and course work told me wasn't accurate. I respectfully disagreed. A moment of silence ensued and I sat terrified, as I realized I had just contradicted a respected psychiatrist during a staff meeting. When he replied, "Benneth, you just made a great point," my confidence grew and my instinct was confirmed. I was on the right path and I would follow it as far as it took me.

Sixteen years ago I sat in the center, first row, directly in front of Mark Sanders in a class of forty students who all hoped to become addictions counselors. Recently Mark told me he could clearly see that I was listening more attentively than the other thirty-nine. He said there was a look in my eye that said, "I really want to learn this stuff."

I guess the same tenacity I applied to my crimes and drug use as a young man served me well while following my dream. There were many times when I wanted to give up, when the obstacles seemed insurmountable and the work too hard, but I knew the choice to keep moving forward was the most important one I would ever make in my life.

I've been sober for twenty years now and in 2000 I received an award for "Counselor of the Year" out of eight thousand addictions counselors in the state of Illinois. I lecture internationally on addictions and criminal justice issues. My work is rewarding and I feel as if I make a difference in the lives of people I touch.

Not long ago, Mark told me that each time he faces a

group—as a teacher, lecturer or speaker—he thinks of me
and looks at each member knowing the potential that lies
dormant in all those who cross his path and asks himself,
Are you the one? I can't thank him enough for knowing that
I was.

Benneth Lee as told to Mark Sanders

Choices

Some people sit, some people try.
Some people laugh, some people cry.

Some people will, some people won't.
Some people do, some people don't.

Some people believe and develop a plan.
Some people doubt never think that they can.

Some people face hurdles and give it their best.
Some people back down when faced with a test.

Some people complain of their miserable lot.
Some people are thankful for all that they've got.

And when it's all over when it comes to an end
Some people lose out and some people win.

We all have a choice, we all have a say.
We are spectators in life or we get in and play.

Whichever we choose how we handle life's game
The choices are ours, no one else is to blame.

Tom Krause

Discards

Hope is faith in the me yet to be.

Treatment Counselor,
Tallahassee Community Hospital

Thinking about who inspired me to do what I do today, well-known names or successful businessmen don't come to mind. My parents taught me my work ethic and I've relied on my school buddies for their friendship and support no matter what was going on in my life. But as I sit in my office and see what I've accomplished over the last thirty-five years, I think I have to thank a bunch of skid row alcoholics and just as importantly, the staff who cared to help them back into society.

When I packed my bags and master's degree to head into the business world, my first significant job was with a very conservative research foundation in Canada. This organization was recognized for being a pioneer in addictions research and they chugged out tons of paperwork filled with statistics and correlations about the impact of alcohol addiction. Drugs were only beginning to become a problem, so the focus was on alcoholism. I chafed at the seriousness of the business, the endless bureaucracy, the tricky politics.

It was here at one of their pilot projects that I first encountered skid row alcoholics—men who had all hit bottom and had been there for some time. They were considered beyond help and this project was their last chance.

They participated in all the clinical studies administered by the research foundation, but seemed to have too much time on their hands despite being "employed" at a farm operation run by the foundation. The directors and staff wanted a more meaningful work program that would both challenge and excite the residents as well as create a variety of tasks requiring different skills. I thought about alternatives, something we could implement that would keep the residents busy, generate more revenue and be less of an issue with safety, which was a problem with the farming activities.

I've always had a love of antiques. What better way to combine my interests and my new challenges at work than to refinish antiques and sell them? I cleared out one of the old barns on the farm, turned it into a showroom, bought a few tools and started accumulating discards—furniture and people, it would seem.

In very little time, I had the workforce well occupied and genuinely interested in their work. Sam was a quiet, reticent man who could hit a baseball a mile. Harold, a rotund, boisterous guy, reminded me of W.C. Fields in more ways than one. And Macky, a wiry little Irishman, blamed his genes for his alcoholism—turns out he wasn't off base with that one. There were a few others, but these guys were the A-team. A storied collection of humanity whose chances at a decent life had all but slipped through their fingers. The program was bringing them back and putting life back into their eyes.

Each day they arrived at the barn for work and tackled the tasks assigned. Harold would be whistling Ellington's "Take the 'A' Train" or humming "Working for the Man" by Roy Orbison while he stripped old varnish and lacquer. Sam paid particular attention to the sanding, careful not to damage the patina of the old wood. Macky had a talent for gluing and dovetailing loose joints, re-caning a seat, using the lathe or the router. Each restored piece became a metaphor for life thrown away that was now salvaged and returned to a desirable, useful, valuable state.

Macky, Sam, Harold and the others found a renewed sense of self-respect and reclaimed a place in productive society. They held jobs, learned and refined new skills and found their misplaced honor again.

I had set up the front of the barn as a showroom where we displayed our collection of restored antiques. The boys were great salesmen, showing off the farm and their work. Sales were steady and we became known around the area. We expanded the program and began manufacturing antique pine reproductions. We became an enterprise. I stayed a couple of more years before moving on to South Florida and founding Health Communications.

As important as the scientific study was in trying to understand and ameliorate the destructive effects of addiction, it was just as important, if not more so, to address the human side of the disease. Giving a person an opportunity to contribute and a chance to heal would keep more people sober than all the research in the world.

As I do whatever I can to make a positive difference in the lives of people I—and we as a company—touch, I often think of the boys, the skid row alcoholics back on the farm and the staff who devoted their lives ever so caringly—and the impact they had on my life. I'm not sure in which moment, with what experience, I went from a bureaucrat to a caring human . . . but it did happen and I wouldn't have it any other way.

Peter Vegso

I Am the Story I Tell Myself

A friend is one who walks in when others walk out.

Walter Winchell

A single note rises, then falls like a raindrop at my feet, shattering into a thousand tiny rainbows. I think there must be an angel caged in the cell next to mine. If I could play the instrument of my voice as miraculously, would I be closer to God? It seems my destiny is to be an ordinary raven, even here, where birds are forbidden to fly.

The jangling of keys and slamming of gates break my reverie. A prison guard bellows, "Get out here, crack head!"

I rise, as do the over forty other women who have shared this cell with me over the past three days. None of us is certain to whom she refers. It is not me, not this time.

I sink back to the floor that has become so cold I could ice skate on it. I seek out the largest woman (the fat ones give off the most body heat), and huddle close to her. In here we have no prejudice or pride. Out there we took each other's money and drugs, in here we give each other warmth and comfort.

A harsh voice shouts, "Barr!" It is my turn. I enter the shower room and strip quickly. I immediately squat and cough while bouncing up and down. I want to please the guards. I have been here before and I know the rules well. I am shoved into an icy shower and sprayed with horrid smelling lotion to "de-louse" me. I wonder why they bother when they don't wash our clothes. I am pushed soaking wet into another freezing cell. I dry off as best as I can with my filthy pants.

Just as sleep comes to steal me from this misery, another voice intrudes, this one much kinder than I am used to.

"Ladies, my name is Mr. Smith. A few years ago I was in a worse position than you, and look at me now. I have a fine job, fine clothes and I'm fine lookin' too. If you want what I've got, you've got to do what I did to get it. I pledge my support to anyone willing to make a change."

I step out of my cell not even flinching when the gate clangs shut behind me. As we are walking to the dormitory where I will be housed I hear shouting and stomping. I am amazed when we arrive and I see that it is military marching and cadence.

"My God, Mr. Smith," I exclaim, "you didn't tell me I was joining the army!"

"There's a lot more to it than this, Mary," he says.

A woman detaches herself from a marching group and comes towards me. "Hi, I'm Lori, the unit captain. In this program it's mandatory that we attend school. We have five minutes to line up so let's go."

We march down the bleak hallways to school shouting an army cadence. I suppress an urge to giggle, especially since the women in general population are watching us with interest. Unlike the adolescent population housed in jail, adults do not get to go to school. It took a lot of work to allow our special program into the computer class. Most of the women in general population spend their days bored and frustrated, sometimes fighting, and getting high. Yes, there are drugs in jail.

After two hours we march back to our dorm where a social worker greets us. She is the only social worker for over two thousand women so we are fortunate to have her tonight. She suggests that we go into residential treatment when we leave, but I can't see myself doing that after being locked up for a year. We meet with her in a group to discuss our issues, which run the gamut from being abused, to being illiterate. This is one time when I am glad there are only one hundred beds available for treatment; I may get a chance to ask her a question.

A lady I don't know starts the group. "I'm lucky they let me back in here," she says through tears. "They told me not to go home, but I missed my kids so much. When I got there they just wanted to go out with friends, and my daughter hid her purse from me when she thought I wasn't looking. I didn't want her to see me crying so I went to a friend's house. Just like when I got busted, she was gettin' high. I was upset so I got high right along with her. This time I am going to take the cotton out of my ears and stick it in my mouth."

God works in mysterious ways. Though our stories are not the same I feel the same way. I have not seen my children or their father for two years. I do not want to make the same mistakes as this woman. I was no longer afraid to die, I was afraid of living my life the way I was. I decided to go to residential treatment when I was released and tried to convince my peers to do the same.

The day of my release has come and I am sent off with hugs. I await the volunteer who will drive me from jail to the program and I laugh aloud when I see that it is Mr. Smith. There is a certain symmetry to arriving at yet another program with Mr. Smith, and I pray I will be as successful in this one.

A single note rises then falls like a raindrop at my feet, shattering into a thousand tiny rainbows. I step up to the cell and say, "Honey, you sing like an angel. A few years ago I was in a worse position than you, and look at me now. Would you like to hear more?" The angel looks at me and smiles.

Mary Barr

Take Care of Yourself

What is most precious becomes memory. Paths not taken are forever gone. The only useless endeavor is to resist the command knit into our very souls, move. Move on.

Unknown

Two nights before our wedding my fiancé, a recovering alcoholic, drank an entire bottle of vodka. His friend found the empty bottle and stated the obvious, "You don't need this in your life," as he showed it to me. I really didn't. I had one dysfunctional marriage behind me and I was taking care of a disabled daughter. But I loved Tom and wanted to marry him.

"I promise I'll never drink again," he said.

How naïve I was to believe him! But I knew very few people who were addicted to alcohol, and no one who was close to me. I really didn't know anything about the disease and I wasn't paying attention to the fact that Tom's first marriage had ended because of alcohol abuse. I ignored family and friends who were trying to dissuade me from marrying him because I wanted someone, and so did he. We were married in November.

The following May he relapsed, drinking off and on until New Year's Day. During that time I attended a few meetings and told him if he didn't stop drinking the marriage was over. He finally stopped, and was dry for three years. I really thought he was on that long road to recovery when he began turning to alcohol to soothe the pain of an arthritic back.

I was sympathetic to his pain, but at the same time I was furious. With all of the treatment programs he had gone through in his first marriage, surely he knew alcohol was poison to his body. And then there was his promise the night before our wedding: "I'll never drink again."

I had married him for better or for worse, as my friends reminded me—the same friends who had told me I shouldn't marry him. And they were right. I was his wife, I did care about him and I was the kind of person who tried to help those she loved. I felt I needed to give him another chance. However, even as I got him into a rehab program, I wasn't sure I wanted to stay with him. Still angry about broken promises, I had no intention of attending the weekly family meetings, but the intake counselor convinced me I should—for myself. I was glad I did.

At the first meeting I was astonished when the family education director said, "It goes against the Christian ethic that says 'Help thy brother' when I tell you to let your brother be and take care of yourself."

Take care of yourself was repeated again and again for four weeks until its bold, black letters were engraved in our brains. The addicted loved one, we were told, was anesthetized; we weren't. We had nothing to dull our emotional pain, and the more we focused on them, the sicker we became. But if we stopped worrying about them and took care of ourselves, there was hope.

Easy to say. Not so easy to do. I soon found myself doing some of the things on the list of enabling behaviors. With one eye I would watch what he ate. I panicked when I saw he was using Nyquil, which contains a lot of alcohol. Occasionally I would look in his car or the shed for an empty bottle when his face was particularly flushed. There were definite signs that he was heading into another major relapse and my searching for empty bottles wasn't going to help him or me. I didn't know what would.

Tom had lost his full-time job, had a new part-time one

but that insurance company wouldn't authorize a full month of rehab and I knew ten days wouldn't help much; he was too sick. I was frantic and he was out of control using credit cards, drinking and driving. I took away the credit cards, but I couldn't stop him from drinking.

I was becoming sick, emotionally and physically. My disabled daughter was distraught as she saw the toll the disease was taking on me. I had to protect her and myself. He would have to leave. To tell him we were separating was going to require more inner strength than I had.

At AA meetings I had found people from all faiths who believed in a Higher Power. My Higher Power was the Heavenly Father, the God of the Christian scriptures. I needed his help to confirm my decision and to comfort me. Searching for that comfort one beautiful afternoon in early August I took my daughter to her sister's and drove to the small cemetery where I sat alone in the shade of a maple tree and prayed. "Heavenly Father, please help me to know what to do."

Birds twittered. Leaves rustled in a breeze. I listened. And then the words, "Take care of yourself," came to my mind. The same words I had heard over and over again in the family education sessions.

I felt peace flow like a river through my body, and knew my prayer was answered.

Getting the answer was the easy part. The difficult part was confronting Tom. I felt so sad. Even though the marriage was crumbling, largely because of alcohol, Tom was a good, kind, very Christian man who had the gift of charity. He had helped my children and me so much I didn't want to hurt him. I hoped he would be able to take care of himself and recover, but deep down I doubted he could. He was sixty-two years old and he had been drinking since his early twenties. His dependency had taken its toll on his body and his spirit. As they say in AA, I had to "Let go and let God."

That Saturday morning we were sitting together in the

van in the grocery store parking lot. I took a deep breath and said in a voice that was amazingly calm and steady, "Listen carefully, Tom. If you take one more drink, we're going to separate."

That afternoon he went out to get a part for the van. He was gone a long time. Too long. I wasn't surprised when through the kitchen window I saw the van weave from side to side as he pulled into the driveway. I wasn't surprised, though I was weak with anxiety, as I saw him stagger when he got out.

He opened the hood of the van and glared at me as I went over to the driver's side and opened the door. My legs were trembling so much I was afraid they wouldn't hold me up as I reached for the paper sack on the floor of the van and found the almost empty bottle of vodka.

"It's an old bottle," he said in a surly voice.

I shook my head. "No, Tom. I was in the car with you this morning. There was no bottle in the van then."

He was silent.

"Do you remember what I said to you this morning?"

"Yes," he said, avoiding my eyes.

"I can't live with this any longer. It's making us sick. Maybe you can live with your daughter until you can get an apartment. You'll have to work it out and then we can see about getting together again. I'm sorry," I said.

"So am I." He raised sad eyes, but this time he didn't beg me to give him another chance. This time he knew I wouldn't.

Feeling relief, feeling pain, I went in my room and cried.

He left, and two weeks later he committed suicide. He wrote a note to his children that said he could see no way out. He couldn't recover.

Loved ones of a suicide often blame themselves but I don't. I know the choices he made in his life were his choices, not mine. Rather, because of my faith in a loving, merciful God and because I have experienced many difficult trials in my sixty-four years, I have learned how to survive and choose to survive well. I have family and friends. I exercise. I write stories and poetry. I am involved in my church. I am fully alive as I believe Tom is also, a man who loved and served his family and who is no longer burdened by a disease that had him in its awful grip.

I was comforted when he died and am still comforted by my faith in a God who says, "Peace I leave with you, my peace I give unto you: not as the world giveth, give I unto you. Let not your heart be troubled, neither let it be afraid" (John 14:27).

I take one day at a time, enjoy the rain and the sun, endure the ice and the freezing winds—and feel peace.

Ann Best

You Become What You Want to Be

The most common sort of lie is the one uttered to one's self.

Nietzsche

Growing up the fifth of six children was a challenge, the struggle for placement and acceptance being the usual issues. Personally, I never felt I needed to be heard or seen. Taught to be seen and not heard from the time we were born, when we broke that rule we were punished severely.

I had several strikes against me growing up. I had very little self-esteem, if any. Our mother had a hair-trigger temper and we constantly had to avoid her wrath, learning to fear and not thrive as children. Even when we weren't in trouble, we felt like we had done something wrong. Talking about love or sex in our house was totally taboo. Our home lacked warmth and my fears of incurring my mother's anger outweighed my desire to talk to her about very important things that should have been dealt with as a child, not as an adult.

My childhood was short. I always say I graduated from the school of hard knocks, and meant it. I was molested between the ages of ten and thirteen by four different family friends and a family member. I was an alcoholic by the time I was fourteen and a frequent user of drugs when I wasn't drunk.

I was not popular in school, my grades were not great and the only thing I excelled at was spelling, which would not carry me far. My mom planted the seeds and watered them daily, telling me I wasn't smart enough or good enough to reach the goals I set for myself in life. I wanted to be a teacher, a stewardess or a nurse. At one time, I had many, many dreams. Not one of them was something my mother encouraged or thought I could accomplish.

I made mistakes, too many to mention and some so humiliating that I cringe inside today as I recall them. The drugs, the alcohol and the self-destructive path I was on were not things I was proud of. I wanted so desperately to change, but I had no idea how. I just wasn't good enough to succeed at anything. The only positive thing left was my desire to try.

I started dating a guy when I was thirteen, falling hopelessly in love with him. True to form, my mother told me I would never do better and on my sixteenth birthday we were engaged. We moved in together after high school and married at nineteen. We had two beautiful kids together, and that was the turning point in my life. Being a good mother was something I could accomplish.

Marrying so young was wrong, we both knew it. We were drawn to each other for all the wrong reasons. It was bad for him, it was bad for me, it was bad for the children, so I started my road to recovery by divorcing him. We never harbored any hate or animosity for each other and frankly I liked him better once we lived apart. He became a better father and a better person and I too became a better human being.

I began to reinvent and get reacquainted with myself. I faced my problems with the help of psychologists and social workers, who taught me healthy parenting and life skills. With their help and encouragement I learned to talk with my kids and to value them for who they were. I am able to guide them toward realizing their full potential through encouragement and emotional support. And, I have stayed clean and sober.

During therapy I remembered the sexual abuse and came forward to have the man arrested and charged with his crimes. I felt wonderful, vindicated and strong when he was convicted twenty years later for the crimes he committed against me.

I look back with 20/20 hindsight and wonder why my educators never picked up on my abuse. The signs were there, I read it in my report cards. About a sullen little girl who sulks and wants to be the center of attention, and cries. *No, I don't want to be the center of attention. I just want to be loved. Can't you see that!* I remember all the incidents as if they were yesterday and have worked hard to move beyond feeling like a victim.

Today I feel lucky. I have a wonderful husband, two more great kids and a home in the country, a life far beyond the dreams of a kid being drowned in the toilet. I have never beaten my children or belittled them. I overcame great odds, faced the loathing and shame, and grieved for the loss of my childhood so that the cycle stopped with me. In its place a life centered on love and nurturing has taken root and I am careful to plant more seeds and water them daily.

Marilyn Joan

Carry On

At times when you feel troubled
When your happiness is gone
Look to the heart within you
for the strength to carry on.

In your heart you will find special virtues
Such as faith and hope and love.
These gifts have been sent down to you
from a Power up above.

It is faith that keeps the soul searching
for the joy the heart hopes for.
It is love that heals the spirit
making it stronger than before.

And if your heart be broken
if your strength should fade away
the power of these virtues
will still win out the day.

So remember when you're troubled
when your happiness is gone
look to the heart within you
for the strength to carry on.

Tom Krause

My Mom's a Party Girl

I will bend like a reed in the wind.

Frank Herbert, *Dune*

"My mom's a party girl," he said matter-of-factly as soon as we stepped outside.

A party girl? I thought. This woman was sliding out of her chair onto the floor and left an empty bottle of gin on the kitchen counter. Party girl?

He must have seen the mortified look on my face that night he brought me home to meet his mom for the first time. She struggled to turn around in her chair, tried to focus her blurry eyes, and began to stutter, "How are . . . how are . . . you?" The lights were all dark in the family room as she sat in front of the TV drinking alone.

"This is my friend, Carla," he said casually as if talking to June Cleaver. "We're going out to grab some burgers, then I'm going to take her home. I won't be late, Mom."

She leaned over the arm of the recliner and tried to form a sentence again.

"Hey! Hey!" she called after us in a much too loud voice. It embarrassed me. What did she want?

"You kids . . . you kids . . . have fun!" she finally said pointing at us and winking.

We stepped out onto the driveway and I looked at his face. There was not a trace of embarrassment. He could have told me she was a drunk, a lush or a boozer. He could have rolled his eyes and made explanations like,

"You'll have to excuse my mom, she's an alcoholic."

He could have made all kinds of excuses, but he didn't. He chose instead to accept her completely and without one hint of an apology to say simply, "My mom's a party girl."

I was a sheltered little goody-two-shoes. My parents were, as his mother would have put it, "teetotalers." I had rarely even seen someone drunk before. I met Rich at my church. He didn't drink or smoke and, after the losers I dated in college, seemed to be the most together guy I had ever met. I had no idea he had come from this kind of a home life. He didn't deny his mother's obvious problem, but he didn't shame her for it either. Not for one minute.

This is a man who accepts his mother for who she is, I thought. *This is a man who respects women.* And that was the night I fell in love with him.

I had never heard the Al-Anon message about having compassion for the alcoholic and accepting them for who they are until many years later, but it came naturally to Rich. When he was growing up, his house was "party central," with people falling over drunk on the front lawn and parking sideways. The neighbors nicknamed his cul-de-sac, "alcoholic's circle." Every week, Rich, the oldest of the five kids, was asked to drive home one of his parents' "drinkin' buddies" who couldn't see straight. When he was nine, his parents taught him how to mix martinis for them when they couldn't stumble into the kitchen anymore. It was only our second date when he opened up and told me about his father.

"My first summer home from college, Mom and Dad went up to the lake with the Johnsons across the street. The Johnsons were big boozers like my parents."

"Your dad drank too?" I asked.

"Are you kidding? We didn't have family dinners. The kids were fed early and the parents had 'toonies' all night."

"So the Johnsons drank with them?"

"Yeah, all the time. Anyway, they were up at the lake

and I'm sure they were all boozing. My dad decided he wanted to go in for a swim. They were on the dock watching him but all of sudden he didn't surface. They waited and kept calling for him but there was no sign of him. Mr. Johnson dove in, but it was too dark to see anything. They found my dad's body the next morning."

"Is that why your mom drinks?" I asked.

"No. My mom drank long before my dad died."

"Why does she drink?"

"I don't know. I have no idea."

"Have you ever tried to confront her about it or get her to stop?"

"Are you kidding? She'd cry and feel absolutely terrible, and then you know what she'd do? She'd make herself a drink."

Rich burst out laughing. I did too. It was amazing how completely unruffled he was by this. What in the world was his secret?

"She's my mom; it's not my job to change her. I just love her, that's all. She's actually a cutie."

The way he smiled when he talked about her amazed me. There was not an ounce of bitterness for her or his dad. Rich was like Teflon. Hurts and disappointments just didn't stick to him.

"You're a lot like my mom," he told me one day.

"Are you kidding me? I don't even drink. I'm the most conservative person you know. How in the world could I be like her?"

"You are." He smiled. "You're funny, and outgoing, and you cheer me on like she does. You're like the real person my mom is. Not the drunk one. She always says to me, 'Richard, I believe you can do anything you put your mind to, darling.' That's who my mom really is. You're like that too," he smiled. "You keep me cheered up."

Rich and I had been married twelve years when his mother had chest pains and fell into a coma. He boarded the next flight to San Francisco and found her lying in the hospital surrounded by machines.

"Can I talk to her?" he asked the nurse.

"She's in a coma, sir, but you can try."

Rich pulled up a chair and prayed for her quietly, holding onto her arm. Then he whispered into her ear. "I love you, Mom, you're the best mother anyone could have had." He held her hand and rubbed it gently. "You raised us five kids even after losing Dad. You made our breakfast every morning—cinnamon toast and cocoa. Remember, Mom? You did all those piles of laundry and you came to all my baseball games. You never missed one. You gave us all a good life. Don't ever feel bad, Mom, you were a great mother."

He stroked her hair back and suddenly noticed a tear rolling down her cheek.

"Nurse? Come here, what's this?"

"It's tears," she said. "I believe she's crying."

"Does that mean she can hear me?"

The nurse came closer and looked at her face, "I'm sure she can."

Rich squeezed her hand and put his head on her arm. "I love you, Mom."

Two days later Rich had to fly home. Her condition did not change, and he called each evening checking on her progress. Then the early morning call came that Saturday.

Mom was gone.

Rich had spent his last hour with his mother the way he had spent his whole life with her: showing compassion.

When other people describe their loved one who drinks and complain how crazy it makes them, I tell them about my husband.

"Quit trying to change them and try some compassion," I say. "You'd be amazed how peaceful your life will become."

Carla Riehl

Twenty-Four Hours to Live

Don't compromise yourself. You're all you've got.

Betty Ford

My relationship with money had always been one filled with a good bit of mystery and intrigue. Mystery because I seldom knew what was going to happen until it happened, and intrigue because I was under the misguided assumption that forces in the universe were conspiring to ensure the money stuff would take care of itself.

I believed that if I worked hard, had good intentions and was a good person, my financial needs would be met. I had taken the law of karma, twisted it a bit for my own purposes and organized my life that way. There was no real need to initiate financial planning if the universe would provide. Rather than taking personal responsibility, I reacted, stumbling from one financial situation to another, without much of a sense of purpose or plan.

Though I had nearly twenty years of recovery under my belt and had seen my relationship with my children, wife, friends, and self grow and mature, I just couldn't seem to wrap my head around how this money thing worked. I just tried not to worry about it.

One chilly Thanksgiving afternoon, I received the news that yet another promising business deal that was supposed to provide for our retirement was not going to work out. With my wife gently weeping on the couch, I stated with more conviction than clarity, "I don't know what I mean or how to fix it, but there is something wrong with my thinking around money and how it works that keeps getting me into situations like this."

I recognized that in my financial life I often found myself at the mercy of someone else's behavior. For the first time I realized there might be something fundamentally wrong with my belief system regarding how money works. I had hit my financial bottom and I had learned enough from other aspects of my recovery process to know that in every painful situation each party brings about 50 percent of the responsibility to the event. I was determined to find out what my part of the equation was.

I began reading all that I could about the psychology of money, talked to everyone who would listen about the subject, began seeking therapeutic support and contacted our CPA. I told him that we were determined to take control of our own financial future, and that we wanted to begin preparing for retirement. We came up with a pretty simple plan. We were to send him a check each month and we could reach our goal in a reasonable amount of time.

Unfortunately, my journey with money was not going to go that smoothly. Though I had it, I could not bring myself to actually send the check. He would call and badger, cajole, plead and beg me to send him the money; I would write out the check, address the envelope and put it on my desk. I just couldn't send it. I had lots of excuses, but the fact was I couldn't do it and I didn't really understand why. My journey to understanding took two more years.

In what I have come to recognize as God's timing, one day I received a note from an acquaintance who I had not heard from in twelve years. He was a financial planner and was recovery. He told me about his work with people around their money issues and asked if I knew of anyone who might be interested in what he was doing, to let him know. Did I know of someone? It was me! In talking with him about the quest I was on and the problems I had in taking care of myself, even though I knew what to do, he very quickly helped me get to the core of my dilemma.

He first asked me to envision what retirement would look like to me. My mind went blank. I really had no immediate picture come to mind, but gradually one began to emerge of me sitting looking out the window in a nice warm place doing nothing. I realized that what retirement meant to me was, "I quit." That vision was quickly followed by the thought *I don't want to quit.* Suddenly it was perfectly clear to me why I wasn't able to send the retirement checks. If quitting is what retirement represented, I didn't want to do it. By not sending the checks in I was guaranteeing that I never could or would be able to quit. I would be one of those people who would be complaining about not being able to quit working in their sixties, as if someone else made that happen.

This realization was followed by a growing awareness that maybe I could make my retirement mean anything I wanted it to. The picture of how my retirement could look began to emerge, and in it I was imagining what it would feel like to only do what I wanted to do, when I wanted, with the people that I wanted to do it with. I really liked that picture. Then I had the thought, *Why wait until then to begin living and working that way?*

Next my friend asked me to identify what my deepest loves and needs were. One part of the discovery process was to imagine that I had only twenty-four hours to live. The twist was instead of figuring out how I would spend my last day, I was to consider what I would regret never having accomplished. I felt good about the fact that because of my recovery I had very few regrets. But that simple exercise motivated me to begin immediately taking care of those I did have. These issues were really about making sure that the three most important people in my life, my wife and two children, knew how much I loved them and how grateful and thankful I was for them being a part of my life.

As a result of the work I did, I began sending checks in for my retirement at twice the rate that I had suggested I was ever capable of. I immediately began sorting out the things about my work that I could let go of so that I could begin living my vision of what retirement is, years before I actually retire. I felt so inspired by my experience that I helped create a workshop where others can address their money issues.

I had never felt better in my life, then during my annual health check-up last April my doctor said, "We will need to start monitoring your health much more closely, it seems your liver disease has progressed to the last stage. We don't believe you have liver cancer yet, but we need to keep a close watch." He said a few other things that I didn't quite catch. We said our good-byes and I left the office. I was stunned by the news. In one brief moment everything changed. I thought about my plans for retirement, wondering if I would live to see that day. I called my wife and told her the news. As I was talking to her, I suddenly remembered the no longer hypothetical "twenty-four hours to live" exercise.

I heard myself saying, "Remember that exercise, the one that asked you to consider what regrets you might have if you had only twenty-four hours to live? Well, I can't think of any. All of the people that I love know I love them and I know that they love and honor me. There's no unfinished business with any of them. I can't tell you how grateful I feel."

As ironic as it may sound, tears of joy began to run down my cheeks. Who would have thought that my journey to understanding my irrational money behaviors would pay off with such dividends?

We have a saying in our work with people, "It is never about the money." For me, it has never been more true.

Ted Klontz

"I do so share my deepest emotions with you!
Hungry and tired are my deepest emotions."

©2003 Randy Glasbergen, www.glasbergen.com

The Camel teaches us to go twice to our knees
Pick up our load with the greatest of ease
And walk through the day with our head held
  high
Staying—for this day—completely dry.

Anonymous

6

OUR COMMUNITY AND DIVERSITY

Never let your head hang down. Never give up and sit down and grieve. Find another way. And don't pray when it rains if you don't pray when the sun shines.

Satchel Paige

Vita

An eye for an eye only makes the whole world blind.

Mahatma Mohandas Gandhi

"You poor old thing," Cassie whispered gently as she softly caressed the mare's lowered head. "I know you have a story to tell if we would only listen . . . I know how you feel," she finished softly.

"Come on, Cass," Jerri said hurriedly. "There's loads more horses to see. And in a much better state than this one," she added.

"I don't need to see any more," replied Cassie, "she's the one I want."

"You're joking, right?" asked Jerri incredulously. Then she saw Cassie's face. "You're not joking are you? I don't believe this, look at her, Cass! You couldn't get more broken down if you tried. With that sway back, potbelly and those hooves, not to mention her age, all she'll ever be is a hay burner!"

"There's more to owning horses than riding," announced Cassie firmly.

"I agree," said Jerri, "but it's sure nice to have the option."

"It's been two weeks and nothing," said Cassie to Jerri. "She's had the best food and she's been groomed every day, not to mention the countless treats. She doesn't care; it's almost as though she's given up, you know?"

She watched the mare slowly amble over to her hay.

There is such indifference even in that, Cassie thought,

and she knew that were she to remove the hay, the old mare probably wouldn't care one iota.

"Why are you doing this to yourself?" asked Jerri with a look of concern on her face. "After all you've been through, why set yourself up for disappointment?"

"I'm not!" declared Cassie. "It's still early days yet . . ."

"Cassie!" Jerri said, "Now more than ever you need positive things, good things in your life, not this," stated Jerri as she pointed at the lackluster equine. "I still can't believe what Jeff did. How could he leave you after . . . after . . . well, everything?" she finished quietly.

"I guess he just couldn't handle it," replied Cassie.

"That doesn't wash with me, Cass," stated Jerri angrily. "That excuse should definitely not be coming out of your mouth. He does not deserve your defense, Cass, not now, not ever."

Cassie sighed; she didn't want to argue, not today. Today wasn't a good day for intensity.

Jerri, however, wouldn't let it drop.

"Look, Cass," Jerri said, trying to sound reasonable. "You've done so much since that whole mess and you've come through amazingly. I don't know how you did it because I'd have been a basket case by now, but you did do it and with a strength I've never seen in anyone before. You amaze me, Cass, and I'm so proud of you . . ."

"I'm not sure it's about strength, at least not most of it," interrupted Cassie. "Life perhaps . . ." and she hesitated a moment grasping at thought. "Yes, perhaps life more than strength, definitely life."

"Well, that makes things all the more puzzling then," stated Jerri matter-of-factly.

"Why?" asked Cassie.

"Because . . ." Jerri said, "that there mare doesn't have any!"

"You don't get it, do you?" said Cassie softly and then added with a touch of sadness, "You don't get it at all."

Days turned into weeks and weeks into months and the

solitary mare still "clung" to life reluctantly. That's the only way that Cassie could describe it. Life enough to still be there but not enough to want to live it. Her demeanor told Cassie that while she might physically be present, life indeed had stopped somewhere in this mare's past. Cassie didn't know if she could help the mare step forward, just one step out of the past that could lead toward a future where she could exist again. She'd even had Jerri haul over one of her older geldings, hoping that the presence of another horse might spark something in the mare.

Cassie had been disappointed. The mare hadn't even whickered at the newcomer and while he ran up and down the adjoining fence calling to her, she merely gave him one ear and cocked a hoof in disinterest. Jerri had hauled him home with a shake of her head, again asking Cassie to quit and find herself a horse that at least acted like one.

Every day, weather willing, Cassie groomed the broken-down mare, speaking softly and gently to her with each stroke of the brush. She was looking better at least. The pot-belly had diminished now that she had been dewormed and, with neatly trimmed hooves, she was filling out nicely thanks to the good senior grain that Cassie had been feeding. All around, the mare physically appeared well. Cassie wondered if she'd ever hear a greeting whicker when she approached the pasture or shook the grain bucket vigorously. Entering the pasture with a pocket full of treats was typically a hazardous experience with healthy horses, but the mare never once approached her nor tried to nuzzle her pockets with interest. Cassie remained at a loss, not sure what to do. But despite Jerri's repeated efforts to have her get rid of the mare, Cassie always refused.

After almost a year Cassie began to feel failure. Despite the schedule and routine that she was insistent on keeping, the mare seemed no better than the day she had arrived. It hurt like heck that she couldn't get through to this mare, but she couldn't let her go. Response or no response, she couldn't desert this horse with her conscience intact. Jerri would call her a soft nut, but even that would be preferable to some of things she'd called her in the past year. Perhaps if she admitted defeat graciously, Jerri would just let the subject drop without too much of an "I told you so . . ."

Sighing, Cassie called Jerri and asked her to stop by after work. She could have done it over the phone, but maybe Jerri would feel less like crowing if they were face-to-face.

Jerri drove up Cassie's long driveway slowly, trying not to throw up dust from the churning gravel. Cassie had sounded serious on the phone earlier and Jerri was a little concerned. The driveway seemed awfully long today.

She allowed the dust to settle before getting out of her truck. Daylight was fading so she went straight up to the house figuring Cassie would be indoors by now. After no answer to her second knock Jerri made her way around to the back of the house more than a little anxious, Cass always went indoors when the light faded unless she had someone there with her. Scanning the pasture, Jerri stopped dead, disbelief spreading across her face. Cassie sat in the middle of the pasture leaning slightly forward in her wheelchair with her forehead resting gently between the mare's eyes. This meeting of the minds, Jerri knew, was not something to be interrupted so she stood quietly, and with amazement watched as the mare began to nuzzle Cassie's hair and then snort ever so softly all over Cassie's face. Cassie was glowing and from the smile on her face, Jerri thought that Cassie had never looked more beautiful.

Jerri stood there for ten minutes before Cassie noticed her and when she did, she beamed even more. Cassie made her way toward the fence and the mare tucked herself between the wheelchair's handle grips and followed quietly and gently behind.

"Well, I'll be darned," said Jerri. "What did you do?"

"I have absolutely no idea," laughed Cassie. "I called you over to admit defeat and I think she knew, somehow she sensed it. When I took her grain to her this evening, she came to me and ate it right out of my lap! Isn't it wonderful?"

"You're wonderful!" gushed Jerri. "Any other person would have given up long ago, myself included," she added with a chastened grin.

"But you never gave up on me, Jerri," Cassie said matter-of-factly.

"What do you mean?" asked Jerri, a touch puzzled.

"Haven't you got it yet?" said Cassie in disbelief, "Gosh, and they say women are so astute!"

"Got what?" said Jerri, even more puzzled.

"She was me," said Cassie softly. "All I went through ... days of despair, not wanting to live, not existing, not caring if I did exist. You never gave up on me. As my friend you did whatever you had to, no matter how long it took, no matter what sacrifices you had to make ... you made them. You helped me live again and I had to do the same for her. I saw myself in her, Jerri; but for you, I might not have been here and but for me she might not have been here either. I had to try, just as you tried, because despite the risk of failure you hung in there for me. I owed her the same and both she and I thank you and, oh yeah, we kinda love you too."

Jerri blinked away tears and tried to swallow the lump that threatened to burst her throat.

"So have you named her yet?" she sniffed.

"Now I have," Cassie answered, "but she had to earn it. Her name is Vita ... it means life."

Elizabeth Batt

My Best Friend, Jack

If I live my life according to my own script there are no surprises.

Theresa Peluso

If there was anyone less likely to become my mentor, it was Smilin' Jack. He was a janitor who had left decades of drunken turmoil in his wake. Yet, by the time we met, Smilin' Jack had transformed his life and radiated with the joy of living.

Raised in the mountains of North Carolina, there was little evidence that anything but a difficult future lay in Jack's path. His formal education ended in the third grade. His father and most of his relatives worked in the local sawmill and it was assumed that he would do the same. The only other option was working with the moon-shiners. By the time he was a young teen, Jack had dis-covered the easy money of running corn liquor. Unfortunately, he also developed a taste for the bottled lightning and became his own best customer. One fall evening, in a car filled with corn squeezings, unable to escape the pursuing revenuers, he was arrested. Sentenced to prison, he spent several years shackled at the ankles, working on a chain gang. Not surprisingly, the days and months of humiliation served only to increase his anger and bitterness at the world.

On his release, determined to escape the boredom of his hometown, he joined the merchant marines. Working aboard cargo ships, he traveled the world. Yet, lost in a haze of whiskey, each port was much the same as the one he'd just left—barrooms and trouble. Eventually the alcohol abuse took its toll and, no longer fit to work, he returned to the familiar mountains of North Carolina. He worked when and where he could, but only long enough to buy another jug of the clear liquid that controlled his life.

A passing carnival hired him as a maintenance mechanic and thus began a drunken tour of small-town America. Weeks, months and years passed in a blur and increasingly he awoke in jail cells with cuts and bruises that he couldn't explain. Eventually fired from the carnival, he found himself in an unfamiliar small town in Pennsylvania. Odd jobs kept him in liquor for a time but as his health deteriorated, he became incapable of even the simplest labor.

In the last, deadly stages of alcoholism he collected welfare and had whiskey delivered to his shabby rented room. When his check was late, drinking after-shave became a reasonable alternative. One evening Jack was found unconscious in an alcohol-induced coma, and rushed to the emergency room.

While in the hospital, doctors convinced him to seek treatment. Having nowhere else to turn he accepted. That became the turning point in his life. By the time I met Jack, it had been several years since he had "taken any liquor."

I had screwed up a good career in New York City. In the process, I'd alienated everyone I knew. Overwhelmed by self-pity and depression, for several years I hid in the bottom of a gin bottle, afraid to live but even more terrified to die. For reasons I still don't understand, Providence stepped in and, after receiving much needed help, I started the difficult task of putting my life back together. I moved to a small town to start over. And more than a year later, my career prospects were improving steadily. But emotionally, I was not doing well.

Then I met Jack.

I had been staring at a lobby office directory for several minutes when a little round man in blue work clothes waddled toward me. Grinning at my confusion, he pointed me in the right direction.

I hadn't taken more than a few steps when, in a friendly Southern drawl, he called after me, "and by the way, son, I can't recall when I've last seen a feller look as down in the mouth as you."

Surprised at this personal observation, I turned towards him. With an almost sad, yet sincere expression, this stranger looked me in the eye and said softly, "Son, if nobody's told you they loved you today . . . I do." With keys jingling, he turned and disappeared through a door into the stairwell.

This warm, smiling janitor touched my heart and I would find excuses to visit "his" office building. Sitting in his cluttered basement office we made small talk. Gradually I came to recognize the priceless experience and wisdom he was imparting to me. When we walked along Main Street, passing cars honked greetings and shop owners stepped out to say hello. I marveled at the magical effect this once hopeless man had on people. "Every day is a blessing," he would tell me. "I shoulda been dead a long time ago, but for some reason the good Lord seen fit to give me a second chance and I aim to use it to help folks."

His philosophy for living was simple: "Live a day at a time and do the best you can. Ask the good Lord to look after you when you wake up; and thank him before you go to sleep." I saw him lend money to people, knowing he would probably not be repaid. If someone admired something he owned, more than likely, he would make them a gift of it.

My career came together and I was again working on Madison Avenue. With Jack's support and friendship, my personal life turned around. I met and fell in love with a remarkable woman and, a year after we met, this beautiful lady agreed to become my wife.

On a breezy, summer afternoon I stood at the altar of a church wearing an ill-fitting tux and a comfortable grin. Accompanied by organ music, the love of my life, resplendent in her lace wedding gown, slowly made her way down the center aisle.

The priest posed the question, "Who gives this woman away?" For a fleeting moment, the altar glowed as if enveloped by a mist of pastels, and the clean, fresh scent of approaching rain drifted through the church. As I took my bride's hand, we looked into the misty blue eyes of the one whose love and guidance had made this day possible.

And my best friend, Jack, smiled at us and responded proudly, "I do."

George Roth

As My Life Turned

I can forgive, but I cannot forget is only another way of saying, "I cannot forgive."

Henry Ward Beecher

"Hurry, get your books, Betty Ann, I'm driving you to school this morning," he said, as I prepared for school at my usual pace.

"How come? It's too early," I said. Besides, I wasn't used to such luxuries.

For most of my classmates and me, walking was a daily ritual—rain or shine. But for some reason today Daddy was eager, even insistent, on driving me. I thought it strange, but then a lot of things appear strange in the world of adults when viewed from the eyes of a nine-year-old.

I told Mom good-bye as I walked out the front door, leaving the air of mystery that hung heavy over the house and my family that spring morning. Sliding into the passenger side of the front seat of our family car, alone with Daddy, I normally would have felt important. Today though, there was something that seemed a bit different, strange even, something I couldn't quite figure out. I sat quietly as Daddy drove the four blocks to Horace Mann School, never imagining in my wildest dreams the turn life would take.

As Daddy approached 20th Street, he circled the block and parked across the street from the school. It seemed as if time stood still. There, in front of the empty barber shop, too soon yet for even its earliest customer, Daddy and I sat alone with awkwardness and an anticipation of something about to happen.

Daddy turned off the key and the motor went quiet, creating a silence that seemed to engulf my whole world. He turned to me, looking serious, and my heart quickened. "I wanted to drive you to school this morning, because I have something to tell you."

What's wrong? I thought to myself: *What's so wrong that he and Mom couldn't tell me together at home?*

"I want you to know, I love you. No matter what anyone ever tells you, I'll always love you. You remember that, as long as you live. You understand? I've always loved you and I always will, no matter what anyone says. Do you understand that?"

Under different circumstances they were words I would have raced to embrace. They were words not part of the everyday vocabulary in our home and I did not know how much they were missed until I heard them uttered from my daddy's lips. They were words I craved nonetheless. I wanted to throw my arms around him, and tell him how much I wanted him to tell me that every day for the rest of my life. I wanted to tell him how very much I loved him, too, but my nine-year-old heart and mind were confused. So I told him only that I understood and I loved him. I kissed him good-bye, opened the car door and crossed the street in utter confusion and loneliness. I was confused and worried all day.

When the final school bell rang out, after the afternoon classes ended, I gathered my books and the rest of my belongings anxious to find some rational explanation for the morning's event. When I got home, Mother was lying down. "What's wrong?" I asked, almost afraid of the answer. There were tears in her eyes that had been there for a while and she looked different.

"Betty Ann," she began, "your dad's gone."

"Gone where?" I asked.

"I don't know," she answered. "He just left this morning after he took you to school."

"Where has he gone?" I pleaded.

I remember Mother telling me Dad was in love with someone else and my tears flowing, a flood of emotion that dampened not only my face but my soul for days, months and years after.

That ride to school changed my life. The circumstances eventually made me stronger and allowed me to grow in ways I never would have if my life had been different. Throughout my life, others' choices, right or wrong, often pushed me into the valleys of life. I began learning at a young age that traversing those valleys could either defeat me, making me less than I could be, or propel me forward, making more of me than I ever dreamt possible.

Toward the end of my father's life I found out he, too, had risen above some of his own personal problems. He went for treatment for an alcohol addiction and never took another drink in his life. He committed his life to Christ and became a changed man.

On his death bed, after cancer had ravished his body, we both talked freely of forgiveness. We both chose to rise above the circumstances of life, and through forgiveness peace settled in upon us both.

He left me again, but this time in death, and we both knew all was forgiven.

Betty King

He Sat Alone

More people would learn from their mistakes if they weren't so busy denying them.

Anonymous

It was an ordinary Saturday at Fenway Park in Boston. The streets were exploding with hoots and hollers. A closer look, however, revealed that no one was engaged in conversation. Men and women alike kept their eyes either on the ground before them, or focused straight ahead. Then I saw him. An elderly man was sitting alone on a stoop. Curious, I wandered over for a better look. A shiver traveled the length of my spine. Unfortunately, the temperature was not the cause of the horrible sensation.

Amidst a flowing river of Nikes and Timberland boots, the nameless man wore shoes that had worn through long ago. Dressed in threadbare rags, he held a silver coffee can in one trembling hand and his sign in the other. It read: Hungry Korean War Vet. As if already dead, the man's yellowed eyes, sunken deep in his head, belied years of alcoholism and a gray tinge painted his somber face. I was reminded of my own sacrifices made for my country in Operation Desert Storm. For a moment, I thought that my stomach might actually kick up the two hot dogs I'd just devoured.

People circumvented the man as if he were a leper. Not one person stopped to help. Obviously, it was easier to assume the man was a con artist than to find the truth in his tormented eyes. I somewhat understood. There were still many truths people did not want to know. In this case, that truth only defined a cold and uncaring society.

Other passersby went above and beyond apathy. They were mean enough to leave behind an insult, or a laugh to stab the poor man's heart. The vet was too old and weary to strike back at the masses. Each time a harsh word was offered him, his eyes closed briefly and then opened again as if he'd completely absorbed the cruelty.

Fifteen endless minutes elapsed and although the coffee can remained empty, I witnessed a fellow human being suffer more embarrassment and humiliation than deserving of an entire lifetime. Whatever dignity remained was greedily and brutally stripped away by those who, somewhere along the line, were hardened and left blind.

Suddenly, another unfortunate soul captured my attention. It was another elderly gentleman; this one, confined to a wheelchair. The man slowly approached a curbstone, and then worked his chair back and forth in a courageous attempt to clear the lip. It was no use. Determination and effort were quickly replaced by frustration and mumbled curses. Through it all, hundreds of patriotic baseball fans herded around him and proceeded on to their different ways. I stood paralyzed with shock.

As the numbness wore off, I took two steps to assist, but was one step too late. The homeless man placed his sign and empty cup on his stoop and went to help another who needed help more. My eyes filled. There was still some good left in the world. Strangely enough, it always seemed to come from those who were in desperate need of what they themselves gave so selflessly. For his trouble, the Korean vet received a donation. The two shared a genuine smile, which apparently only those in need could understand. The pauper returned to his stoop and the judgmental gaze of a million cruel eyes. The man in the wheelchair pumped his arms to another of life's obstacles. I stood amazed. The same chill returned down my spine.

After placing a crisp twenty-dollar bill in the beggar's

can, I received a nod for my generosity, and then a tap on the shoulder. My brother Randy's raised eyelids told me that he didn't approve.

During the lengthy ride home, I explained the tragic scene and the topic led to some unusually deep discussion. Though we were in complete agreement on most points, not supporting a person's drug or alcohol habits and the genuine possibility of being scammed, I found that Randy shared the strong opinions of most. I, on the other hand, was less suspicious. There didn't seem a need for it.

We traveled a good distance in silence. I decided that as long as my own intentions of helping were pure, then I didn't see any risk of injury to anyone. For the price of a scratch ticket, I'd rather give the man the benefit of the doubt. The odds seemed better. Besides, it was one of society's problems that more people should be taking personally. With thousands being swallowed up by substance abuse, alcoholism, unemployment and homelessness each day, it could have easily been anyone sitting on that same lonely stoop. Then, placing myself in that man's worn shoes, I only hoped that someone would be kind enough to take a chance on me rather than the state's lottery.

Reaching Fall River, my traveling companion broke the silence with a very innocent question. Though he expected no answer, Randy asked, "Steve, don't you ever wonder why God has given so much to so few, and so little to so many?"

Surprised that my brother's thoughts mirrored my own, I smiled. The answer seemed so easy, so obvious. To Randy's surprise, I responded sincerely, "I think that God has given enough. The problem is that people have forgotten how to share his generous gifts!"

Needless to say, the rest of the journey was driven in silence, the Boston Red Sox continued to lose and somewhere on a very cold stoop a needy man sat alone.

Steven Manchester

Stress Management 101

I am always ready to learn, although I do not always like being taught.

Sir Winston Churchill

Have you had days when Murphy's Law was in full swing? Well, this was one of them. I had to be in Manhattan, which is an ordeal in itself. A flat tire, a jack-knifed tractor-trailer on the highway, a ticket by a police officer who saw red when I saw yellow . . . you get the picture. By noontime I was a candidate for the funny farm.

When I feel stressed out, I go to an AA meeting. Through my involvement in treating alcoholics I knew this was a group of people who had used alcohol to escape stress. I reasoned that since they were now sober, they must have found new ways to cope with it and I concluded the principles and practices of Alcoholics Anonymous were the key.

When I finally reached Manhattan I found several noon-time AA meetings within a radius of a few blocks and chose one. A young woman was the speaker. She had begun drinking at thirteen, added marijuana at fourteen and a variety of drugs after that. Eventually she began selling herself to procure drugs. At twenty-six, someone got her into Alcoholics Anonymous, and she was now nine years sober, happy, working and in a good relationship.

Her story was no different than the many others I had heard. So far, no relief from my misery. Then she said,

"Oh, there is one more thing I must tell you before I finish.

"I am a rabid football fan. The New York Jets are my team, and I'll never miss a game. One weekend I had to be out of town, so I asked a friend to record the game for me on her VCR. When I returned, she gave me the video tape and said, 'By the way, the Jets won.'

"I started watching the tape, and things were just terrible! The Jets were losing badly. At halftime, my team was twenty points behind. Under other circumstances, I would have been a nervous wreck, pacing the floor, biting my fingernails and raiding the refrigerator. But not this time. I was perfectly calm. I knew they were going to win.

"Ever since I came to AA and made a conscious decision to turn my life over to God, I know that it'll turn out good in the end. So even if I'm twenty points behind at halftime, I don't lose my bearings. It'll turn out alright."

I knew then why I was at that meeting.

This young woman not only eliminated all the agitation engendered by Murphy's Law that day, but also provided me with a powerful coping tool. There have been times when the stress I was under would have brought me near the breaking point, but then I remembered her teaching: "If you turn it over to God, it will be okay at the end, even if you're twenty points behind at halftime."

Abraham J. Twerski, M.D.

Build It and They Will Come

No passion so effectually robs the mind of all its powers of acting and reasoning as fear.

Edmund Burke

In the ten years from 1989 to 1999, I went through alcohol treatment four times. Once at the Betty Ford Center, twice at Serenity Knolls and finally at the Sierra Tucson Treatment Center. All fine centers that gave me everything I needed to know about battling chemical dependence. And I worked hard at recovery. Each month-long session in rehab toughened my resolve to make it—to overcome my terrible disease—but somehow, each time I failed.

After rehab visit number four, the one at Sierra Tucson, things in my life improved in many ways, but eventually and what seemed like inevitably, I began drinking again. This time however I embarked on a spiraling journey downward that culminated in my standing in front of a plate glass window in the penthouse suite of a luxury hotel and seriously contemplating whether I should jump.

My story starts in 1956, the year I was born. My parents were married . . . but not to each other. I was the product of an affair that broke up two families and earned me the deep and often violent resentment of all of my half-siblings. My father never married my mother and my mother and I struggled financially the whole time that I lived at home.

To say that my childhood was dysfunctional is an understatement. The lasting two legacies of my upbringing were a lifelong struggle with depression and my core belief that material success is the most important thing in life and the key to happiness.

This belief contributed to my recurring relapses since oddly enough, drinking had no consequences for me professionally. I was a highly successful attorney and although my personal life was a mess, I was a material success and that, I believed, was what mattered.

My slide to the brink began nine months after my stay at Sierra Tucson. Even though things on the surface seemed good—I was wildly successful in my career and my son was planning to come to live with me for high school—deep inside myself I was still depressed.

Drinking helped me deal with my depression in two ways: Either I would drink myself into a stupor and stay in my house, finally numb to my internal pain, or I would go out seeking distraction—visiting nightclubs, casinos and bars in a whirl of high-rolling gambling and continuous drinking.

This time I chose to seek excitement. I checked in to the penthouse suite of a Nevada casino and proceeded to drink nonstop for two weeks. I didn't eat and hardly slept. I drank and gambled and caroused. Stuck in high gear, I felt like king of the world. If my high started to slip, I drank some more.

Finally, my body couldn't take anymore of this abuse. When I couldn't even hold down any liquor, I crashed. I remember sitting in a bathrobe on the leather couch of the Safari Suite emotionally spent, spiritually bankrupt and disgusted with myself in every way possible. It was sunset and I was looking out the window at the mountains in the distance. Sunk in despair, the question that kept chasing itself through my head was, *Should I end it?*

I stood up and walked over to the window. It was a heavy plate glass window and in order to jump I would have to break the glass first. I turned and saw a trio of bronze statues of naked women by the Jacuzzi. That would work. I picked one up in my arms and turned back to the window. I stood staring down, weighing whether I would be better to my family alive or dead. It was the thought of my family, of my son Charlie, that made me put the statue down and walk back to the couch to consider the situation more carefully.

Collapsing on the leather seat, I sat for a few minutes, thinking of Charlie. I was physically sick and more desperate in my spirit than I had ever been in my life. Night had fallen and I was enveloped in darkness, inside and out.

Suddenly, a light came on inside me. In the next moment, I felt a wave of energy begin in my head. It moved down, resonating in my chest and then radiated down the length of my body. I remember the feeling of relief as a sensation of well-being began to spread inside me. It was such a startling contrast to everything I had been feeling just a minute before. Then the clear thought came, *I'm not ready to die—this is NOT what I am supposed to do.*

I knew I had a purpose in being here and for that I wanted to get better. Although I felt lifted up with this new idea, my body was still in terrible shape. I literally didn't have the strength to make all the phone calls necessary to get me to a rehab center.

I rolled over on the couch and picked up the phone. I called the head of the casino and told him, "I need your help. I'm either going out your front door or I'm going out your eighteenth floor window. I need you to arrange for me to enter treatment. Now." I asked him to call Sierra Tucson.

With great difficulty, I managed to take a shower, dress, get in the limo and catch a plane to Arizona. En route, my body literally shut down and when I finally reached Sierra Tucson, they rolled me in on a gurney.

It took about ten days for my body to recover from the poisoning I had put it through. I didn't speak and hardly remember anything about that miserable time. Yet, as soon as I was finished being sick, I noticed immediately that my sense of well-being was back. I also noticed a feeling of fearlessness inside of me. All my life I had lived with fear—fear of losing what I had, of losing relationships—but now it was gone. I thought, *I should be dead. I've lost everything, but I'm here. There's nothing left to fear, because I can get through these things. I am a stronger person now.* It sounds odd, but I had to get sick before I could get well.

Although I was back at Sierra Tucson, things were very different this time. Every other time I had been through rehab, I had been treated for chemical dependency. This time I was admitted to the Trauma Unit. My counselor told me, "We know you know all about treatment for chemical dependency. This time we are going to deal with your family of origin issues. We are going to address your depression."

He felt that all the alcohol treatment in the world wouldn't help me until I addressed the underlying causes for my alcoholism. This approach, combined with the new feeling of spiritual energy I experienced inside of me, worked. Yet when I left Sierra Tucson thirty-two days later, I knew that the only way I was going to be successful in my recovery was (1) to become more involved in the recovery community and (2) to do something in my life that made me happy.

When I got home, I enrolled in California State University's Alcohol and Other Drug Studies Certification Program to better understand the mechanics of addiction and recovery. One day as I sat listening in class, I began to have a familiar sensation. Out of the blue, I experienced a wave of energy that started in my head and radiated down the length of my body. The thought accompanying this energy was, *I need to open a treatment center.*

The excitement was electric inside me. I knew that I was going to create the most advanced, innovative, cutting-edge, multidisciplinary recovery center to treat people with the same disease I had. In that moment, the Bayside Marin Recovery Center was born in my mind. It didn't matter that I didn't know how to build a treatment center or that I wasn't a professional counselor. I knew what they had taught me in AA was true: If I'm going to keep what I've got, I need to give it away.

Since that day, the creation of Bayside Marin has become the focus of my life. I am involved in every aspect of the process from construction to landscaping to staff selection. I still successfully practice law, though now as a mediator.

Even more important, I have no desire to drink. My days are filled with enthusiasm, purpose and a sense of significance. I have never felt so connected to a Higher Power. In the past, no matter how much money I made, I never felt this way.

The remarkable way things have just fallen into place make it clear that Bayside Marin is being created through me. To start, the whole construction process has been remarkably smooth. What normally would have taken two years has been completed in six months. And when I began contacting top professionals in the field to ask them to join Bayside Marin's staff, the response was always the same: "This opportunity is what I have been waiting for all my life." So many wonderful people have left long-standing positions to work at the center.

On June 5, 2004, I received my certification from the Alcohol and Drug Studies program, fulfilling my goal to better understand my disease and myself. In addition, it has made me a better administrator for the programs offered at the center that was born of my transformation. Bayside Marin, a place to heal and turn lives around—named for the center's idyllic location next to the San Francisco Bay in beautiful Marin County—opened its doors two weeks later. Within one month, it was full.

I went back to Sierra Tucson recently, but not on a gurney and not as a patient. I wasn't greeted by the detox staff or shown to my room. Instead I was greeted with hugs and a big sign saying: Welcome Perry! Everyone told me how proud they were of what I'd done. This time I was there because I had meetings scheduled with the senior staff of Sierra Tucson to talk about a collaborative relationship with Bayside Marin.

To top things off, Charlie is coming this summer and I'll be there to spend lots of time with him.

I remember standing at that hotel window wondering if life was worth living. Now I know.

Perry D. Litchfield

Black Is a Primary Color

A true friend never gets in your way—unless you happen to be going down.

Anonymous

Choices people make and circumstances in their life sometimes conspire to teach lessons in the most difficult ways. Finding myself in prison was both the worst and the best thing that ever happened to me. Following the path of my addiction put me there, and a court-ordered drug program set me free.

For two hours every day over a period of nine months we would meet. Weekly we broke up into small groups of six to ten women and went through a process of intense intervention facilitated by one of the five counselors, known as primaries in the prison system.

Each of us received individual treatment plans based on our entry interview. We wrote papers, read books, watched videos, did our homework and passed our tests, but what counted the most toward completing the program was class participation.

The significance and depth of each woman's story differed vastly. We came from all walks of life, spanned every racial, religious and age boundary. The one thing we all had in common was we were addicts. Whether it was alcohol, drugs or drug dealing, addiction had become an overwhelming, destructive force in our lives.

I had always thought my life experiences were unique but after listening to the other women's stories, I knew I wasn't alone. Realizing that was powerful for me. We shared things about ourselves that no one, no matter how close they were to us, would ever have known. Some of our experiences had never been said aloud for fear that doing so somehow made it too real for us to deal with.

My primary was a black woman who carried herself proudly, head high and poised. When Carla Davis spoke, her words were strong and direct. She moved around the classroom with the gracefulness of a rose swaying to a summer breeze. I was grateful in so many ways that she was my primary. I admired her; I wanted to emulate her and devote myself to helping people. Unfortunately I was sitting on the wrong side of the desk.

I was nothing but a number to the prison system, but Ms. Davis always treated me with respect and spoke with words that allowed me to maintain my dignity. Her advice was given with the wisdom of a thousand scholars and she could identify and sympathize with my internal turmoil over my biracial son. Her kind, caring eyes never left my face when I would go on and on about my problems. Sometimes I'd look up and see tears brimming over her bottom lids, ready to slide down over her high cheekbones the next time she blinked. Tissues were always a part of her desktop décor.

Nine months later it was graduation day. A person from each small group was selected for having improved the most. I glanced around the room, silently tallying who had opened up the most, had shared their deepest darkest feelings and worked the hardest.

Before I completed my mental score sheet everyone was clapping and looking at me. My name had been called. I stood up and moved slowly to the front of the room in disbelief. When I raised my head and looked into Carla's eyes tears were once again brimming over her bottom lids. She stretched out her arms and wrapped them around me. Her hug was as loving as if she were my own mother. She whispered in my ear, "I am so proud of you, you've earned this."

When the day finally came to walk out of prison I was convinced once I was on the other side of that fence I would never look back. I would put that part of my life completely out of my mind. It hasn't quite worked out that way. In my day-to-day living I still hear Carla giving me advice, and when I become a little shaky in my recovery I just think of that day and the warmth of that hug and it gets me through "one day at a time."

Christine Learmonth

And the Wisdom to Know the Difference

Convincing yourself does not win the argument.

Robert Half

"Don't worry about Mark. You go to Al-Anon."

I stared at my doctor in disbelief. "Me? I'm not the one with the drinking problem."

"I know that, Carol. But someone you love drinks and it's affecting your health in ways you don't even realize."

I hurried to the car, climbed in and slammed the door. Imagine him telling me I need help.

I turned the key over and gunned the accelerator. Crunch. My head jerked. Behind me sat another car, its red fender bunched up like a wadded piece of paper.

"Hey, lady, are you blind?" A tall, lanky teenager with orange-streaked hair jumped from his car and faced me. "You didn't even look before you pulled out."

I scanned his outfit. Baggy jeans that scraped the cement, a T-shirt that read, "I was born to party," and an image of a cobra ready to strike, tattooed on his left arm.

"Do you actually have a mother or were you hatched?" I barked.

After a lengthy confrontation that would have made a juicy piece for the Jerry Springer show, I drove home. Mark's car was in the driveway.

I plopped a sack of groceries on the kitchen counter. "What time did you get in last night?"

"I don't know," he mumbled, pawing through the refrigerator.

"Well, I do. It was after one o'clock. Your curfew is ten on a school night."

"So?"

"So you're grounded."

Mark rolled his eyes. "I'm already grounded."

"Then you're double grounded."

"Get a life, Mom," he scoffed, and shuffled toward his bedroom. I heard the door slam.

I reached for the bottle of Tums and downed a handful. What am I going to do?

The following week went reasonably smoothly. My hopes begin to rise. *It's just a phase,* I told myself. He'll snap out of it. A late-night call brought an abrupt end to my expectations.

"Mrs. Davis?" A deep voice resounded on the end of the line.

"Yes."

"Is your son Mark Davis?"

"Yes." I gripped the phone, fearful of what was coming next. A car accident? A death?

"Mark was found passed out at the mall parking lot. He's been drinking."

"Oh, no. What shall I do?"

"I'll drive him home. But he will have to appear in juvenile court for sentencing. If he has no prior record the judge usually mandates a period of time in a treatment center or AA."

I paced the floor until I heard the police car pull into the driveway. I'd thought of a million things to say to Mark, but when he walked in I burst into tears. He looked terrible. There was vomit on his shirt, and one shoe was missing. I led him to the bathroom and told him to clean up. He was in no condition to talk or listen to me. Later, when he had collapsed into bed, I knelt beside him and stroked his hair.

"Please, God, help us," was all I could manage to pray.

The following morning I was up early. It had been a fit-ful night of sleep and my eyes were red and puffy from cry-ing. My mind raced for a solution. Grounding him didn't work. He was too big to spank. Talking, scolding, preach-ing. . . . I'd tried it all. Perhaps if he spent time in jail. The thought terrorized me. A rehabilitation center? I had just begun a new job and the insurance wouldn't kick in for another three months. Mark's father had abandoned us years earlier. I knew very little about Alcoholics Anonymous except it was for drunken bums. At least that's what I thought. How could they possibly help my son?

Mark stood before the judge and heard his sentence: "Alcoholics Anonymous three times a week for one year." A counselor was assigned to his case.

The first meeting I waited in the parking lot. *There must be a lot of alcoholics in our town,* I thought. The parking lot was jammed. A group of women, talking and laughing walked toward the building. They seemed to be enjoying themselves.

An hour later, Mark slid in next to me.

"How was it?"

"Okay."

We drove home in silence.

The routine continued. Three times a week I drove Mark to AA meetings. I'd grounded him from using his car for six months. Now as I sat in my car watching the snow blanket the ground, I began to have second thoughts. I saw subtle changes taking place in Mark. He kept his curfew. He stayed home more. But he was still sullen and unresponsive to my questions.

One cold icy night, a turn of events changed my life for-ever. As usual, I was sitting in the car with the motor run-ning, trying to keep warm. A young woman knocked on my window.

"Why don't you come in and share a cup of coffee with us?"

"No, thanks. I'm not an alcoholic."

She laughed. "Neither am I. But I do attend Al-Anon. Wanna give it a shot?"

Anything was better than this freezing car, I thought. I climbed out and we hurried inside.

The Al-Anon room was at the end of the hall. The front room was for AA. I seated myself at a long table and gratefully accepted a cup of coffee.

"My name is Alice," the young woman smiled. Several other women welcomed me. I noticed one woman who looked my age, and also an older gentleman.

The meeting opened with the Serenity Prayer:

> *God, grant me the serenity*
> *to accept the things I cannot change,*
> *the courage to change the things I can,*
> *and the wisdom to know the difference.*

I immediately felt more peaceful. *What's going on?* I wondered.

The topic was "detachment." I didn't have a clue what that meant, but as I listened to the group share their stories, and apply one of the Twelve Steps to their situation, an overwhelming sense of belonging washed over me. I was not alone. I was not crazy. My doctor's words flashed before me. "Don't worry about Mark, you go to Al-Anon."

From then on, I was hooked. I couldn't get information fast enough. I learned that I was an enabler, someone who saves the alcoholic from the consequences of his own behavior. How many times had I laid down a rule and then backed off when Mark begged for another chance? I'd even finished his school work when he was too tired. When he said he'd lost his paper route money I bailed him out. How could I be so blind? The group assured me they had all been where I was and to just keep coming back.

The next thing I did was to get a sponsor, another woman who had been in the program for at least a year and who seriously applied the Twelve Steps to her life. I asked Ellen to be my sponsor. She was close to my age and her son was an alcoholic. She agreed and we met each week over coffee. It was wonderful to have a friend who knew exactly how I felt. Ellen was not afraid to correct me if she saw me slipping back into my old ways of thinking. And often times she asked for my advice.

A strange reversal began to take shape. It dawned on me one morning that I wasn't obsessing about Mark's drinking. Not so long ago that's all I thought of. Now, it was me I was focusing on, and it felt wonderful. My biggest pat on the back came from Mark. One night after coming home from a football game he paused on the way to his bedroom.

"Thanks for not grilling me about what I did tonight."

I look up and smiled. "Ultimately, I have no control over your choices, Mark. But regardless of what you do, I will always love you."

Where did that come from? Al-Anon. It was kicking in.

Mark had a couple of slips. Through it all I clung to my support group and my sponsor. The day came when Mark was admitted to a long-term halfway house in Minnesota. It was there he faced his demons. Tough? Yes. For both of us. But we survived. Today, he is a grown man with a successful business and a loving family. Me? I'm still attending Al-Anon. A friend asked me why I was still a member seeing that Mark was sober now. "Because," I replied, "it's not about Mark. It's about me. Sometimes I get the two mixed up and I need the wisdom to know the difference."

Carol Davis Gustke

Not a "Piece of Cake" for Me

If you chase two rabbits, both will escape.

Russian proverb

Having a disease like diabetes can really make you feel left out and different. Just enjoying a simple thing like eating a piece of cake is complicated. Diabetes is a disease where your pancreas doesn't produce insulin. Insulin turns the sugar that comes from food into energy. Without insulin, you would die. To get insulin, diabetics have to take an injection every time they eat.

Having diabetes is really difficult when I go to parties or when we get treats in school, like cookies or cupcakes. There have been a lot of TV commercials that make it seem as if caring for diabetes is quick and easy, but it's not. First, I have to draw blood from my finger and put it into a machine to find out my blood sugar number. Then I call my parents, tell them my number, and we calculate how much insulin to take. After that, I draw the insulin from a vial into a needle, and I give myself the shot. Finally, I can eat that one piece of cake, and that is all I can eat. I can't have any more than what I took insulin for, because of my blood-sugar levels.

I wind up taking four or more shots a day. I draw blood five or more times a day. It just never ends. I have been doing this every day for over ten years, since I was twenty-two months old. I have to go through that whole process, and it takes so long sometimes. At parties I feel like I'm holding everyone up. I can't be like the other girls who can just sit down and enjoy a meal or a treat. I wish I could have a piece of cake and just relax and enjoy eating it right away.

I was recently at a birthday party where we were having cake and pizza. I had drawn the blood from my finger and was trying to reach my parents on their cell phones. "Come on, Emily, hurry up!" someone said. They were all seated at the table and waiting for me. I was going as fast as I could. "Emily, come on," someone else said a few minutes later. It wasn't fair! Why did I have to hold up my friends' meals like this?

I was taking my injection when another friend walked into the room and said, "Sorry to rush you, but can you go any faster?" That was when I realized how much this happens to me and how it affects my feelings. How this process I have to go through makes me feel so sad and so different from my friends. I also realized that it will always be this way, no matter what I do or how bad I feel, it will not change, and I will have to understand that.

Even though I can't prevent myself from having diabetes, I have learned what it means to have great friends and a family who is always there to help. More and more often, when I am having fun, I find myself forgetting that I even have diabetes. I feel like a normal eleven-year-old girl enjoying life the way it was meant to be enjoyed. I guess I can still have my cake and eat it too, with the support of my family and friends!

Emily Schroder

"Ever have one of those days when you're not sure whether you're in the zone, out of the box, under the gun, over the hump or behind the curve?"

©2003 Randy Glasbergen, www.glasbergen.com

The Indestructible Dignity of Humankind

The best solution for little problems is to help people with big problems.

Rabbi Kalman Packouz

I was a fledgling psychiatric resident when I was called to see a patient who requested an emergency appointment.

Isabel was sixty-one. She related that she was one of three daughters of an Episcopalian priest. Her family disowned her when she was an alcoholic at age twenty. She married, and when their child was three, her husband said, "Choose. It's the family or the booze." Isabel said, "I knew I could not stop drinking and that I was not being a wife nor a mother. I gave him a divorce."

Stunningly attractive and unattached, Isabel began serving high-society types as an escort. She was provided with a fine apartment, furs and all the alcohol she desired. As the alcohol eventually took its toll on her behavior and her customers dropped her, she began serving a clientele of lesser stature. She rather quickly hit the skids, leading a dissolute life in fleabag hotels. When she was found unconscious from drinking, she would be admitted to a hospital for several days.

She attended AA meetings in the hospital, but got drunk soon after discharge. During a period of twenty-five years, Isabel had seventy hospital admissions for "drying-out."

At age fifty-six, Isabel prevailed upon an attorney

friend to have her committed to the state mental hospital for a year. The day she was discharged, she attended an AA meeting. She soon found a job as a caretaker for a prominent physician who was alcoholic.

I knew nothing about alcoholism. I was so intrigued by this story that I never asked Isabel what the "emergency" was. However, as a psychiatrist, I knew that people do not change without motivation. What could have possibly motivated Isabel to put herself into a mental hospital for a year? There was no one in the world who cared about her. Desirous of discovering the secret of her motivation, I told Isabel to come back for another appointment. I continued to see her weekly for the next thirteen years in a futile attempt to learn her motivation.

Isabel had told me she stayed sober by attending AA. Curious to know what treatment AA provided that surpassed anything psychiatry could offer, I asked Isabel to take me to an open meeting. It was immediately evident to me that the Twelve Steps toward recovery were not specific for alcoholism, but were a formula for character improvement and spirituality that could benefit every man, woman and child. Although not an alcoholic, I have continued my AA attendance for over forty years.

Isabel died peacefully in her sleep at age seventy-three, without having revealed her motivation for recovery. Inasmuch as Isabel had no external advantages to be gained from sobriety, I came to the following conclusion.

Within every human being there is a nucleus of dignity and self-respect. Circumstances in life might cause this nucleus to be buried under layers of grime. However, this sense of dignity pushes its way up for recognition, and one day breaks through the surface. The person is then aware that, "I am too good for this. This behavior is beneath my dignity." At that moment, the miracle of recovery can begin.

I believe it was this moment of truth that made Isabel reach out desperately for help. The only facility then available to protect her from compulsive drinking was the state hospital. She committed herself to preserve her human dignity.

Isabel taught me that this nucleus of dignity and self-respect is within every person, albeit deeply buried. If a person can be made aware of it, he can recover from alcoholism and other self-destructive behaviors.

This conviction led me to open the Gateway Rehabilitation Center in Pittsburgh, which has branched out in the past thirty years to provide services to some 1,800 people daily. I don't know whether anyone put a headstone on Isabel's grave, but the Gateway Rehabilitation Center is her living monument, and thousands of people owe their lives and happiness to a woman who had no reason on earth to recover, other than because every human being has an inherent sense of dignity, which needs only to be exposed.

Abraham J. Twerski, M.D.

Gratitude

People have a way of becoming what you encourage them to be—not what you nag them to be.

Scudder N. Parker

Early in my career I took a position as a music therapist for a prison mental health unit. While "serving" my time in the system, I worked with an inmate whose story touched my life. This man, whom I'll call Steven, decided against going straight home from the office one day. Instead he stopped for a few cold ones at a club close to his place of employment. Steve left the bar later than he had planned and in a hurry to get home flew through a red light, broadsided another car and killed the passengers instantly. That tragic evening was his third DUI. That fateful night not only ended the lives of the passengers in that car but cost Steven twenty years of his freedom.

Prior to trading in his polo shirts for drab brown overalls, Steven had been an architect for a prestigious company living a comfortable suburban life with his wife and two beautiful children. Losing his freedom and acquiring a taste for prison food were adjustments he found difficult, but living with his guilt and having his family disown him threw him into the depths of depression and several suicide attempts.

By the time we met, Steven was in the tenth year of his sentence and his third year of recovery.

Steven was a quiet man during the five years that I

knew him. He kept to himself and said very little unless spoken to first. He caused no trouble, never had a disagreement or altercation with other inmates and shared personal information with only two close friends; one of whom I later learned was his sponsor. He attended the required groups and went to his AA meetings religiously. To the nontherapeutic staff he most likely appeared as just another one of the nameless inmates.

On one particular day, the staff was keeping a careful eye on Steven. He was up before the parole board and we, the staff, were already aware that his parole would be denied and that he would have to serve out the remaining five years of his sentence. Because of Steven's history of suicide attempts, the staff paid extra attention to Steven to be sure that this blow would not be too much for him to bear.

Arriving for work the morning following Steven's hearing, I spoke to the overnight staff who reported no problems that evening or the previous day. I then saw Steven for our session. He appeared to be in good spirits even though he knew he would not be seeing the walls outside of the penitentiary for another five years. I had expected to see that morning a morose man with a long drawn face who had probably not slept at all the prior night. Instead I was met by someone who looked well-rested and freshly shaven. He greeted me with a chipper, "Good morning," and I tentatively asked how he was doing.

"Did you happen to notice the beautiful sunrise this morning on your way into work?" he asked.

I shook my head no.

"Well, I just watched it from my cell and realized how grateful I am that I can see the sunrise through the bars on my window. It is an especially beautiful morning. And, I just had breakfast. Today my oatmeal wasn't as cold today as it often is which makes it a good day."

As I thought about his comment, he paused ever so briefly before continuing, "Yesterday's news was disappointing but I realized I have a choice. For today I am choosing to focus on the things that I do have instead of those which I don't. So in answer to your question of how I am doing today, I *really am* doing all right."

The statement and the sincerity in his voice stopped me in my tracks. Could I believe that after getting "hit" with another five years in jail that he really was all right? Hearing the resolve in his voice and the simplicity with which he spoke, I realized yes, he would be okay. In the following days and weeks Steven seemed to glow with an inner peace and serenity.

After I left the position at the prison I had no further contact with the inmates, but I never forgot what I learned about acceptance and appreciation from Steven. I am certain he's completed his sentence and has been released, but where he is today, I don't know. I wonder where he is living and if he continued on his journey of recovery.

Today when I start throwing a pity party for myself about things I lack or feeling overwhelmed, I remember that I, too, can choose what to focus on in my life. However bad things appear to be, I have the opportunity to watch every sunrise unobstructed by prison bars and I don't have to worry about cold oatmeal. I *really am* doing all right. It's going to be a good day.

Lisa Kugler

By the Dawn's Early Light

I count him braver who overcomes his desires than him who conquers his enemies; for the hardest victory is over self.

Aristotle

The air was stifling in the small, dimly lit room. The aging General in the red bathrobe said in heavily accented English, "My finest campaign was invading Hungary in the fifties." Anger filled my throat with hot bile as I remembered my Hungarian neighbor back in the United States whose family had been victims of that invasion.

It was November 1990. Perestroika and Gorbachev's temperance campaign were in full swing. I was one of five Americans invited to spend the night in the detox ward of Moscow Hospital #19 where 6,000 beds were filled with alcoholics being subjected to liver washings and other physical procedures. They would be sent home "cured." All would drink again and most would die alcoholics.

Wanda, Nancy, Bob, Dick and I were members of the Soviet-American Conference on Alcoholism, sharing our stories of staying sober in AA. Most of our audiences the past week had shed tears of gratitude as we shared our way to freedom from addiction. Here it was different. An air of disbelief and arrogance filled the overheated space. I looked to the small, high window for some relief from the fatigue of a long day. I found none in the snow piled against the darkness.

After we spoke and the General had finished, two

strapping Soviet athletes explained confidently, "We've been here before. We'll be out in five days and back to our hockey team." The young doctor in charge of the detox unit proffered his opinion, "Our people are just now able to have some privacy and you think they'll sit in a room and tell about their lives?" When I introduced myself in the little Russian I knew, "Ya Terry. Ya alcoholique," the head nurse replied, "No, no, too healthy, too pretty."

The General continued, "I had to come here." His rheumy eyes slid over us and I shivered in disgust. "I had no place where they would let me stay." Self-pity poured out over his expensive leather slippers now worn and scuffed. "With all my medals and successes, this is where they finish me. My career . . ." And he put his hand to his face in the gesture we had seen many times that week: tip of thumb to lips, head back as if draining a glass, the sign of an alcoholic. So this was the enemy I had grown up fearing, the red menace, the communist set to rule the world.

I shot my eyes to our group leader. A successful lawyer in the States, she was most comfortable in tight situations. "Thank you, General, and all who shared this evening," Wanda said. "We end our meetings with The Lord's Prayer, if you wish to join us." All stood and reached out to hold hands. The General took mine. His hand was cold and wet. Shame and guilt filled me. Mumbled English and Russian mingled in hurried prayer and hasty good nights.

The rough cotton pillowcase rubbed cool against my cheek. I could hear an occasional sigh or deep breath from Wanda and Nancy and just make out the shapes of our high metal beds, lining three walls of the large, square room. Looking into the darkness above me, I could not see the tin ceiling I had noticed as I undressed for bed. We had said little after good-night hugs to Dick and Bob, who now slept in the next room.

So exhausted, I could not think, an unidentified heaviness weighed upon me until I pleaded "Whatever it is,

Lord, I give it to you. I need to sleep."

It seemed only a few minutes later that I woke suddenly, cloaked in fear. Low Russian voices and the squeak of rolling cart wheels wrenched me back to where I was. Another alcoholic was being admitted to the detox unit. "Lord," I breathed, "what a lousy disease." A chill ran through me. Pulling the covers up to my ears, I closed my eyes and saw the General. Shame and guilt mixed with the memory of his cold, sweaty hand.

"We have a disease, cunning, baffling and powerful," *The Big Book* of AA says. And last night, I judged the General, refusing to identify with him as a fellow sufferer. No wonder I felt guilt and shame when he took my hand for The Lord's Prayer. If I had allowed myself, I would have remembered that my hands were cold and wet many days early in sobriety when I was desperate for a drink but equally desperate not to be a drunk. And I would have said to him. "It's okay. We have a choice. We don't have to drink tonight."

A loud knock and the nurse opened the door a crack.

"Hurry. The hospital ambulance is waiting to take you back to the hotel for the conference breakfast meeting."

I wouldn't have a chance to correct my mistakes. I dressed quickly as I whispered a prayer. "Please, Holy Spirit, help me here." Searching for my gloves, I put my hand in the pocket of my jacket and found several small pins I had brought from home to trade. I picked out three and joined my friends in the narrow hallway. We filed slowly past the members of our meeting last night. The snow was blowing in the open door beyond them and the ambulance driver was motioning us to hurry.

One after the other, the athletes kissed me on each cheek. I placed a New York Yankees pin in their trembling hands and got big grins in return. The doctor shook my hand and smiled and the nurse hugged me. "Alcoholique," she said. "Healthy. Pretty." We hugged again.

The General stood last, near the open door, his red wool

bathrobe tight around his bulging middle, silk pajama pants flowing over and nearly hiding his slippers. I opened my hand to show him the red and white crossed flags of the U.S. Army Signal Corps and slipped the pin into his hand. "My father fought for his country, too," I said. "You and I, we fight together." I put the tip of my thumb to my lips and tilted my head back. We laughed and our teary smiles mingled as we hugged.

Terry P.

Wise Beyond His Years

The weak can never forgive. Forgiveness is the attribute of the strong.

Mahatma Gandhi

When he was only twelve, Danny chose to come to one of our treatment programs. He had been inspired by his older brother's progress in dealing with anger, which was also a significant issue for Danny.

Although Danny's father was sober, Danny hated Dad more now than when he was drinking. When his father was drinking, Danny understood a disease was involved and that his father couldn't make loving choices. Now that Dad was sober he still didn't reach out, which confused and hurt Danny.

Dad had replaced his alcohol with his recovery program but life hadn't changed for Danny. When he approached his father with fears about getting beat up in school, Dad just looked at him and said, "Easy does it, son. You've got to learn to let go of these fears." Danny wanted some reassurance and a hug, a little understanding from his father. But what Danny got was a recovery slogan.

While Danny was with us he found lots of surrogate dads and got lots of hugs. By the time he completed the program it was less important to him that his father wasn't able to give him the attention or affection he needed. Danny learned to ask for support wherever he could find it.

I was at a conference several months later and Danny

was in the audience. During a break I asked him whether his dad was now hugging him and unfortunately he said no. He went on to tell me that during the recent holidays his grandparents had come to visit and Danny watched the interaction between his father and his grandpa. "I noticed that Grandpa never touched or hugged, or even talked nice to Dad. No wonder Dad didn't know how to treat me," he said with wisdom beyond his years.

With his abundance of treatment hugs and his new ability to get more, Danny became more confident and began to initiate the hugs. An interesting thing happened.

As Danny explained it, "It doesn't matter who starts a hug—just as long as you make a connection with the other person. I've been in my dad's arms thirty-seven times over the past few months and I'm going to keep giving my dad hugs until someday he learns and has so many, he can afford to give one away. I want to be nearby and get the first one."

This young man, only twelve, had learned to forgive and use his energy for getting his needs met. With fulfilled needs he can afford to help someone else, in this case his father. Feeling all the feelings and forgiving someone else is a gift we give to ourselves. It's called serenity. When we let go of the energy it takes to hold on to anger, blame and resentment, we have the energy to get our own needs met.

Like Danny we can all learn to plant our own garden instead of waiting for someone to send us flowers.

Sharon Wegscheider-Cruse

7

RECOVERING JOY

Healing does not mean the damage never existed. It means the effects of the damage no longer control our lives.

Earnie Larsen

Bill Saves the Bill

They can because they think they can.

Virgil

In April 2000 we sat together in a packed room surrounded by state legislators, lobbyists and lawyers. Bill, my
ten-year-old son, could sense that I was nervous and
squeezed my hand. He looked up at me with his azure blue
eyes and smiled in his reassuring way. I once again reflected
on how lucky I was to have such a beautiful, loving child.
We were in the State Senate Chambers at the Capitol
Building in Sacramento, California. Senator Wesley Chesbro
(D) was sponsoring a bill that would require health insurance companies to offer treatment for substance abuse. I
was preparing to offer personal testimony as to the effectiveness of treatment on alcohol and drug addiction.

As a recovering addict, my whole life had suddenly
turned around two years before when I stumbled into
substance abuse treatment at Kaiser Permanente—a large
HMO in California. I was lucky to have health insurance
that covered treatment for drug addiction. Many people
are not so fortunate.

As we sat waiting my turn, we listened to the insurance
company representatives and lobbyists testify against the
bill. The arguments were persuasive claiming treatment
was expensive and not cost effective. It was fairly clear
from the Senate Commission's comments that the bill
would not pass. My son was listening too.

He squeezed my hand at one point and whispered,

"Mom, let me talk." I was a bit confused and asked him, "Do you mean up there . . . at the podium . . . in front of all these people?" He simply nodded and said, "Yes, I want to talk."

I sat back in surprise and then I whispered, "What are you going to say?" He replied, "Just wait, you'll see." He reached for my purse and got out a pencil. On the back of the Senate agenda he started writing notes to himself.

In no time at all it was my turn to speak. Bill insisted on coming to the podium with me. I gave my two-minute testimonial and then asked permission from the floor for my son to say a few words. He was so small he could barely reach the microphone. He took a moment to look at each member of the Senate Commission, put aside his notes and began.

"My name is Bill Lee and I am ten years old. Up until I was seven, my mom was really addicted to drugs. Sometimes I couldn't wake her up. Sometimes I was hungry and had to try to cook my own food. One time we were homeless. I remember thinking maybe she wasn't really my mom anymore, maybe there was an alien inside her. I didn't know it was because of drugs."

The Senate Commission was giving him their full attention as he continued, "She finally told me that she was addicted to drugs but that she would get better because she was getting treatment. She promised that everything would be different. And today my life is different. Now my mom is always there to help me. We go everywhere together. She takes me to Water World, we go skiing, she helps at my school and she comes to all my soccer games. No matter what we do, we have fun and we laugh."

Bill paused just a moment to collect his final thoughts. "I love my mom more than anything. If she didn't get treatment I think she would be dead. And where would I be? I just know there are other kids out there with a mom or dad who needs treatment. That's why I hope you vote YES on this bill—because every kid deserves to have a mom and dad who can get treatment if they need it. Thank you."

The packed room was utterly still for a moment. Then one by one everyone stood and clapped and cheered. He took my hand and I gave him a reassuring smile as we turned and faced the crowd. I thought my heart would burst. It was truly a moment I will never forget. To this day I am in awe of Bill's courage and I wonder at the marvelous force that prompted him to address the crowd that day. Senator Chesbro proclaimed that Bill saved the bill—and on that day—indeed he did!

Tracey Lee-Coen

My Father's Eyes

Do not look back in anger, or forward in fear, but around in awareness.

James Thurber

My brother and I arrived home from a New Year's Eve of broomball on a sub-zero Minnesota night. It was shortly after midnight, and we felt perfectly confident we had honored our parents' request for our New Year's Eve festivities. Into the kitchen we breezed, quickly shocked to be met by an anxious mother and furious father. Time seemed to slow down as my brother slipped by them both and my stepfather zeroed in on me.

"You are a lousy, no-good daughter!" he shouted. I was silent. "You sneak around causing trouble. Are you trying to tear this family apart?"

Why didn't he seem to see me, even though he was now only a few feet away?

"All you do is manipulate!" my stepfather continued. "You sneak around smoking, drinking and causing trouble." I stood open-mouthed as I listened to him describe someone who could have been my stepsister, but certainly wasn't me, the overachiever who tried to prove her worth through being the perfect child. I got excellent grades, was an officer for my church youth group, won state and national academic awards, worked more than one job to cover my own expenses, avoided drugs of all kinds, and whatever else I thought might help me become the model child.

The tirade continued, though we somehow managed to

work our way into the next room, closer to the stairs that would provide my escape.

I no longer stood silently. I verbally fought back. I looked to my seemingly helpless mother for assistance. I defended and justified myself, as well as the others I felt he mistreated in the family. My mother stepped between us for a moment, but he wasn't about to let anyone intervene.

The most puzzling thing to me was that he was looking right at me, into my face, yet his eyes were glazed over, and it didn't seem he saw me standing there at all. None of the accusations fit. Was he shouting at the wrong person?

Eventually I escaped to my room, where my mother comforted me in my heaving sobs. I had played tough in his presence, but the words deeply wounded me.

Things had been traumatic with my stepfather ever since the night my mother forced me to call him "Dad" back in elementary school. Because my biological father seemed rather absent, I longed to have a father around every day, but I never seemed to acquire daughter status, at least judging from our daily interactions. At the point of that traumatic New Year's Eve, I felt pretty hopeless that things would ever be healthy between us.

I had about two years left under my parents' roof. I spent those years continuing my pursuit of perfection. I continued sacrificing things of youth in order to be mature and responsible. But in the process, somehow I also managed to grow, and somehow I never lost hope that things could be okay between my fathers and me.

I started to understand things like the power of forgiveness. I saw that my fathers had already hurt me, but by holding on to bitterness, I was only allowing them to have further power over me. I recognized that there was nothing I could ever do to change their behavior. The only person whose behavior I could alter was me. I began to believe that if I continued to love them in healthy, balanced ways, at the very least their mistreatment of me would be seen for how unjust it was. At the most their hearts would begin to soften.

After my junior year of high school I spent most of my summer working at a camp in central Minnesota. As my stepdad's birthday approached I realized I probably should get him a card, since I would be seeing him on that day. I stopped by a Christian bookstore and perused the selections, feeling pretty hopeless about the whole situation. Finally, I found a meaningful one that represented all the hopes of my heart to be my stepfather's daughter. I purchased it and, in my emotional exhaustion, simply signed my name, rather than adding personal notes like I usually do. I felt a little like I was taking a risk. The card was emotional and expressive. If I laid out my heart before him and was rejected, I wasn't sure what impact that would have on our relationship. But I took the risk.

On the evening of his birthday, I gathered around the table with the handful of other immediate family members who were available to eat cake. I added my card to the pile and patiently watched as my stepdad opened gifts and read cards.

I froze in my seat as he quietly read my card. Then he looked up, and I was shaken to my core. Those eyes . . . those eyes of indifference, those eyes of fury, those eyes that had looked right past me on that New Year's Eve . . . they saw me, they looked right into me. His eyes searched mine as he asked simply, "Do you really mean that?" I couldn't even speak; I just nodded.

A few days later, I found a note from my stepdad on that same kitchen table. It was the only thing up to that point I could recall being written in his hand to me. It was a cheap little card that matched the wrapping paper it was purchased with. It said, "Surprise!" on the outside, which ended up being an ironically fitting word. Inside my stepdad had written: "Erin, Thanks very much for the card. Those words meant a lot to me. Love, Dad." That was it, but it represented a whole lot to me. It confirmed what I had suspected his eyes were telling me on that birthday evening, that he would meet me halfway in our journey toward a healthy relationship.

And he did. In the spirit of made-for-TV movies, our relationship changed almost overnight. My final year under my parents' roof was bewilderingly blissful at times. My parents acknowledged my achievements. They threw a small and wonderful birthday party for me. They talked with me about the things that mattered most. And I carried that little note from my stepdad around in my purse wherever I went. The only time I took it out for anything besides appreciating it was to include it in a collage I had to create for an English class about the story of my life, for which it was a central feature.

Had his heart finally softened? Had mine? I never did figure out the key to what happened for us, but I do thank God that I have very healthy relationships with both my fathers today. I continue to seek growth in forgiveness and in my own character, rather than trying to fix or improve others. And when I speak to my small children, I often get down on my knees and look into their eyes.

Erin Hagman

Legacy

However long the night, the dawn will break.

African proverb

My brother, Kelsey, once told me he could not remember a time when our mother wasn't sick. He was six years old when she was first diagnosed with breast cancer. I was eleven. Neither of us could fully comprehend the seriousness of the situation, although each time she went in for a doctor's visit, my parents would try to explain to us what he had said. We believed that she was just sick, the way we sometimes got sick, and that the doctor would give her medicine to make her better.

We lived in a small farming community and people knew Beverly Trimmer. They knew her because she was an active part of our community, teaching Sunday school to four-year-olds at the First Baptist Church, playing an active role in the PTA and teaching computer literacy to junior high school students. People didn't just know her, they loved her. She was passionate about life, about raising me and my brother, about teaching, about making a difference. Her warm and caring nature drew others to her and she did make a difference in the lives of more people than she will ever know.

Just as my brother and I had hoped, our mother got well. She was scheduled for a mastectomy and it seemed as suddenly as we had learned of the cancer, it was gone. Our family rejoiced. Unfortunately, our victory was short-lived and by the time I was a teenager, the cancer had returned with a vengeance. Despite excruciating treatments of radiation therapy and chemotherapy, the cancer continued to spread. My mother never complained. She went on about life as if nothing was wrong. She continued to teach, in addition to maintaining our household and caring for me, Kelsey and my dad, Eddie. She fought the cancer with every ounce of her being, but to no avail. The only way we could tell how much pain she was in was by looking at her face. Her frown lines deepened and her smiles were forced. Looking back, I am now amazed that she could even smile at all.

Before long, Mrs. Trimmer was replaced by a substitute teacher at the junior high school. She no longer had the strength to teach her computer class. Her students missed her terribly and although I was a high school student by this time, younger children asked me about her all the time. "How is Mrs. Trimmer feeling?" they would ask. "When will she back at school?" I would always tell them she was feeling better, that she missed them, too, and that she would be back as soon as she could. The truth was, she would never be back.

Things took a drastic turn on the home front, too. My mother, the loving, sacrificing caregiver, was now relying on us to take care of her. My father quit his job in order to stay at home and take care of my mother full time, my grandmothers were at our house daily, helping to bathe and dress my mother, and I and my brother also did what we could to help. Our family pulled together to take care of my mother, who had told my father that she wished to die in her home. On February 13, 1989, the cancer granted her wish.

I was eighteen years old, a freshman in college and a motherless daughter. My mother's death was a tremendous obstacle for me to face. As a young adult trying to find my place in the world, I'd just lost my greatest human source of love, comfort and encouragement. With the realization that my mother wouldn't be there to attend my college graduation, my wedding, the births of my children (just to mention the "biggies") came the realization that I had to make some choices. I didn't make all of those choices right away, some I may not have even made consciously. I began by making the choice not to let my emotions prevent me from graduating from college. Because my mother had been so passionate about education, I knew it would be a great disappointment to her if I allowed my grief to stand in the way of my success. I earned a B.S. degree in biology in just three years, graduating with honors from Wayland Baptist University.

I made a decision not to allow myself to be victimized by the loss of my mother. I learned quickly that being angry or questioning God left me feeling emptier than ever, so I chose to instead have unwavering faith in him and trust in his greater purpose. Once I made this choice, it opened up all kinds of opportunities for me to recover from the death of my mother.

The first thing I did after putting my faith in God was start talking about Beverly Trimmer, my mother. I made a decision that I wasn't going to forget about her and I wasn't going to let other people forget her, either. I chose to help her live on by honoring her memory through sharing details of her life with others, even those who never knew her. As my children, who are now two and three years old, grow older, they will know their grandmother. They will hear stories and see pictures and they will learn what a wonderful person their grandmother was.

The next thing I did was embrace the good things that had evolved from this tragedy. My father, who I had gained a tremendous amount of respect for as I watched him care for his dying wife, was blessed with yet another loving, compassionate and giving spouse. My stepmother, Jackie, joined a grieving family and stood by not only my father, but me and my brother, as well. As we worked through our loss, the adjustments that had to be made and the evolution of a new family unit, I grew to love, admire and respect Jackie. Instead of resenting her, I have found in her a trusted friend, advisor and one of my greatest sources of encouragement. She is not my mother's replacement and she has never tried to be. She holds a different place in my heart, and it is right next to my mother's.

Perhaps the greatest good of all that has come from the loss of my mother has been the new lives that would have never been had she survived. My dad and Jackie have two children of their own, Linsey and McKenzie—my half-sisters. I love them immensely and they help me to accept the fact that some people have to leave this world in order for others to enter it. I am grateful that I have them in my life and they are constant reminders that God does indeed have a divine plan. There is good to be found in the worst of situations if only we can gather the strength to look for it.

Last of all, I find that reaching out to others is a great source of healing for me. Whether it is helping someone financially, providing emotional support for someone else who has experienced loss, contributing to cancer research, or whatever the opportunity may be, it helps me to put my own loss into perspective. There are others out there who suffer, many of them much more than I have, so seizing the unique opportunity to be a source of comfort to them or make a difference in some way is monumental in the constant healing process I go through daily.

It is up to each of us to determine how we are going to react, in fact, how we are going to recover, from adversity or tragedy in our lives. It is easy to fall victim to the tragedy or loss yourself. It is easy to use it as an excuse for personal failure, emotional problems and social problems. However, I've found that it is easier to take control over your perspective of the loss. I choose to honor my mother's memory by being the person she raised me to be—the person she invested her life in. I am now a wife and a mother and I am also her legacy. I strive to be the best person I can be, a daughter she would be proud of.

Letitia Trimmer Meeks

Bare Bottoms and Dancing Toes

You grow up the day you have your first real laugh—at yourself.

Ethel Barrymore

The close of the front door ended the abuse.

I watched my husband, once my best friend and the father of my children, walk out of our lives. Tears of relief and a trickle of regret emptied down my cheeks.

"It's okay. I'll sleep with you tonight." My eight-year-old son, Karl, wrapped his arms around my waist and offered comfort. I looked down into his innocence and held on tightly.

The October wind whistled down the chimney and rattled the windowpanes. Outside, leaves tumbled down the quiet street. Inside, I tumbled to the couch and pondered my new life and future.

We settled into our family of four and soon my kids fantasized about Halloween. I quickly made costumes, casting a crew of motley pirates.

"Unhand the treasure or die," Karl said, waving his rubber sword and swatting his younger brother on the backside. Challenged, Grant drew his plastic saber from his buccaneer belt. His oversized pants slipped down and he tugged one-handed for the sagging drawers. I looked for a safety pin.

Entranced in a dance, Erin flipped her flimsy nylon

skirt, twirled in circles and chanted in kindergarten rhymes, "I'm a wrench."

Tangled in his costume, Grant toppled to the floor, screaming in the high soprano known only to three-year-olds as Karl, foot planted on Grant's chest, bellowed, "Take that."

The dogs howled. Chaos reigned. I covered my ears and shouted, "Mutiny!"

I laughed with them but behind the mask I worried about the realities. I had no job and no credit cards—my options limited for now. I smiled and snapped a picture of my rowdy crew. Amid life's changes, one constant remained: I was still Mom.

"Let's go," I said, as I gathered glow sticks and pillowcases to hoard the waiting treasures. A chill kissed our cheeks as we rang doorbells and collected fortunes of sugar. Overhead, rain threatened.

Onward we trudged, our bounty mounting with each "trick-or-treat." With the sidewalks empty of masked children, and only a few glow sticks glimmering in the distance, we headed home.

The first raindrops fell as I bent down and blew out the candle in the jack-o-lantern. A trail of smoke snaked out of the carved eyes and crooked mouth; a trickle of juice dripped down the steps.

Karl laughed and said, "Jack's smoking."

"And peeing." Grant covered his mouth and snickered.

I left Jack to piddle on the porch and unlocked the front door. Kids flopped to the floor, turned pillowcases upside down and dove into the assortment of miniature treats.

"Let's clean up first," I said.

Into the bathroom we marched. Costumes dropped to the floor beside the three pairs of shoes. Soap a friendly companion, I washed the makeup off Erin's cheeks as the boys stood like soldiers at the toilet, a tight formation of side-by-side spouts.

A family in unison, I scrubbed. She squirmed. They flushed.

Startled the boys jumped back as water flowed over the brim and flooded the floor. Bare-bottomed, they ran out of the bathroom as the water nipped at their naked dancing toes. I frantically jiggled the handle and commanded the toilet to stop.

"No," I pleaded, grasping for the plunger and plunging repeatedly. I flushed again. Defeated, the water over-flowed and crept between my toes.

"Don't worry," I told the kids. Silently, I assessed the situation. For little boys a backyard bush was a welcome target but what of the girls? My neighbor gone on vacation, I refused to resort to door-to-door solicitation for bathroom privileges. I decided we'd use the bathroom at the grocery store.

For a couple of days, the plan worked. Boys and dogs peed in the backyard. The ladies drove to the corner store. Greeted by suspicious glances from the checkers, guilt bore a nasty wound and I felt obligated to buy something in exchange for the double-ply tissue and a Tidee Bowl flush. Low on funds, we conceded to one-ply and to squat in a pot.

Desperate for money, we emptied change bottles and scrounged for dollars. The children counted pennies and rolled coins. Urine spots burned the camellia leaves. My fingers flipped the Yellow Pages for a plumber. A gardener could wait.

Every plumber I contacted was booked or wanted money, a lot of green up front.

Slamming down the receiver, I snarled, "Bet your kids aren't peeing in the rain."

While rain cascaded down the front gutters, my tears dropped onto the kitchen table. Discouraged, I cradled my head between my hands and mumbled, "We're tired of piddling in a pot."

I recounted the rolls of coins. Still short. Lost in my dilemma, I heard footsteps on the linoleum. Lifting my head, I turned to my oldest son.

"It'll be all right," Karl assured me with a supportive smile.

Bundled in a black jacket, Karl stood by my chair, a decision sealed on his freckled face. Thin gloves covered his hands; a red and blue knit hat hid his curly hair.

"Where're you going?" I pointed to the rake in his grip.

"I'm going to help."

"Karl, no—" I objected, but he ran out the door before I could stop him.

"Boys," I sighed and returned to search for my plumber in shining armor.

"Sorry, lady."

"Not tonight—"

"Get real!"

Wearily, I dialed one more time. A burly voice answered. Exhaling slowly, I started to go through my saga.

A gust of wind whipped around my ankles as the front door opened and shut. Karl tore into the kitchen, muddy, wet and wind-blown, his shoes dripping puddles on the floor.

"Just a moment," I asked of the waiting voice on the other end.

Grinning proudly, he put a crumbled one-dollar bill in my hand.

"Where'd you get this?" I stared at the soggy dollar.

"Mr. Ballard hired me to rake his lawn." He dropped his hat on the table and ripped open the snaps of his jacket.

I traced the curve of his cheeks: chilled and bluish. Pictures reeled in my mind. I envisioned my son running porch to porch, knocking on doors and asking to rake leaves in the pouring rain. I could only imagine the reactions.

"How many houses did you go to?"

"Five!" His face beamed brighter than the Halloween pumpkin. "But I only needed one. He paid me a whole dollar. Now we can get the toilet fixed."

Hugging my son tightly, his rain-saturated jacket soaked into my shirt. I held his hands in mine and realized they weren't so small after all.

"Lady, lady..." I heard a muffled call.

"I'm here," I struggled to find my voice.

"Cash only," he growled.

"No problem," I unfolded the dollar, added George to the toilet fund, and hung up the phone.

"Guess what?" I said. "A man's coming to fix the toilet."

A smile burst across his face.

I bent down, squeezed his shoulders and said, "Guess what else?"

His eyes broadened with curiosity.

"Your mom's a very rich woman, the richest of all."

I cupped his hand in mine and we jumped in the puddles, survivors of the storm.

Cynthia Borris

"I Love My Body!" When Do You Ever Hear Women Say That?!

It is the mind that makes the body.

Sojourner Truth

Who decided that it is more virtuous to be skinny than to be a good person? I almost died acting out this tragic reversal of values. And furthermore, who decided that small is good and big is bad? My madly driven quest to shrink my 5'7", 155-pound frame led me down a long, hard road of self-loathing, struggling, denial and finally acceptance.

It all started in the early eighties when my parents suddenly started dieting and strapping on their new Nike shoes to jog around the block. Their new fixation with thinness immediately sparked an insatiable thirst in me that would soon destructively infiltrate my soul.

Right about that time, I decided there was something wrong with my body that a diet or exercise could fix. Unfortunately, diets just weren't for me. I found this out through many years of diet-related circus acts that failed miserably. Try as I may, and believe me, I tried with the very best of them, diets and me, well we just didn't get along.

My dieting schemes were quite unique, or so I thought. I went through all sorts of ritualistic tricks to tease myself into thinking I wanted less food or foods that didn't taste very good, but promised a magical transformation into Madonna's physique. My first attempts at control were simply cutting my portions in half and pushing the undesired half in front of my father. He could always be counted on to eat anything unattached to the table. One foolish phase had me deciding that as long as I didn't eat a "main dish," I would lose weight. That directly translated into lettuce and sugar as my targeted nutrition.

I cleverly devised many more strategies of masking diets into desirable behaviors, so driven was I to reduce myself into someone else's body type. The usual suspects read something like this: all protein, no protein, all carbs, no carbs, all cooked, all raw, only green, not in the morning, only in the morning, not after 7 P.M., only when sitting, only when standing . . . *ad nauseum*. You get the drift.

My food superstitions were only superseded by my insidious exercise contortions. I wrote the book on ways to drive your body into the ground, all in the name of fitness and health. I speed-walked so many neurotic times around the block that my neighbors got dizzy, logged countless hours on the stair-stepper leaving my quads too burnt to climb my porch stoop, and actually turned down dates because I had to jog. I knew something was wrong when I chose to gratuitously exercise over enjoying the very prize I was supposedly torturing myself for.

This stringent devotion to altering my body combined with an inborn ingenuity led me into a successful career as a fitness and dance professional. I figured I might as well capitalize on my obsession. So I cashed in on my compulsion in the fitness industry, teaching an obscene number of classes and consuming an illegal number of protein bars. The dynamic duo of food and exercise went hand in hand. I couldn't do one without the other. As soon as I ate, I had to exercise. As soon as I exercised, I ate. I began walking an impossibly precarious tightrope every day trying to balance the two in a desperate effort to maintain my physique.

Having hopelessly tried every trick in the book to no avail, I hit a wall, a point of no return, that I bless to this day. That moment happened when I was a fitness and dance instructor in Tokyo and couldn't stop eating and exercising obsessively. Food control and exercise discipline elevated into a full-time war, leaving me exhausted at the very thought of starting a new day. My body was in revolt with a failing digestive tract due to all the sugar and excess food, and hip, knee and ankle joints that threatened to quit at any moment.

One anxiety-ridden day I was toiling away on one of those gliding stationary machines in the gym, between the two aerobics classes I taught, thinking incessantly about the sugary treat I was going to consume whole the minute I finished. Something remarkable happened in that circuit-blowing moment. Something snapped. I had a visceral experience I will never forget. In my mind I suddenly had the grim reaper's mighty scythe in my hand and was violently hacking away at the iron cage of regimen that was holding me imprisoned in this murderous gridlock of food and exercise.

I stopped the machine, started crying, and didn't stop for a long, long time. Through the help of an interpreter, I forged an unprecedented breach of contract and begged the Japanese club to let me go home. They posted shaming signs saying I was leaving due to psychological illness, and reluctantly let me leave the country. I ran to the airport and landed home humble, broken and tired.

That's when I could no longer deny it: I had a full-blown eating and exercise disorder. I ate compulsively, voraciously and secretly, and then purged through excessive exercise. My every day would start in a panic about what to eat and how to exercise it off, and end identically, usually laced in guilt and shame. Thank goodness for a compassionate friend who led me to my first eating disorder support group meeting. This was the beginning of a new life. I quit my highly coveted career as a fitness instructor at a prestigious West Hollywood gym, and took up full-time recovery for my addictive behaviors.

My counselor's first question was, "Are you willing to take a day off a week from exercise?" I replied, "No." She said, "Okay," and we went on to work the steps. Initially, I was willing to take off one day a week, but suffered from immense feelings of guilt every twenty minutes. Eventually one day off a week turned into every-other-day moderate exercise. She then asked if I was willing to quit sugar. I again replied, "No." The imperfect road to sanity with my food has been messy and illogical at times, but progressively improves each day. Instead of my demoralizing weight-control track record of one step forward, two steps back, I now experience a positive momentum of two steps forward, one step back in living a balanced life with food.

I spent many years unsuccessfully struggling to change the size and shape of my body. They say the definition of insanity is doing the same thing over and over again and expecting different results. Although my dieting and exercise innovations all disguised themselves as my latest enthusiastic hobby, they all had one thing in common: They were all attempts to change the size and shape of my body. Therein lay the spark for change, the point of departure. The new idea, the only fad I hadn't tried, was to love and accept my body unconditionally at the size and shape it was. Period.

This newfound acceptance of my body was the revolutionary act that led me on a new path to unprecedented freedom from obsession and dangerous behaviors. I've found that fixation on my body size only increases the problem, while acceptance eradicates the problem.

It's taken many years to undo the damage I incurred with my food and exercise abuse. My digestive system has sputtered, kicked and bucked for years from all the fake fuel and sugar overload. It's taken equally as long to redefine moderation with exercise that works. Formerly, food and exercise were my foes. I used them to punish, restrict, measure and rate. My new lifestyle embraces an unprecedented, loving attitude towards these life-sustaining activities.

My bottom line commitment is that I no longer harm myself with food or exercise. As well, I no longer use food or exercise to try to change the size or shape of my body.

These two groundbreaking principles have revolutionized my ability to not only experience freedom from the grips of insanity, but have also granted me an increased capacity to experience love and joy every day of my life.

Many gracious revelations have enriched my life, instigated by this change. I now know that beauty is not a size, and fitness is not a shape. I can blaze up canyon trails, hold a mean Warrior Pose and spread joy with my vibrant smile, all in my natural-sized body. I've come to realize that there is nothing inherently good or bad about a size. A size isn't good or bad. A size is just a size. Period.

As well, I've finally come to know beyond a shadow of a doubt that there is nothing wrong with me. Nothing needs to be changed. My size is just right no matter what. I have no further need to try to change something that is not broken.

What a relief to never have to count another carb or lap again! I love my body and look forward to the day I hear this chorus echoing loud and proud from women of all shapes and sizes, far and near!

Rachel Caplin

The Dead Zone

We could never learn to be brave and patient if there were only joy in the world.

Helen Keller

My name is Debbie and I'm an alcoholic. It took me years, four failed marriages and a complete loss of family before I could make that statement.

I don't remember crossing the line and going from a heavy drinker to an alcoholic. All I know is that by the time I was twenty-four, alcohol ruled my life. I couldn't work or sleep, let alone raise my twin sons.

I walked out on my first three husbands because they were closet alcoholics. I drank constantly, but in my mind I was not an alcoholic.

I eventually moved to a smaller town to attend a community college and to put as many miles as I could between my three former spouses and myself. I had been in school for a month when I began to experience severe stomach cramps and other flu-like symptoms. My doctor performed every test that my insurance would allow and yet failed to diagnose anything tangible. When he asked me if I drank, I said, "Absolutely not. I have children to take care of." That answer worked as well for, do you smoke? Have you been depressed or considered suicide at any time? "No, doctor, never. I have children to care for." I was diagnosed with manic-depressive disorder and was started on antidepressants.

After three months the doctors could not explain why I was in worse condition than before I went in for treatment.

I continued to drink and fantasize about death. Everybody could see that I was losing weight. I could not hold anything down and I was lucky if I could sleep two hours a night. They decided it was the stress of the move and the return to college, all while trying to work full-time and raise twin sons.

In 1991 I married my fourth husband and by 1992, I was back into an established routine that I could manage. I was drinking heavily. I had quit my classes because they interfered with my drinking, but I told everyone that the program I was in didn't fit my needs. My new husband and I were communicating well enough to survive and my sons, who were now twelve, had adjusted well to their new home and stepfather. Life was just a bowl of cherries.

Six months later, my drinking was out of control. One night I drank enough liqueur to give me the false courage to admit to my husband that I'd had some intimate sexual encounters just for fun with some of my coworkers over lunch, six of my male coworkers to be precise. He listened to what I had to say and then went for a walk. Four days later I finally sobered up enough to realize he had not come home. How could he walk out on me? Didn't he take seriously the vow to love me for better or worse? Wasn't love supposed to be unconditional?

It took him another week to tell me he had no intention of ever returning and that he wanted the hell out of this marriage. Then my sons dropped a bombshell on me. They both decided that they would rather live with my sister. They blamed me for running off the best father figure that I had ever given them.

That's when I fell apart. Thoughts of suicide ran rampant in my head, but I couldn't find the courage to act upon them. Besides, love aside, I had decided that I would not make it easy for my husband to acquire his freedom. The longer I lived, the more miserable I could make his life. I was beyond angry and I failed to see his hurt because I was too busy feeding my own pain. That's when I recognized that I needed help and not from a

bottle. Where would I go? My husband and sons had
abandoned me and wanted nothing more to do with me,
my friends had disappeared almost overnight; I had no
family that I was close to. I was alone for the first time in
my life. Welcome to the dead zone.

It was a few days after my sons left that I remembered
reading something about Alcoholics Anonymous. I punched
the number quickly, before my courage could dissolve, and
acquired a list of meetings.

That night I did attend a meeting, and I was petrified. I
went in expecting to hear people lecture me, but no one
did. I remember people talking about themselves, their
problems, their accomplishments, their families and the
happiness that they had found. I remember someone
handing me a white poker chip, thirty-five cents and a
meeting card with names and phone numbers of some of
the women at the meeting. I remember someone saying
welcome and come back. Someone patted me on the
shoulder and said ninety meetings in ninety days.

When it came my time to speak, I remember saying, "I'm
an alcoholic and I need to be here so I can get sober and get
my husband back." I honestly believed joining Alcoholics
Anonymous would be enough for my husband to stop the
divorce and come running back to me.

By the end of October, I was forced to accept the fact
that I was going to be single again, like it or not. I decided
I would be wasting time getting sober for a man, so I
would get sober for myself. My sons had returned home
and I wanted to be their sober mother. They deserved
that. I realized I was not the only one hurt by my drinking; my sons had been traumatized as well. Deep down I
knew my husband was hurt but I was still angry with him
for abandoning me in my time of need.

I wanted to work the Steps and make an honest effort
but I did not have a sponsor and I was a confirmed athe-
ist. I had dedicated my life to the belief that God did not
exist. There was no way anyone was going to get me to
believe otherwise. How could these people be ignorant

enough to put their faith in a fable? And since he didn't exist, why should I put all of my dreams and hopes into believing that he possessed the ability to restore my sanity? Besides, what had he ever done for me? In my mind, he had carelessly allowed me to become an alcoholic. I damn well did not need any more of his help.

I had been in AA for three months when I finally admitted during a meeting that I did not, could not and would not believe in God. After the meeting I was told that I did not belong in AA and that I had no business whatsoever to be at that particular meeting. I went straight to the store, bought a bottle of Jack Daniels and proceeded to get drunk. While I was at work the next day my sons found the bottle and emptied the contents into the sink. I knew then that I had to go back to AA. I had to give this God thing a shot, or I was not going to ever be sober.

I found a sponsor, one who understood what I was dealing with and who was willing to work with me. I was willing to try to work the Steps and I was willing to try to find faith in a higher power greater than myself. I just didn't know who that would be or where I was going to find it. I had been working Step Two for a month and still could not find a higher power I could relate to when my sponsor asked if I wanted to borrow hers. She described him and I agreed to take him home with me. She instructed me to make a list of all the characteristics I wanted my own higher power to have. Driving to a morning meeting three days later, something incredible happened. I had been going over my list of higher power characteristics; he had to be supportive, caring, forgiving, understanding, patient and noncontrolling. Suddenly I heard a voice say, "You already have me with you." There was no one in the car but me. My radio was broken and, a quick glance through my rearview mirror verified that I was the only one on the road.

There was no other explanation for the voice except that it was my higher power. Who else could it have been? I felt as though a heavy weight had been lifted off my shoulders. I could stand straight and hold my head up proudly. Without really trying, I had found exactly what I was looking for, or more to the point, he had found me. Before I knew it, I was calling him my God. Years of hiding from and denying his existence were swiped away with those six little words.

Not too long after that, I forgave my soon-to-be ex-husband and we established a friendship. He has been supportive of my AA alliance from the beginning. He kept telling me over and over that I could do it. He must have seen the change in me because in December, he asked me to be his wife again. I agreed to his proposal under three conditions: (1) it had to be what he really wanted, (2) we had to attend marriage counseling and 3) he had to allow me to remain in AA with no interference. I was actually working my program and I was not about to give up what I had already accomplished.

I have been sober for seven years now, I am working my Steps and God has worked more miracles than I can count in the past several years. My husband and I spent two years in counseling and we finally renewed our marriage vows last year. I'm sure we'll have challenges, what union doesn't? But we are stronger and have the tools within our reach to get through them.

I have formed a new relationship with my twin sons. They are proud of me and shame no longer exists between us. I have earned back the lost trust, respect and love of family members and I have new friends. My husband has a job, we have bought our house and we have our health. I have pride and confidence in who and what I am now. I have learned to smile and laugh again. I have the power to make choices and to do things I did not dream would be possible for me. I have the power to stay sober and by the grace of God, I will never walk alone again.

My name is Debbie and I am in recovery.

Debbie Heaton

Late Night Movies

Your pain is the breaking of the shell that encloses your understanding.

Kahlil Gibran

"Hey babe, pancakes are ready," my husband called from the kitchen.

I walked in to find the table set with all the necessary plates, silverware, butter, syrup and napkins in place. However, my eyes could only focus on the countertop with its spilled batter, dirty griddle and gooey milk puddle.

"You could have cleaned up your mess," was all I said.

The hurt look on my husband's face flashed and then he said, "Well, thank you too!"

We were off and running. Why couldn't I keep my big mouth shut? My anger flared like a fire suddenly out of control, his defensiveness coming right back at me. Our fight ended in the usual way. There were the angry recriminations, then silence and finally, several hours later, we kissed and made up. Lately, the "I love yous" came farther and farther apart.

What was wrong with me? Paul had been sober for fifteen years and I was acting as if he was still drinking. Why couldn't I see what a changed person he had become and appreciate all the little things he did to let me know he loved me? He was trying so hard to make up for lost years and I was thwarting him at every turn.

"Dear God, please remove this anger from my heart," I

prayed daily. I didn't understand why he wasn't answering my prayers. No matter how hard I tried to keep from being an angry woman, some little thing would set me off.

Our customary way of spending Saturday night was to rent a movie and cuddle in front of the television, fire in the fireplace, drinking Diet Pepsi and eating popcorn. With the children all grown up and living their own lives, our ritual seemed soothing and a way to try and reconnect. That weekend we rented *On Golden Pond.* In this touching movie, Katharine Hepburn and Henry Fonda play an older couple with a grown daughter who is somewhat estranged from the father she loves.

In one particular scene, the daughter tells her mother she wants to make peace and forgive her older, ailing father. Katharine Hepburn asks her, "Well, when do think you might start?"

All evening that line kept going around in my head. *Well, Sallie, when do you think you might start?* Was I going to stay angry with my husband for the rest of my life?

Later that night, unable to sleep, I lay awake thinking. As tears rolled down my face, I realized I could not release this anger until I forgave him. The more I pondered this, the more lighthearted and free I felt. I realized I was not the judge and jury, God was. I could not continue to judge my husband, only to love and forgive him. *Well, Sallie, when do you think you might start? Right now,* I thought, *right now,* and I said a silent, "Thank you, God," rolled over and fell into a peaceful sleep.

Now I'm not saying that night was a total epiphany. We're now approaching our thirty-fifth wedding anniversary and I sometimes still fall back into my old ways, but when I do, I ask myself, *Well, Sallie, when do you think you might start?*

Sallie A. Rodman

Recovery's Unlikely Destination

*The surest way to happiness is to lose yourself in
a cause greater than yourself.*

Unknown

Recovery is a life's work, a journey, not a destination.
Being on this journey for all of my adult life, and a good
chunk of my teenage years, I have found that recovery
comes in many guises: our self-help programs, our readings, our writings, our friends and for some of us also our
work. As a psychologist who spends a great deal of time
with children whose lives have been unalterably changed
by alcohol and drug addiction, I have found my own path
deepened, challenged and ultimately redeemed by the
children I work with.

Those of us who are in recovery are comfortable, to a
greater or lesser degree, with the concept of a Higher
Power. I found this concept profoundly moving as a
teenager and throughout my adulthood, so much so that
I have written books speaking about our Higher "Parent,"
a positive force that we have internalized that can and
does guide us. So when tragedy struck in my family's life,
and my sister who suffered from both addiction and mental illness was murdered, I turned to my Higher Parent
and asked that simple question: Why?

I thought, *Hadn't I learned enough?* Why did I need to suffer in this way? Why did my mother need to have yet
another loss? I questioned, listened and felt the enormity
of this vacuum of silence. There was no epiphany that

allowed me to begin to grab hold of my life, no lesson learned that I could share, only an emptiness, a growing numbness that, when I began to feel again, became another source of pain.

Those of us who live with family members who are so very ill know that there will be no happy ending. We know there will be no miracle cure, no happily ever after. We watch someone we cherish disappear, slowly, bit-by-bit, while still in the prime of their life and feel powerless to stop it. But that does not mean we are prepared for the end. And we can never be prepared for such a tragic ending as a murder. I know I wasn't. And I wasn't sure how to try to recover, or even if it was possible.

First Step work, a little voice inside of me said. I went to meetings, read, prayed, cried and spent long periods of time not speaking or thinking. After a lifetime of being resilient, I no longer felt any connection to this part of who I thought I was.

I had written a new book on women and resilience, I was lecturing and had a full-time private practice as a psychologist. In my worst moments I read the book I had written as if someone else had authored it. It was a reminder of my former self, with an emphasis on former. I needed something different if I was to heal. In the midst of my pain I realized I needed a change, something dramatic, something that lifted me out of the known and pushed me to an edge that I could master. I understood that I needed to be in this pain, and understand it, and I needed to give back, to reach those who were, like my sister, abandoned. Those who society shunned, those for whom there was little sympathy and not much hope. I realized I needed to do Twelfth-Step work.

That's when my Higher Power went to work. Out of the blue I was approached to work at a statewide child welfare agency. Here would be a place to reach in and bring the strengths of these youth to light. So abused and so hurt, these are children from families frequently in

despair. Many have no family at all, few biological con-
nections to any other adult, youth who claimed family
friends as family as no other family was available. In some
ways they paralleled my sister's life. My sister lacked an
anchor. She was also homeless. These are youth who are
struggling, in pain and angry. Angry that they had no
answer, angry that no one could make it stop, angry.
Angry as hell. So much so, they had been placed outside
of their community. I knew this type of anger with one
difference; I hadn't been placed outside of my community. I had chosen to go, so I could again find myself.

I once worked clinically with a teacher who was so
relieved when a student she had was arrested. She said, "I
am so happy he threw the brick through the window in
the school, because now we have to pay attention to him,
now we have to figure out why he is failing." I understood
that comment when I came to work with "my boys."

The children in child welfare are there in large part
because no one, not the school that they often skipped, or
the mental health clinics where they went for treatment,
not the child abuse hotlines where their desperation got
attention, not the emergency room where their injuries
were nursed, nor the judge that they appeared before,
could figure out why they were failing. These children are
placed away from their communities, away from their
family if they have one, so that someone can figure out
what is going on.

As painful as it was for me to try to understand why
what happened to my sister happened, it was infinitely
easier for me, for I was an adult. I had a recovery program.
I had seen and lived through other tragedies. But try
explaining to a fourteen-year-old why his brother is dead
from a drug deal gone bad, why his best friend just committed suicide by drinking and taking pills of an
unknown origin, why his father killed his mother, or why
he is freed for adoption and has been for some time, but
there is no one interested. The kind of relentless suffering

these kids have experienced puts tragedy on a whole new plane. It also broadens what recovery is really about.

I realized when I committed myself to this work that I was not, as friends said, "being so wonderful by working with these youth." I was doing this in order to heal. I was doing this in order to learn about the resilience that kept these kids getting up in the morning, let alone the strength that it took to get through a day. I wanted to be with those who knew the misery I was experiencing, who shared the pain that I knew so well, a pain I couldn't run from, a pain I had to go through, and for which I had no path.

There is such hope radiating from these kids. Despite everything that life has dished out to them they refuse to throw down their cards. They keep striving. They keep dreaming. I needed to remember how to do this, and I have. Together we have healed. And I am so much the wiser for this.

I had a session yesterday with one of the boys I see clinically. I was slowly walking him back to his cottage. It is one of the simple pleasures of working here, the ability to be outside, walking in the country, enjoying the air, the wind on my face and the light. Unlike many staff, who drive from building to building in a mad dash to save a minute, I walk whenever I can. It is a way of taking care of myself between sessions, of having a moment of peace, a moment to remember.

We had spent our time talking about choices, choices he had made that he now regrets. *Oh yes, I know those,* my little voice says. Choices he now sees. *Yes,* I say again inside of myself. He wants help in making better choices. "That's why I'm here, that's what I need help with," he says, smiling at me from under hooded eyes. He has a brilliant logic. On the way back to the cottage he accepts my offer to help me write a curriculum about making choices. I know writing is therapeutic for me, and I know it will be for him.

In his cottage another boy starts teasing him about

having no family. Kids in here will take whatever advantage life offers them, not unlike life outside. This boy, not nearly as personable as the child I see clinically, knows where this child is vulnerable. Baiting goes back and forth. But the child I have just seen smiles at me and says, "Choices. . . . I'm not going to hit him." I nod. He's getting it. And so am I.

Patricia O'Gorman, Ph.D.

The Journey to Me

Kites rise highest against the wind—not with it.

Sir Winston Churchill

Sixteen years old and I had all the answers to life; I quit school and got married. I didn't "have to"—I wasn't pregnant—I just wanted to be a wife. I thought that was all I needed to make my life complete.

I knew the nineteen-year-old "man" I married had abused his former girlfriend, but I also knew why. She cheated on him. She deserved it. End of story. And since I would never do anything like that, of course he would never hit me, right?

And so began seven long years of physical, verbal and emotional abuse. My new husband slapped me for the first time on our first wedding anniversary. That was the beginning. It got worse, so much worse, but it took me nearly three years to truly understand that it was never going to get better. By that time, I had become an emotional zombie. It was safer that way, feelings made me vulnerable; feelings gave him a weapon against me; feelings hurt.

My husband also would not let me do anything that would make me "better" than him. In his eyes, that meant that I could not go back to school, get my GED or get a job. Because he didn't much care for working either, our financial state was pathetic.

We were evicted from more places than I care to remember. We lived with my family. We lived with his family. We lived with friends. And there was even one night, when nobody wanted to deal with the bullshit anymore, that we were actually homeless.

From time to time, my husband would leave and I would get a chance to take control of the situation. I would find a job, pay some bills and start to get on my feet. But then he would come back and take it all away. Within a short time we would be back to square one. The cycle would continue and he would leave again. After awhile I started to hope that he wouldn't come back, but he always did.

I know people wondered why it took me so long to get out of such a sorry situation. What they didn't know is that I tried for almost four years and more than once I almost died for my efforts. The man I married didn't like being rejected. When he returned from a two-week jaunt to Chicago and wanted to come home, I refused. He persuaded me to change my mind by slamming me on the floor hard enough to knock me unconscious; just one example of the many arguments I could never win.

But ultimately he did leave for the last time. He went far enough away that I knew he wasn't coming back any time soon. I wasted no time. I filed for divorce the very next day and then started to think about rebuilding my life.

I wasn't sure I could do it. As bad as the physical abuse was, the emotional assaults had been even worse. By the time of my divorce at the young/old age of twenty-three, I knew I was worthless; believed I was useless; and I totally accepted the fact that I didn't deserve even the slightest attention. However, I also had two young children to support and I realized I couldn't do it on minimum wage; so I decided to go back to school.

I worked at a fast food restaurant during the day and enrolled in an evening study class to get my GED. A few months later, I felt incredibly proud when I held that little certificate in my hands. Like a small child, I felt like I had something I could show to the world and say, "See what

I did?" And then I realized . . . I actually could "feel"!

But it wasn't enough. My next step was to find a local trade school designed for people like me, people who needed to learn a skill in a hurry. I enrolled in the secretarial program and spent the next six months learning to type, file and do basic computing. It was rough at first because typing was supposed to be a prerequisite for the course. They made an exception for me and I was determined to succeed. And succeed I did; at the end of the course, I not only graduated, I did so with the Outstanding Student Award for that class.

In addition to getting an education, something else significant happened while attending that school—one day another student talked to me! I was stupefied and confused. Didn't she know that I was nobody anyone would want to be friends with? It wasn't possible! And yet it was happening!

I finally realized what it meant; I was on my way to becoming a real human being. And I was pretty sure it felt good!

About a year later, another new chapter in my life began. I started dating again, painfully and awkwardly. One night I ran into a man I had met several years before, during one of my brief periods of employment. We began dating. Our relationship would last for several years, but the first six months were a little rocky.

One night we had a quarrel and the argument triggered something inside me. I literally went crazy; I physically attacked him, screaming and punching, scratching and kicking. I was totally out of my mind. I had never done anything like that before!

Much to my amazement, he didn't hit me back. Instead, he simply left and the next day calmly "suggested" that perhaps I should seek some counseling. I took his advice and spent the next eight months seeing a wonderful therapist.

After explaining what had brought me there, I was a

little surprised when the therapist insisted that we dig through all the drama in my childhood. Drama? To me, it was just "life." Didn't everyone have branches of alcoholism, obsessive behavior and child molestation in their family tree?

Eventually we progressed to the subject of my marriage. By that time, I understood that I had married so young because I was searching for the love and nurturing that I had not received at home. I realized that my self-esteem had already been low because of the misuse and neglect I had suffered as a child, as well as the financial side effects that often accompany alcoholism. Following that kind of childhood with an abusive marriage was, to use a very stale analogy, like pouring gasoline on an already raging fire. The resulting inferno threatened to consume everything in its path, most especially me!

Next, she taught me to look deep inside myself and find that tiny, sheltered core where I still believed I was a wonderful, worthy person. I learned to nurture that tiny core and help it to grow, little by little, until one day it flourished and I realized that I liked myself; I respected myself. Soon I became strong enough to tell anybody who felt differently that his or her opinion had no bearing on my life or my self-image.

I felt different on the inside and it showed on the outside. I stood up straighter, I looked people in the eye and I even became able to walk into a room full of people without cringing. Simple things that might sound trivial to a "normal" person and yet meant the world to someone like me, who had once considered herself to be one degree less than nothing.

Two years later, I decided to upgrade my skills, so once again I went back to school. This time I chose a business college with a one-year course in accounting. I also took computer classes in spreadsheets and word processing; the end result was a highly marketable combination when I started looking for a job.

My confidence soared when I discovered that my skills and knowledge gave me my choice of jobs! I didn't have a degree and I would probably never be rich, but I would never have to work for minimum wage again!

Now, I look back at the life I lived over twenty years ago, and it seems like it was another person. In a way, it was. I remember the person who lived that life, but I have not seen her in a very long time. She is not who I see in the mirror today. The person I see today is young and free inside. I look forward to "life" and "tomorrow" and the "future," all words that once upon a time had lost all meaning for me.

And looking at what I have accomplished, I see that it is monumental, and yet not incredible. There is nothing that I have done that is not within the reach of anyone who wants it. Although it is never easy to get out of an abusive relationship, once you are out, the sky is the limit! There are therapists and counseling programs that operate on a sliding scale fee; support groups that don't cost anything at all; programs that pay for childcare while you attend school and even after you go to work; monetary aid to help support you while you go to school; student grants and loans to pay for tuition and books. Whatever your situation—whatever you need—there is some kind of helping hand. All you have to do is reach out for it!

That is my rags to riches story . . . are you ready to write your own?

Linda S. Day

From Victim to Victory

In the depth of winter I finally learned there was in me invincible summer.

Albert Camus

What am I doing here? Why am I in this place? What did I do to deserve this? I was a good wife! No, I was a great wife! So what am I doing without a home, no job and with three frightened, displaced children in a women's shelter?

The room began to fill up with bewildered, battered women and children. The shelter was packed to overflowing that Thursday morning. The Bible says, "There is a time for everything"; apparently that week in January 1981 was a time to run.

Just the day before, one of my daughters had confessed to me that my husband of ten years was molesting her. My backbone melted. I felt hot and cold. I was going to vomit, but I called the Sheriff's Department instead. I had to wait for the deputy in charge to call me back. It was not a long wait.

Her voice was compassionate and her instructions brief.

"You must leave with the children and get to a safe place. I'll make the arrangements. Gather a few things for a couple of nights. Leave a note that you and the children are safe, and you will call him at a specified time. Then leave."

She gave me the shelter address, and I began calling my close friends. Within twenty minutes I found out that I didn't have any. Finally I called someone whom I barely knew. She dropped everything, asking no questions, and she turned out to be one of the greatest blessings of my life. Within an hour and a half, we were at Butler House.

So there I sat, on a cold January morning, wondering what twist of fate had brought me to this place, to spend an hour with homeless women and listening to a stranger tell me about my life. What could she possibly tell me that I didn't already know? I had spent ten years dodging shouts and blows, trying with all my might to "make nice" a life that had become a nightmare. I had lied to everyone, especially myself, about what a "saint" my husband was. I had insinuated myself between my husband and my children, trying to keep them safe, and I had obviously failed at that. I was as low and as lost as I've ever been in my life.

The meeting began with short introductions and brief histories all around. We all gasped over the woman who had been set on fire, and there were groans over the women who insisted they still wanted to go back with their husbands or boyfriends, no matter how heinous their actions. Finally I told my story, swearing never to go back and believing down to my bones that I would carry on.

Eventually, the leader of the group began to speak. She told of stories of other women, some who had succeeded and some who had failed. It never occurred to me that I would fail. With courage, strength and endurance, I was certain I would succeed in freeing my children, and myself, from the bondage that had paralyzed us for ten years.

Finally, the leader came to the climax of her speech. She searched every face in that room. I remember her gaze resting upon me, compassionate and determined.

"There is a reason," she said, "that you are all here. Something very specific has brought you to this day. We know all the stories of love, betrayal, brutality and grief, but do we know the question that will answer all your questions?" She looked again, from face to face. No one knew the question that would answer the question. I, for one, was a little irritated, feeling a bit "jerked around."

She continued, "Each one of you must ask yourself one question: 'What are the choices that I have made in my life that have brought me to this moment?' Only you can answer that question."

The room filled immediately with murmurs, then whispering, then shouted remarks. A few of us remained silent. Moments passed, then all of a sudden, the fog in my mind cleared, and I got it! I really got it!

It was the most important turning point of my life. It had never occurred to me that I had made choices. Choices not to finish school, choices to marry a man I didn't know, choices to bring children into my uncertain world. My children were everything to me, and if saving them meant taking that first long, hard look at myself, then so be it.

From the moment of that first tentative look, my life began to change. I understood that everything that happened from that time forward would be the result of my personal choices. It was the first small step for me, as I began to understand how to change my life and the lives of my children. In looking forward, I had to take a terrifying journey into my past, so that I could understand where I had given up my freedom to choose.

I'm still taking that journey, even as I write. In the past twenty-five years, I have made good and bad choices. All mine. And, yes, I take that journey into my past, every day, pulling up the blinds and unlocking the doors. I let the sun shine in; chasing away the shadows from my soul, and every day the journey becomes more victorious. Each day, I come closer to understanding my true self. Laughter comes easily. I'm no longer frightened. I'm happy. I can see, by the grace of God, that I am a victim no longer, for I have been given the victory.

Jaye Lewis

Miracle at Wal-Mart

What gift has Providence bestowed on man that is so dear to him as his children?

Cicero

At ten weeks our little Beau was our pride and joy, my husband's first child, our only son. He was such a beautiful, sweet baby I thought my heart would burst with love every time I looked at him. I anticipated the years ahead, the birthdays, the skinned knees, the guidance his dad and I would give to his life. But my anticipation was made of stuff fragile as a dream.

On one beautiful sunny day I talked quietly to my son as we left the house and I secured him in his infant carrier in the car. All too soon, I dropped Beau off at the baby-sitter's house, a woman who had tended the children of both my family and friends. She took Beau from my arms, marveling at his beauty.

Hours later, at work, the call came. Words can't describe the terror, anguish, grief and disbelief my husband and I felt. Our beautiful baby became a victim of SIDS (Sudden Infant Death Syndrome) that day and I became a mother with empty arms.

One year, four months later I have a daughter seven months old. Josie is beyond adorable and shares a generous place in my heart with Beau and her older sister, Riley. I never want to put her down. She goes everywhere with me.

Josie was only two months old when I strapped her into her infant carrier for a trip to Wal-Mart. The day was unusual on many counts. It was Tuesday, and Saturday is my usual shopping day. I shop in the afternoon and here it was still morning. Josie slept peacefully in her carrier, secured in the shopping cart, as I walked up and down the aisles accumulating my purchases.

Pleased to be ahead of schedule that week, Josie and I waited in line, but when I started to pay for my purchases, I realized I didn't have my wallet. Seeing my frustration, the woman at the checkout counter offered to hold my things while I returned home for money. About forty-five minutes later Josie and I were back at Wal-Mart, wallet in hand. We joined the line of waiting customers, Josie resting in her plaid covered infant seat. A grandmother and her granddaughter of about three years were ahead of us in line. This little girl was insistent in her demands to see Josie and was relentless in her determination. I smiled as she tugged at her grandmother's skirt, begging to see my baby. Finally the grandmother lifted her up to look at Josie.

In her unsure baby language the little girl asked, "The ovver baby die?"

Bells went off in my brain. The shocked grandmother paled and asked, "What did you say?"

"The ovver baby. It die?" she repeated.

By now I was crying like a baby myself, explaining that I had recently lost a child to SIDS. The grandmother was embarrassed and apologetic, but she needn't have been. Her grandchild had given me a beautiful gift. Somehow this little girl saw what I couldn't, that our darling Beau was there with us.

When we left the store, I discovered I'd even parked next to their car. Had I not gone to Wal-Mart on an "off" day, had I not forgotten my wallet I might never have met this child who could see Beau, my little son, there beside Josie. I can't prove divine intervention but I'm convinced ours was a meeting that was meant to be.

I secured Josie's carrier in the backseat of the car and

shivered. I looked around. *I know you're here, Beau. I just wish I could hold you, darling baby.* I took out my cell phone and made an important call. My mother answered on the first ring and was alarmed by my tears. I quickly assured her everything was okay and explained that Beau had been returned to me in a way I'd never expected.

I wish all families who have lost children could have an experience such as mine, but in lieu of that, my hope is that sharing my experience will bring comfort to those who have suffered losses, to know their infants are with them in a different way.

Beau will never blow out candles on a birthday cake or cry over a skinned knee any more than the ache in my heart will ever leave. I still have sleepless nights but a miracle has given me a very real presence of my son, "the ovver baby," in my life.

Sherry Diedrich as told to Ruth Coe Chambers

"I got in touch with my feminine side.
She's suing me for custody of my inner child."

©2003 Randy Glasbergen, www.glasbergen.com

8

FULLY RECOVERING, FULLY ALIVE

*You gain strength, courage and confidence
by every experience in which you really stop
to look fear in the face. You are able to say
to yourself, "I lived through this horror. I can
take the next thing that comes along." You
must do the thing you think you cannot do.*

Eleanor Roosevelt

The Red Peanut

Shared joy is joy doubled. Shared sorrow is sor-row halved.

Anonymous

One of my favorite places to spend the night as a child was my friend Lucy's house. I liked the family, the pets and Lucy's father kissed me goodnight. I could fall asleep content as I did in my own home. At Lucy's eighth birthday we had a peanut hunt. As I was approaching a very large tree I felt someone behind me and heard her brother's voice, "Pretend you can't hear me. I followed my mother around all morning and the red peanut is in the tree right in front of you. Just keep walking you can't miss it."

I followed his instructions exactly, not daring to disobey such a direct order and soon the red peanut materialized, practically iridescent in my line of vision. I reached for it feeling guilty but excited, as though I were picking a piece of magic fruit from a giving tree.

I won six packages of pink bubble bath which I can still see and smell in my imagination.

A few months later I got a love letter from Lucy's brother telling me I was "a very nice girl," he loved me and promised gum and money in the next letter. I wrote him back and never heard from him again.

Each of our families went down life's altering paths. Each had the family disease of alcoholism, which slowly changed once-happy families into hurting ones. Our families became factories that manufactured and maintained alcoholic family dynamics. Words like trauma, grief, denial, minimization, rage, fusion and cut off no longer belonged to other people, they described us.

The black and white thinking, feeling and behavior so much a part of any alcoholic dynamic slowly subsumed our own families. Our families burned slow fuses until the security and warmth we had learned to call home blew up. Each of our parents divorced after a quarter of a century of marriage. Just at the point where some families and marriages consolidate and coalesce their learning on how to have successful relationships, we were coalescing our learning on how to have dysfunctional ones. That is the map we took with us into adulthood, along with a ton of unnamed, unprocessed pain. Each of us went into young adulthood carrying huge emotional and psychological burdens that we didn't know what to do with.

We met each other again at my stepcousin's wedding. As soon as I saw Brandt I knew I was seeing someone close to me. When we danced I felt a current between our hearts that made everything all right, that put my world into balance. That was thirty years ago and we have been together ever since. We have each adopted the idea that something was wrong with us. That what happened to us, though it may not have been our fault, was our responsibility to deal with. That we were sick and needed to get better and that to get better we would have to be as aggressive and methodical about addressing our disease of codependency as we would if we had cancer. We took treatment very seriously and devoted no less than fifteen years of serious work to turning around dysfunctional dynamics that family systems experts generally agree take three generations to heal without aggressive intervention.

Yesterday we celebrated our twenty-eighth wedding anniversary. After twenty-four I felt we had conquered our legacy. We have two children, Marina, who is twenty-six, and Alex, who is twenty-three. Both thriving and wonderful and the lights of our lives. We are thankful each and every day and do not take these blessings for granted. They have been hard won and we've each logged more time in therapy and Twelve-Step programs than anyone (except ourselves) would ever believe.

We have had many difficult times that we have gotten through and because we got through them they eventually made us stronger. My son reminds me of the Italian proverb, "What doesn't kill you makes you stronger." We feel so lucky, grateful and proud of ourselves that we had the sense to get the help we needed when we needed it and equally blessed by our other family members who have too. And we are so deeply happy that we didn't throw in the towel on ourselves, the ideal of marriage, family and each other. Our children have been our motivators. We chose to recover rather than repeat to the best of our abilities, knowing that nothing and no one is perfect and that our task was to learn to meet life on life's terms and learn to be happy with what we have and work to make it better.

This is what I have learned.

I believe in love. I believe that life wants to work out if we let it. I believe that there are no dead spots in the universe and that if we whisper into it at any place, anywhere, our prayers will be carried straight to God's ears. I believe that God is in charge and that if we hold that thought and release it every time it occurs to us good things will follow.

I believe as my grandmother told me that, "Troubles are God's way of calling us to Him," and that if we meet them with a humble heart, place our faith in God and take the next right action, we will come through them better and stronger. If we look for silver linings they will always be there.

I believe that I am growing and evolving and so is this universe, that I am a part of something special, something called life. I believe that life is a gift and that it is my responsibility to work it till it works. I believe that if we put enough good into the world the world will eventually put it right back into us if we are patient and know how to watch for it. I believe that the secrets of life are sewn into the lining of the universe for us to tease out one at a time.

I believe that a good attitude is worth more than money, a good heart is worth more than a high birth and that a good character is a foundation upon which at least three generations can be built. I believe that appreciation is how to deepen our experience of the beauty that is always somewhere around us. I believe in children, that they are God's way of giving us a second chance at living. I believe that a good marriage is not only about finding the right person but also about being the right person, that broken hearts can mend and broken lives can find meaning and purpose again.

I believe in love and its power to heal, restore and reveal our next lessons; that for every one step we take towards God, God takes four towards us. I believe that promises really do come true, that if we work our program with sincere and open hearts and do our best to align our will with God's, that life will work out and we will find inner peace.

I believe that the trials of my own life were how I got here and just for today "I do not regret the past nor wish to close the door on it." Just for today I am grateful for all of it. I believe that God has been guiding my steps in each and every way, even when I didn't know that for sure.

I believe in the gift of recovery in my life.

Tian Dayton, Ph.D., T.E.P.

The Faces of Heroes

Tell me who you live with and I will tell you who you are.

Spanish proverb

The truth is, cancer affects us all. In fact, there are few lives that have not been visited, in one form or another, by the horrifying specter of this disease. Many have sat by the bedside of a neighbor, a child or a parent struggling with this illness. We have talked to misty-eyed coworkers about their prognoses and treatments. There are old friends we have lost to cancer. And new friends we have made during the battle.

When my wife was diagnosed with breast cancer in October of 2002, we were a typical midlife couple, raising respectable kids in the suburbs, paying off a mortgage, working our jobs with an equal mix of enjoyment and stress. But the advent of cancer changed all that. Cancer changed us. Or, I should say, survival changed us. For it was the recovery, the struggle against the unseen adversary, that made our good marriage even stronger, enabled us to reevaluate our goals, and gave us new opportunities to help others.

When my wife first called with the news, her voice stretching out to me over the telephone a thousand miles away, I could scarcely believe the words.

"I have cancer," she said softly, "I have cancer."

Sitting alone by the phone in Indianapolis that evening, I felt my spirit winging its way to my wife's side as she sobbed in Orlando. "It will be all right," I tried to assure her. "Don't worry."

"I love you," she told me. "I want to come home."

"I love you, too," I said.

A few hours later, after a quick flight back to Indy, we embraced and wept together. But our journey was just beginning.

Consultations followed. Tests. Books and magazines by the stack. Meetings with specialists and surgeons. Our minds swam in a boiling sea of information and uncertainty. There were other discussions, and decisions to be made.

Eventually my wife opted for a mastectomy. The die was cast.

But thankfully, we emerged whole on the other side of this experience. We learned much about ourselves and about each other. Everything we experienced with cancer has only served to make us stronger people and more compassionate and caring.

I think of these things whenever I meet someone who is recovering from an illness or from some dreaded disease of the heart or mind—from alcoholism, drug addiction or abuse. These experiences can scar us, but they cannot destroy our spirit, not if we refuse to allow it.

Walking through the cancer experience with my wife, I learned that it takes great courage to believe that we can overcome. There is a certain bravery in facing up to our own weaknesses, to our own mortality, to all of the possibilities that might be visited upon us. Anyone who has survived an illness, who has recovered from an addiction, is living testimony to the resiliency of the human spirit, to the courageous hope that resides within us.

Now, seeing the people around me through new eyes, I realize that there are many survivors in this life. There are those who have survived a childhood in the presence of an alcoholic parent who have gone on to live loving and productive lives. There are those who have survived drug addictions, or depression, or child abuse who have managed their pain in such a way that they are able to leave that suffering behind them, and then journey on, day by day, into the bright and welcoming embrace of family and friendship. There are others who have survived defeat, illness, even the face of death and endured through faith and hope in God.

These heroes are with us every day—sitting beside us at work, in the classroom, in the cafeteria, or in the intimacy of the living room. We may not see them as such, but their lives are much bigger because they have walked through the valley of pain and emerged whole on the other side.

There is so much truth here.

We can encounter the heroic in so many of the people who bless our lives.

All we have to do is look closely. And if we do, we are bound to meet a hero or two. That's what I learned.

After my wife's recovery from breast cancer, I came to realize that I was a survivor, too. Not in the same fashion, perhaps; but I had stood by my wife's side, held her hand, and made that part of her healing possible. We had survived the threat of cancer together.

And in the end, that's what life is all about. Life is taking a stand with someone, sitting beside a friend, talking to a neighbor, encouraging the defeated, teaching the young, loving through the hardships of the journey of life. And in the simple touch of a hand or a warm embrace, we are healing each other, too.

One person at a time.

Todd Outcalt

The Dying Battery and
the Recovering Codependent

When love and skill work together, expect a masterpiece.

John Ruskin

It is December 1985 and I drive a diesel automobile. Diesels are notorious for slow starts in cold weather and so a dying battery has become a regular part of my daily life. Like a good scout, I have been prepared. Before my wife, Dede, leaves for work each morning, I go out and jump-start my car using my cables and her battery. I just hook the two up and it's as easy as pie. Routine. Normal. At least it has been. Until this morning.

This morning Dede confronted me. She had consulted an expert, an objective third party she informed me solemnly, "and you're not going to like what I have to say," she continued. Silence followed as we sat there, knee to knee and eye to eye.

"What is it?" I asked, already scared, already angry.

You see, lately Dede had been asking questions such as: "Is it harmful to my battery to be used so often to jump-start your car?" Of course I told her that was ridiculous. I told her that she needed to learn to give. Yesterday she said she was thinking of asking a mechanic her question. I was shocked and told her so. "You are making this a relationship issue! You don't trust me."

So there we sat, me angry just from hearing her

confrontive tone. Dede was direct and her position was well thought out. The mechanic had told her that it was not good for her battery to be used so often to start my car. He told her that if it continued, we would soon be in the market for two new batteries.

She said that she believed that I truly had not known this before, but in light of this new, more reliable information, she wanted me to be responsible for taking my car in for the necessary repairs. Dede wasn't going to stand by and watch her battery die.

I was furious. "I cannot believe this! You really are making this into a relationship issue!"

"I'm not saying that, Thom . . . " she began.

"Yes you are. You act like I'm trying to treat you like a doormat, like I'm abusing you in some way." I was exaggerating. I was distracting, trying to get the focus back on her, where it belonged.

Dede left for work. I stewed. I thought of my alternatives. I thought of friends I could call on to come over and help me jump-start my car. A different friend every day? How exhausting. I thought of how guilty I would feel if I now used one friend regularly for this, in light of the new information Dede had presented me about the potential drain to my friend's battery.

I thought of making a point each night of getting out of bed every two hours or so, going out in the cold night to start my car in order to keep the battery charged. Dede would surely feel sorry for me then and insist that I use her car to start mine. But with the new information, I would feel guilty. Damn.

And then it occurred to me—one of those rare moments of true inspiration. The proverbial light bulb went on. By George, I had it! I would make time to take my car to the shop for repairs. I would take responsibility for my car. I would make it a top priority. I felt absolutely brilliant.

Acting on my new plan, I took the car in for service. Within an hour, a brand new battery had been installed and I was on my way. *Maybe Dede is not as ridiculous as I have thought,* I thought as I drove home that evening, excited to tell her that getting a new battery isn't really such a big deal.

The episode with my car battery was a metaphor for our life at the time; the recovering codependent woman in a relationship with an actively addicted man. In January 1986, with the same firmness described in the dying battery episode, Dede confronted me about my alcoholism. Six months sober herself, she said, "You're drunk. You'll need to do something about that if you want our relationship to last." I knew just what she meant. I didn't like it, but I knew.

So I began recovery from alcoholism. I have not had a drink since that January evening and today we are two fully charged batteries. One day at a time. Thanks, Dede.

Someone told me the other day that abstinence from addictive behaviors is really just the positive application of procrastination. I like that.

Lying in bed the night before my eighteenth anniversary with abstinence, I said to Dede, "Now let me see if I remember this correctly. Eighteen years ago you told me in no uncertain terms that I should not have another drink for eighteen years. Is that right?"

She laughed. "No, you are not remembering that correctly."

"Okay. Just checking," I said.

Thom Rutledge

Legacies Left Behind

It is easier to build strong children than to repair broken men.

Frederick Douglass

As a child growing up, fear was a way of life. Then came the sadness and pain; the loneliness was pervasive. Living in a small logging community of fewer than five hundred people in the Pacific Northwest, drinking, and even more so—alcoholism—was a way of life. My parents' tavern was the hub of the community for most. Certainly drinking was central to my family because my father was alcoholic.

My parents taught me to be grateful for what I had—a house, food and parents who cared. And I was, and am, grateful. But what I remember most was the confusion as to why my father behaved as he did and the chronic fear he would die in a car wreck. He was forever taking off in the car with a half case of beer and me next to him. I thought if I went with him, he might come home earlier.

Why did I want him home? It was all such a fantasy—so maybe he would relieve my mom from work so she could fix dinner for us, or even be home at night before we went to bed. Maybe because I thought my brother and sister would be less upset.

My brother was terminally ill. By age nine, he could not walk; he crawled and then soon he went into a wheelchair. At seventeen, he died. By then my father was becoming quite scary. He was losing any of the control he had been trying to maintain. Today I believe he was having psychotic episodes caused by his alcoholism. At this time in his alcoholism he became quite violent. The fear of him killing my mother, or some combination of my mother, my sister or me became paramount. Who was this man who I have loved, I knew once loved all of us—why and how could he do this to us?

My father, having grown up in Appalachian poverty, wanted so much for me to go to college—a big feat at this time for a little girl from this town. I wanted to live out his dream; it gave me value to him, so I focused hard in school and told myself what he told me, "You have got to go to college." The only way I knew that could happen was to beat the odds of another social dynamic and that meant not getting pregnant. With those two goals, school and not getting pregnant, I ventured forth underneath a cloud of fear, trying not to rock the boat any more than it was already rolling.

Having learned so much about how to survive by taking charge, initiating and being goal oriented, I became a successful student and leader while screaming on the inside as my family was being torn apart by addiction. With my brother's death and my family's inability to cope, the alcoholism weighed heavily on our grief. Funny how those who learn not to speak the truth of their lives, can ultimately find voices in other arenas.

As I went on to college, my parents divorced. By then I was numb. I became invisible on a large college campus. The nightmares began and persisted for many years. I had visions of watching my father kill himself or us; visions of not being able to save my brother from tidal waves. I was unable to wear turtlenecks because of the sensation of being choked. I would spend my waking hours driven and goal-focused—anything to keep busy and distract myself from feeling incredible pain.

God's gift to me was sending me on a journey that led me to my first job as a social worker in an alcoholism treatment program. I knew nothing about treatment but what I did know is that most addicts were people like my dad—good people overcome by something outside of their control. I had spent my life surrounded by good people whose lives had gone very awry due to their addictions.

I was asked to develop a family program but I neglected to ask what they meant by "family." I invited the children of the alcoholics to the treatment program, yet at this time, the mid-to-late 1970s, there was no concept of adult children and the word codependency did not yet exist. I wasn't sure what to do with all of these kids, young or adult, but common sense told me that if they lived with addiction they had the right to understand it. And intuitively, I knew group would help them lessen their profound sense of being unique in their pain, that they were not alone in their experiences.

I began to see that the pain of human experiences is universal and that with a safe setting and a language through which to talk about one's experiences, people could begin to speak their truth, to own their reality. They could ultimately come to put the past behind, to let go of painful familial scripts and be accountable for their own choices. To this day, I maintain a belief I internalized at a young age, "No one deserved to live as we had." Not me, my brother, sister, mother or my father. No one deserves to live a life of fear, pain and shame. Of that, I was and am passionate.

Through this process, I found my way to a self-help group. It was not long before both my personal recovery and my professional direction began to unfold.

Today I am honored to carry this message of healing and recovery throughout the world. I have taken the experiences of growing up in an isolated, tough little community—where alcoholism was a way of life—and become a part of a worldwide community of healing and recovery.

I no longer live in fear, confusion or pain. Secrets and shame are a part of my past. I allow myself to experience what I am feeling when I feel it and I trust my own perceptions. I have tapped into a fun-loving person within me. I can ask for help; I don't need to be rigidly self-sufficient. I find joy in the present and I surround myself with people who respect and treat me well.

In some ways, my recovery is summarized with two beautiful pieces of art in my home with messages that say, "You deserve to no longer live your life in fear," and "Does the pain ever go away? . . . Yes."

Claudia Black

A Light Touch

Weeds are flowers, too, once you get to know them.

A.A. Milne, Eeyore from *Winnie the Pooh*

There are low bottom drunks, low bottom meetings and places where low bottom folks get treatment. I am a critical care nurse. I guess you'd call where I work a low bottom hospital. Not that we deliver inferior care. We don't. It's just that large percentages of the people we treat are homeless or in a position where they easily fall through the cracks of the cracks of the kind of care other people enjoy. Drugs and/or alcohol are major components of nearly all our business on any given night in urgent care.

I know this is where I am supposed to be even though it gets tough around here. As often as not I end up in a wrestling match with men who are already full of drugs and booze who then have other drugs put into them so we can operate or do whatever is necessary to save their lives.

I think I am supposed to be here because I know what they are going through. No matter how ugly the situation gets or what the streets have done to them, it is my job to deliver a light touch to those who are already so broken. I always see the person behind the dirt and blood because I was once on the street just like they are now.

My first drink was at about eleven years old. It took me to a place I always wanted to go. I found an escape through booze from an alcoholic home and all that goes with it. Soon I was out of control. By sixteen I was on the street making a living by exotic dancing, selling drugs and anything else anyone would give me money for. You know the story.

I tried different low bottom treatment places. They always threw me out. If I were in charge of those places, I'd have thrown myself out too. Finally everyone I ever knew slammed the door in my face. All except Tony and Frank.

Tony and Frank were two beautiful, old guys who had survived the street, found sobriety and sanity through AA and now lived together. When I had fallen way past the worst I could imagine they always left the door open for me. They'd give me a place to crash, give me food and tell me about how it didn't have to be this way. There was a way out, they said; all I had to do was want it. Tony and Frank meant business but they always had a light touch.

One day I did want it. My two old angels took me to my first meeting. I had been to AA meetings before, of course. I say this was my first meeting with them because this was the first time I ever went to get help. It was the first meeting I ever went to where I listened. That was the meeting where I started upward.

Like everyone's story, mine was and is up and down. My life isn't perfect but it is a far cry from what it was. After ten years in program I decided to go back to school. I found out I was good at school—amazing how much easier learning was being sober. So I just kept going. At one time I thought I wanted to be a psychiatrist but everyone we studied in abnormal psychology sounded like me. I knew all the people the books were talking about. What they described didn't sound so abnormal to me. So I figured psychiatry was getting too close so I quit and became a nurse.

That was ten years ago. I've been in urgent care eight years. I know why I am here. To give the light touch to those who need it so badly, just as I needed it in that other life. Tony and Frank put me in debt. This is how I am paying back.

Anonymous as told to Earnie Larsen

Fat, Stupid, Ugly

We have it in our power to start the world again.

Thomas Paine

Lucky. Blessed. Optimistic. Happy. These are new words in my vocabulary. They taste sweet and juicy, like exotic fruit in my mouth as I practice saying them.

Things didn't start out well. When I was born, my mother didn't want to hold me. In my baby book, she wrote, "Debbie was a fat, unattractive baby." My father started abusing me before I could talk. My grandparents, parents and sisters were small, beautiful and smart; I was reminded again and again that I was Fat, Stupid and Ugly. By the time I entered puberty I was smoking, drinking and taking diet pills prescribed by the doctor my mother took me to. My schoolwork was dismal. Married at seventeen to a batterer, by nineteen I was divorced and dead inside.

I was married two more times and had a precious son, and kept right on drinking. When my drunkenness all but ruined my sister's wedding, I had to confront my demons. I entered a hospital rehab program and forty days later emerged raw and vulnerable, a sober alcoholic. That was nineteen years ago and I haven't had a drink since.

That was just the beginning of my recovery. I went to AA meetings every day, worked the steps and made my amends. But I was so damaged, still the Fat, Stupid, Ugly girl that I had always been. My father, now long dead, came back to haunt me, urging me to slice open my throat rather than look at the truth of his abuse.

Remarkably I found my life's work, imagining and then creating a youth center in South Central Los Angeles—A Place Called Home (APCH). But even this rich, fulfilling work didn't prevent me from falling into yet another abusive relationship, this time with a man who was later convicted of rape and murder. I escaped; I was luckier than his next girlfriend.

Eight years ago, I struck up a friendship with an artist named Diana and before long we were best friends. We went to Twelve-Step meetings together, wrote together, and after a long time and to our mutual surprise, fell in love. Life was finally starting to feel good, when, in a horrible car crash, I nearly died. During the month I was in the hospital, my profound wounds were complicated by a stroke and a heart attack. Diana never left my side.

Once she brought me home, the truly horrendous work of recovering started in earnest. I had broken bones, a serious head wound and brain damage, but absolutely no idea what had happened to me or how injured I was. Diana and I went from being equals to being mother and balky teenager. Our relationship went from being about us to being about me. She nurtured and protected; I resisted and rebelled.

Together and separately, we saw our therapist. The trauma had unlocked a Pandora's box of emotions, memories and unfamiliar feelings of vulnerability. I began to examine and write about my earliest experiences of abuse. I wrote and remembered. The process was excruciating and progress was infinitesimal. I took my memories to my therapist and worked to untangle the twisted, knotted threads of my personal history. I started to confront my fears—and my mistakes.

Miraculously, Diana and I fought our way back to being equals, respectful and loving, each taking responsibility for ourselves, encouraging the other, and guarding the rare and beautiful life we have discovered together.

Therapy is still painful. I want to pull away from the

memories, to deny my mistakes, and let them slip back into the shadows. But today I have the loving support that allows me to face the real ugliness of my past, to look at it, talk about it and let it go. Today, I have a son, sisters, friends and a partner who accept me as I am and whom I love without reservation. Very slowly I am coming to see that although I will probably always be on a diet, and my thoughts and words are sometimes scrambled, and I'll never look like a magazine model, my name is not Fat, Stupid, Ugly. My name is Debrah.

When I got sober nineteen years ago, I thought I had gone through recovery. Little did I know how many challenges lay ahead and how many layers I would have to peel away before I began to feel okay with myself. Today I find myself using these words: *lucky, blessed, open, optimistic, satisfied, content, happy* and very, very *grateful.*

This must be what recovery feels like.

Debrah Constance as told to J.I. Kleinberg

I Will Not Give Up

A person who seeks help for a friend, while needy himself, will be answered first.

The Talmud

We found her on the floor of her living room, sprawled on her stomach next to the sofa. She was still conscious but just barely. Together, Suzanne and I lifted her up on the couch. I sat next to her and took her hand. "Karen. You are going to be all right. We're going to take care of you. It's going to be okay."

I can still remember her face, looking up at me but not seeing. She wanted out, and she was almost there. She tried to speak, but there was only the sound of incoherent mumbles.

Suzanne went to find Karen's keys, coat and shoes. I went into the kitchen and poured out the unfinished glass of wine and the rest of the five-gallon box. Suzanne found the empty bottle of sleeping pills. I found the suicide notes on the kitchen table. I folded them up to take with me. I didn't want Karen to find them when she came home again.

She made it almost seven months without a drink this time. She had called Suzanne in her stupor to say good-bye.

We dragged her lifeless body down the stairs and into my car and headed to the emergency room. I drove and Suzanne sat with Karen in the backseat, desperately trying to keep her awake.

I was "on" that night, very efficient. I turned off my own

feelings, and I tried to be strong for Karen. The next few days, though, were a blur. Karen was going to be okay, but I was still really shaken up.

I needed something. I needed to run. A winter of running on the treadmill watching ESPN wouldn't work this time. I needed to run outside.

I laced up my shoes and bundled up against the cold. I ran through my neighborhood, the crisp cold air burned my lungs.

I thought back to sixteen years ago when I discovered running and drinking. I fell in love with both. I learned to high jump and hurdle. I was part of a team. I spent long Saturdays at track meets, learning how to compete. Then there were the glory days of winning medals and trophies, chasing and breaking school records.

I spent Saturday nights in parks and in friends' homes when their parents were away, guzzling beer, discovering vodka, whiskey, tequila and grain alcohol. I laughed with a recklessness I had never felt before. The pressures were gone. I was relaxed. I rebelled in my own quiet way. I voraciously smoked cigarettes. I kissed boys.

And then I got sick, over and over. I emerged from blackouts in unfamiliar places, in smoke-filled rooms. I shut down emotionally. I stopped remembering.

I was on two separate paths. I was Dr. Jekyll and Mr. Hyde. I continued to high jump but not as high. I continued to long jump but not as far. I continued to live but not fully. At twenty-one years old, I was a zombie, the walking dead. My soul had become fragile. I didn't want to die, but I didn't want to live. I just didn't want to feel.

I had a few close friends who were there throughout my struggles, and they reached out and rescued me. They got me into treatment, and I surrendered to my alcoholism.

That was almost eight years ago.

Now here I am, no longer drinking but still running. I

reached the track and stopped to stretch. I hadn't been to the track in awhile. I decided I was going to run a timed mile, just to see where I was at.

The track was covered with snow and ice in areas. I jogged to the starting line and then started my watch.

Go! Focus on the run. I established my rhythm as I came off the first turn and headed into the back straightaway. I dodged the icy patches and noted their locations for the next time around. I sailed into the second lap and continued to press forward. As I headed into the third, I was hurting. I didn't want to stop, but I wanted to slow down.

"Going into the third lap is where you need to pick up the pace. That is where the others slow down." I could hear the words of my high school coach. I focused on my form and pushed through the pain.

Down the straightaway I imagined I heard my dad cheering. I heard my college coaches clapping. I saw my college teammates who helped me get sober waving me on.

And then on the backstretch, another voice. My own. "I will not give up."

My lungs were screaming. My legs felt heavy. "I will not give up."

I thought of Karen, imagining her in the high security-detox, where they took away her belt and shoelaces, just in case.

"I will not give up."

I thought of Karen hooked up to tubes that pumped in charcoal to absorb the poison of the alcohol and the sleeping pills.

"I will not give up."

I headed into the last turn, picking up speed.

I thought of myself at thirteen years old, a young girl full of curiosity and wonder, full of so much potential, so much promise. And also a girl tripped up by fear and insecurity, who tried to find herself by escaping in alcohol. A troubled girl who grew up to be a woman who wanted herself back.

"I will not give up."

As I crossed the finish line, I pressed the stop button on my watch. I looked at the time, and I smiled. Thank you Karen, for the lesson. I hope you learn it too.

Deirdre Morris

Now I Am Whole

I have come a long way, struggling,
finding my way, through the darkness,
each step labored, under attack.

I've progressed, if not in body
then in the stretch of the mind
with a smile on my face ignoring the pain.

Look past what I show you,
to what I have become;
there is more, my friend, than this shell;
there is the essence of who I am.

For you, who did not know me before,
you are lucky.
For then, I was part, and now, I am whole.

Betty King

Out of the Mouths of Babes

Answers are like butterflies. They most often come when we are doing something else.

Earnie Larsen

It was early Saturday morning—a rare weekend off. I was heading home to celebrate Dad's birthday. As I settled into my seat it was still dark outside. I closed my eyes and drifted off to sleep, awakened occasionally as a bag bumped against the seat or someone slammed shut an overhead bin.

Suddenly I heard a distinctive, familiar voice. It had to be Reggie. He and his three siblings had been through the Betty Ford Center Children's Program a couple of times and were regulars at the Wednesday evening continuing care program. The whole family worked hard to overcome Dad and Mom's addiction to alcohol and other drugs. Along the way there had been many setbacks, pitfalls and disappointments, but they never gave up. Though I cared deeply about each member of this family, Reggie had stolen my heart. The youngest, he was friendly and outspoken, greeting the world with love and joy. Though he joked, giggled and laughed most of the time, Reggie occasionally stopped people in their tracks by speaking the truth with the terseness of a true warrior.

I opened my eyes to see the whole family awkwardly negotiating the aisle with way too much carry-on baggage. It was 6:30 A.M., on a day off—way too early for this!

I instinctively reached for my newspaper and opened it wide to conceal my identity. Children freak out when we meet unexpectedly away from work. "What are you doing here?" they may blurt out in disbelief. Many assume that I just live at the center and patiently wait for them to return to group, answer their phone calls during times of trouble or quickly respond to their e-mails. That day I felt incapable of interacting without at least one cup of coffee in my system.

They settled in two rows ahead of me. What a gift to hear their banter and discourse throughout the hour-long flight! As the plane pulled up to the Jetway in San Francisco I truly thought I had escaped. Little did I realize that the plane being only half full would give me away. When the bell signaled our safe arrival Reggie, forgetting his backpack underneath the seat, bolted toward the door. As he came back to retrieve it he saw me and shrieked loudly, "Jerry!"

He moved with a speed, force and purpose of an Olympic sprinter. Other passengers were swept aside as he made his way back and jumped into my arms—it looked like he was parting the Red Sea. There was a collective sigh from everyone, a Hallmark moment.

Reggie turned around to face everyone in front of him and proudly declared, "He's my therapist." He briefly turned toward me with a mischievous look in his eye then whirled back around declaring, "He keeps teaching me it's not my fault." As he finally headed off the plane he flashed me a huge smile and giggled one more time.

Jerry Moe

Through the Eyes of My Heart

Holding on to anger is like grasping a hot coal with the intent of throwing it at someone else; you are the one getting burned.

Buddha

Torrential rains soaked me to the bone. I stood watching as somber people threw flowers on the wooden coffin barely visible at the bottom of a cold, wet hole. I wondered if my heart would drown in the rain.

I followed the slow parade of black-clad people out of the dreary cemetery into the noisy restaurant. The room was damp, the kind that seeps though your skin, creeping to the very core of you. Self-conscious about my dainty high-heeled shoes heavy with mud, I sipped on hot, strong coffee, hoping for a jolt of energy deep down in my soul. With a smile only as deep as my lips, I listened in on conversations about the weather and the upcoming elections.

My wet feet were very much on my mind, and I wished for fluffy slippers that would make me feel warm all over. And cozy. Because there is nothing cozy about burying the man who gave you life, no matter what kind of man he had been.

As far back in my childhood as I can remember, I had understood that my father wasn't "nice." To all who knew him, he was clueless at his best, purposefully cruel at his worst. Absolutely self-centered, he did exactly what pleased him and nothing more, nothing less. He was a genius professionally, but a failure at home, unable to successfully relate even to his own children—we were a distraction, mostly unwelcome. There was a time when I thought that the man had no heart.

After dutifully paying their respects, the people left one by one, drifting back to their own lives. I took my mother home and tucked her into bed with loads of feathery blankets; maybe that would make her feel warm all over. And cozy.

I discarded the dainty, muddy shoes and put on my faithful old sneakers. I grabbed my father's woolen checkered shirt hanging there by the door and slipped out for a walk—comfort food for my soul.

I moved quickly until I was out of the village. When the horizon was filled with an expanse of fields, I stopped. The sky had poured out its anger and seemed appeased now, having replaced darkness with fluffy clouds and a few rays of sun peeking through. I closed my eyes, marveling at the peaceful quiet. I breathed deeply. Beginning to walk again, I let my slower steps lead me back to the cemetery. It was deserted by now, heaps of flowers covering the freshly filled hole. I picked up a single yellow rose that had fallen out of a bouquet.

Hugging myself in my father's checkered shirt, I reveled in the smell of it, old cigarette smoke with a nauseating tinge of alcohol. And I let my heart remember.

I must have been eleven and he waltzed with me to a tune of Schubert's. We bumped into furniture and I giggled and giggled and giggled. My mind understands now that there is a strong possibility he had been drunk but that isn't what my soul recollects; it senses the joy of being twirled around in my daddy's arms.

And my memory goes back to the day I woke up from surgery to a huge basket of fruits, which I couldn't eat of course, yet the message was clear: My dad had been there.

I let myself relive the day he walked me down the aisle some twenty-two years ago. He wore his starched dress uniform; all the decorations pinned perfectly on his shoulder and breast pocket. I chose to lean on him as we began our long walk to the altar. They buried his rigid body in the same starched dress uniform. Quite a dignified look.

My father surely gave my life an edge. How many daughters have the privilege of learning love when there seems to be nothing lovely? I was forced to read him with the eyes of my heart.

"I love you, Daddy," I whispered. Oh! For one more eccentric waltz, one more useless fruit basket, one more walk with him. But his baby-blue eyes were forever closed.

I brushed my lips to the yellow rose and gently laid it on top of the many flowers. It stood out. And at that moment I knew deep within my soul that a fraction of me would forever stand out because of who he had made me to be.

Barbara A. Croce

Fully Alive

The rung of a ladder was never meant to rest upon, but only hold a man's foot long enough to enable him to put the other somewhat higher.

Thomas Henry Huxley

When I was a child, there were two secrets that I was supposed to keep. I think Mom hoped I would dispose of them as easily as my Rainbow Brite dolls and horrendous shoe-string barrettes. The first secret was what I had done that day on the playground; the second was what had happened with him. I never realized how intertwined the two were.

I cut. The first memory I have of my self-destructive behavior dates back to second grade. With my thick glasses and terrific shyness, I was the loner of my class. That day—the one I'm supposed to erase from my mind—Lester Sloan and his gang were being particularly cruel on the playground. I blocked out their taunts by squeezing a jagged pebble until my hand bled. The feel of my blood trickling down my palm fascinated and empowered me: The boys' taunts may hurt me, yet this was a pain I could control.

Despite Mom's warning never to harm myself again, I could not forget my discovery. Mom may dismiss my crying with the sticks-and-stones line, but she didn't know how cruel my classmates could be. When the kids' tormenting would become too severe, I would turn to physical pain. Most often, I'd dig my nails into my palm, something that could be done without anyone else seeing, as soon as I heard "Hey, four eyes!" Soon, I didn't need to cry anymore.

It wasn't until junior high, when certain physical changes caused memories to resurface as guilt, that my destructive behavior became severe. Ironically, the other secret Mom hoped I would leave behind with my childhood was what I thought about most. She wasn't the only one who wished that I could forget: Every time I harmed myself, I was trying to shove away thoughts of him.

Like every addiction, achieving the high took greater and greater measures. The pebble in the schoolyard evolved to pins, knives and razors. By high school, I cut any part of body covered by clothes, although my wrists were my body part of choice. The slashes became my words, the only way I knew to express myself. Above all, I cut not to feel. Even if the control fix was only temporary, it took precedence over any overwhelming confusion and pain. For me, cutting was a way of denying my sexual abuse, a very effective means to shove back every horrible remembrance that tried to surface. I cut when I could feel his heft on top of me and his warm dry lips against my own. I cut when Mom sighed heavily and wouldn't look away from the TV the few times I tried to talk about what had happened. I do not blame her—no mother wants to face that she couldn't protect her daughter from her own brother. I didn't want to confront the reality that I had had sex with my uncle. Sure, anyone else would have called it incest or rape, but since I didn't talk about the abuse, I had no one to contradict my belief that I had been a seven-year-old whore.

I began having horrible anxieties over failing. I believed that I had everyone fooled. Sure, I may get A's now and seem likeable enough, but I truly believed that I was holding on to my successes by a single thread, and it was only a matter of time before everything would fall apart. Once everyone discovered the fraud I was, I knew they would abandon me. That became my greatest fear: being utterly alone. When the anxiety became too overwhelming, I started to have episodes when everything—the room around me, the rushing in my ears, the thoughts in my head—started spinning, and I would feel as though I were suffocating. Cutting became the only way to stop the spinning and restore order to my life. Afterwards I'd sit in a dull trance, entirely calm, numb and empty.

By the time I left for college, I was cutting two, three, sometimes four times a week. My legs and arms were a mess of scar tissue, and I was wearing long sleeves in the heat of summer. I knew that this was not a life, but I had no idea how to stop.

* * *

My name is Elizabeth Walton. I have not cut myself in three years, seven months and twenty-one days, but that is not the only reason I know I am recovered. I know I am recovered because days, even weeks, can go by when I will not even think about cutting. What once was an obsession that cast a dark shadow over every part of my life, now no longer has the slightest appeal. I know I am recovered because I can be around my uncle and not revert to the timid, insecure girl who blamed herself for everything.

I know I am recovered because I am fully aware that people in my life may read this, yet I am not ashamed for them to know my journey. My mother's warning from that afternoon so long ago had remained with me: Don't ever tell anyone you did this to yourself. She only had meant to protect me. If a pebble on the schoolyard would disgust people, what were they going to think of me slicing my wrist with razors? For years, I allowed myself to be trapped by silence and shame. Now, I realize that silence was part of the problem. What I had done may not have been normal, but it certainly didn't make me some kind of disgusting monster. Even in a society where so much has lost its shock value, cutting not only remains scandalous, but also a topic people rather would pretend didn't even exist. For years, I didn't think it existed. I believed I had to be some kind of freak, a sicko in the most negative connotation. The truth is, there are plenty of people silently suffering from the same addiction, as I had been, who are in much greater need of a confidant than a razor.

I did not reach this wonderful, liberating state alone. God has blessed me with caring and supportive parents, a fiancé who would do anything to see me truly happy, and so many other compassionate hearts. These individuals have given up their lunch breaks for me, cried with me, stayed up until 4:30 in the morning talking to me when they really should have been resting up for their 8:00 A.M. physics exam, and loved me even when stepping away would have been far less painful. They have helped me peel away my layers of defenses, until I understood what was at the root of my fears and pain.

I remember something one of the first people to touch my life said to me years ago: Someday, you will feel as though you are looking at a picture, instead of actually suffering through all this. I had nodded, but truly had believed that he was wrong. I never thought that I could have reached a state where I would not be overwhelmed by a tremendous lack of self-worth and fears of failure and abandonment, nor that I ever would be able to go a week, let alone over three-and-a-half years, without even having the slightest urge to harm myself.

Most important, I know I am recovered because I can love myself. I spent the better part of my childhood desperately trying to win the good favor of an admired adult whom I never could please, and the next thirteen years believing that what I had done with him was entirely my fault. Now, I do not need to mask my insecurities and pain under a mess of slashes on my wrist. I know that I am strong enough to be able to confront my issues in a constructive manner, worthy of other people's help, and above all, a good person. I can enjoy life, laugh without reserve, find joy in even the simplest pleasures and love fully. I finally am alive.

Elizabeth Walton

More Chicken Soup?

We would love to hear your reactions to the stories in this book. Please let us know what your favorite stories were and how they affected you.

Many of the stories and poems you have read in this book were submitted by readers like you who had read earlier *Chicken Soup for the Soul* books. We publish at least five or six *Chicken Soup for the Soul* books every year. We invite you to contribute a story to one of these future volumes.

Stories may be up to 1,200 words and must uplift or inspire. You may submit an original piece, something you have read or your favorite quotation on your refrigerator door.

To obtain a copy of our submission guidelines and a listing of upcoming *Chicken Soup* books, please write, fax or check our Web sites.

Please send your submissions to:

Chicken Soup for the Soul
P.O. Box 30880, Santa Barbara, CA 93130
fax: 805-563-2945
Web site: *www.chickensoupforthesoul.com*

Just send a copy of your stories and other pieces to the above address.

We will be sure that both you and the author are credited for your submission.

For information about speaking engagements, other books, audiotapes, workshops and training programs, please contact any of our authors directly.

Breaking the Cycle, Building the Future

A portion of the proceeds from the sale of each copy of *Chicken Soup for the Recovering Soul* will be donated to:

The National Association for Children of Alcoholics (NACoA)
11426 Rockville Pike, # 100 • Rockville, MD 20852
phone: 301-468-0985 • fax: 301-468-0987
www.nacoa.org • *nacoa@nacoa.org*

One in four children in the United States under the age of 18 is now living in a home with alcoholism or alcohol abuse and countless others are hurt by a parent's drug addiction. While these children cannot speak for themselves, NACoA is their voice of hope, help and healing. These children have a great risk of becoming tomorrow's alcoholics, drug-addicted persons or of developing mental health problems. Without intervention and support when they are young, the pain too often continues into adulthood and cycles into the next generation.

NACoA is a nonprofit membership and affiliate organization founded in 1983. Through its many programs, NACoA's work to break the cycle of addiction on behalf of these children includes:

• Training and tools for professionals who touch children's lives. NACoA partners with organizations that represent and train teachers, social workers, physicians and clergy to help them identify and support children of addicted parents.

• Advocacy, newsletters and networking to support programs to help affected children across the nation and across systems that impact them.

• Information and resources available by toll-free telephone at 1-888-554-COAS (2627) or online at *www.nacoa.org*.

People in recovery often are the strongest advocates for these millions of children affected by parental alcoholism or substance abuse. Breaking the cycle of addiction in families is crucial. Please, consider doing what you can to support the work of NACoA to break this cycle, offer hope, promote recovery and improve the lives of these children.

Who Is Jack Canfield?

Jack Canfield is one of America's leading experts in the development of human potential and personal effectiveness. He is both a dynamic, entertaining speaker and a highly sought-after trainer. Jack has a wonderful ability to inform and inspire audiences toward increased levels of self-esteem and peak performance.

Jack currently has three wonderful horses living in his stable and rides with his wife, Inga, his son Christopher, and his stepdaughter Riley.

He is the author and narrator of several bestselling audio- and videocassette programs, including *Self-Esteem and Peak Performance, How to Build High Self-Esteem, Self-Esteem in the Classroom* and *Chicken Soup for the Soul—Live.* He is regularly seen on television shows such as *Good Morning America, 20/20* and *NBC Nightly News.* Jack has co-authored numerous books, including the *Chicken Soup for the Soul* series, *Dare to Win* and *The Aladdin Factor* (all with Mark Victor Hansen), *100 Ways to Build Self-Concept in the Classroom* (with Harold C. Wells), *Heart at Work* (with Jacqueline Miller) and *The Power of Focus* (with Les Hewitt and Mark Victor Hansen).

Jack is a regularly featured speaker for professional associations, school districts, government agencies, churches, hospitals, sales organizations and corporations. His clients have included the American Dental Association, the American Management Association, AT&T, Campbell's Soup, Clairol, Domino's Pizza, GE, ITT, Hartford Insurance, Johnson & Johnson, the Million Dollar Roundtable, NCR, New England Telephone, Re/Max, Scott Paper, TRW and Virgin Records. Jack is also on the faculty of Income Builders International, a school for entrepreneurs.

Jack conducts an annual eight-day Training of Trainers program in the areas of self-esteem and peak performance. It attracts educators, counselors, parenting trainers, corporate trainers, professional speakers, ministers and others interested in developing their speaking and seminar-leading skills.

For further information about Jack's books, tapes and training programs, or to schedule him for a presentation, please contact:

Self-Esteem Seminars
P.O. Box 30880
Santa Barbara, CA 93130
phone: 805-563-2935 • fax: 805-563-2945
Web site: *www.chickensoupforthesoul.com*

Who Is Mark Victor Hansen?

In the area of human potential, no one is better known and more respected than Mark Victor Hansen. For more than thirty years, Mark has focused solely on helping people from all walks of life reshape their personal vision of what's possible. His powerful messages of possibility, opportunity and action have helped create startling and powerful change in thousands of organizations and millions of individuals worldwide.

He is a sought-after keynote speaker, bestselling author and marketing maven. Mark's credentials include a lifetime of entrepreneurial success, in addition to an extensive academic background. He is a prolific writer with many bestselling books such as *The One Minute Millionaire, The Power of Focus, The Aladdin Factor* and *Dare to Win,* in addition to the *Chicken Soup for the Soul* series. Mark has also made a profound influence through his extensive library of audio programs, video programs and enriching articles in the areas of big thinking, sales achievement, wealth building, publishing success, and personal and professional development.

Mark is also the founder of MEGA Book Marketing University and Building Your MEGA Speaking Empire. Both are annual conferences where Mark coaches and teaches new and aspiring authors, speakers and experts on building lucrative publishing and speaking careers.

His energy and exuberance travel still further through mediums such as television (*Oprah,* CNN and the *Today Show*), print (*Time, U.S. News & World Report, USA Today, New York Times* and *Entrepreneur*) and countless radio and newspaper interviews as he assures our planet's people that *"You can easily create the life you deserve."*

As a passionate philanthropist and humanitarian, he's been the recipient of numerous awards that honor his entrepreneurial spirit, philanthropic heart and business acumen, including the prestigious Horatio Alger Award for his extraordinary life achievements, which stand as a powerful example that the free enterprise system still offers opportunity to all.

Mark Victor Hansen is an enthusiastic crusader of what's possible and is *driven* to make the world a better place.

Mark Victor Hansen & Associates, Inc.
P.O. Box 7665 • Newport Beach, CA 92658
phone: 949-764-2640 • fax: 949-722-6912
FREE resources online at: *www.markvictorhansen.com*

Who Is Robert J. Ackerman, Ph.D.?

Dr. Robert J. Ackerman is Professor of Sociology and Director of the Mid-Atlantic Addiction Training Institute (MAATI) at Indiana University of Pennsylvania (IUP) and a cofounder of the National Association for Children of Alcoholics (NACoA).

As an author he has published numerous articles and research findings and is best known for writing the first book in the United States on children of alcoholics in 1978. Twelve books, many television appearances and countless speaking engagements later he has become internationally known for his work with families and children of all ages. Dr. Ackerman has served on many advisory boards and worked with numerous government agencies and task forces. The recipient of many awards including the 2003 Swinyard Award for his work in alcohol and drug abuse, he is a veteran of numerous TV appearances and has been featured on *CNN Headline News,* the *Today Show,* and in *USA Today* newspaper and *Newsweek Magazine.*

Dr. Robert J. Ackerman

MAATI, IUP • 1098 Oakland Avenue • Indiana, PA 15705

phone: 724-357-4405 • fax: 724-357-3944

e-mail: *Ackerman@iup.edu*

Who Is Theresa Peluso?

Theresa joined Health Communications, Inc. (HCI) in 1981 where she was introduced to the work of Dr. Ackerman and many of the pioneers of the contemporary recovery movement. That journey, which started over twenty years ago, has come full circle with her collaboration on *Chicken Soup for the Recovering Soul,* but it is far from over.

While developing special projects for HCI, Theresa enjoys life in South Florida with her husband, Brian, and follows her creative spirit wherever it takes her.

Theresa Peluso

HCI • 3201 S.W. 15th Street • Deerfield Beach, FL 33442

e-mail: *teri@recoveringsoul.com*

Who Is Gary Seidler?

Born in Shanghai, China, and raised in London, England, Gary immigrated to Toronto, Canada, in his late teens. While working as a journalist at the Alcoholism and Drug Addiction Research Foundation of Ontario, he met Peter Vegso. In 1976 they formed a partnership and relocated to Miami, Florida, to establish their publishing enterprise: The U.S. Journal of Drug and Alcohol Dependence (USJ), Health Communications, Inc., (HCI) and The U.S. Journal Training Inc. (USJT). Gary now lives in Beverly Hills, California, with his wife, Lana. Together they sponsor an annual summer experience, Camp Hope, for at-risk inner-city kids and their families. Gary has three children, Mandy, Oliver and Robert. His passions include thoroughbred horse racing and his own personal growth/spiritual recovery.

Gary Seidler
US JT • 3201 S.W. 15th Street • Deerfield Beach, FL 33442
e-mail: *bellaboy@aol.com*

Who Is Peter Vegso?

Peter Vegso arrived in the United States in 1976 with Gary Seidler to cofound The U.S. Journal, Inc. (USJ), Health Communications, Inc. (HCI) and The U.S. Journal Training, Inc. (USJT). Since then his entre-preneurial vision has left an indelible mark on the recovery move-ment and the "self-help" genre.

HCI's first breakthrough came in 1983 with the release of *Adult Children of Alcoholics* by Dr. Janet G. Woititz, which remained on the *New York Times* Bestseller list for 51 weeks in 1985 and was followed by John Bradshaw's *Bradshaw On: The Family* and *Healing the Shame That Binds You* in 1987. HCI continued its successful track record in 1993 with the *Chicken Soup for the Soul* series and dozens of other national bestsellers. Peter and Gary's early commitment to serve professionals in the treatment community contin-ues today through *Counselor Magazine* and The U.S. Journal Training, which offer high quality information and training opportunities.

Peter lives in South Florida with his wife, Anne, and has two daugh-ters, Melinda and Hayley. He continues to guide HCI and its affiliated companies in making a difference in the lives of everyone touched by their work.

Peter Vegso
HCI • 3201 S.W. 15th Street • Deerfield Beach, FL 33442
e-mail: *peter@recoveringsoul.com*

Contributors

The stories in this book are original pieces or taken from previously published sources, such as books, magazines and newspapers. If you would like to contact any of the contributors for information about their writing or would like to invite them to speak in your community, look for their contact information included in their biography.

The **Anonymous** contributor of the story, *Angels Dancing,* is a gifted entertainer who participated in an Onsite Workshops Financial Integration program. For more information on the program, visit *www.onsiteworkshops.com.*

Mary Barr's insights on addictions have been featured in conferences, media and universities internationally. Her self-empowerment series is shown in various correctional facilities. Mary helped develop the first transitional program in the former Soviet Union and traveled to South America to research counter-narcotics issues. She has overcome abuse, addictions, homelessness and imprisonment.

Godwin H. Barton is a North American Indian who spent his childhood living on the reserve. Now a resident of Vancouver, British Columbia, Godwin works in the area of education. He is an aspiring writer of poetry and nonfiction who is currently working on his book *I Once Stood Over . . . An Eagle in the Wild.*

Elizabeth Batt is a writer and academic advisor for Suite University. A qualified animal nurse, Elizabeth teaches several online horse-related courses. She lives in Montana where she plays with horses and runs her equine business, Natural Halters. Contact Elizabeth at *elizabethbatt@naturalhalters.com.*

Ann Best is a freelance writer and caregiver to a daughter disabled from a car crash. They live in St. George, Utah, where she writes stories, articles, screenplays and poetry. Over the years she has been published in various magazines and journals, won awards and self-published two books. You can contact Ann and find her books at *www.inspirational-book-source.com.*

Loretta McCann Bjorvik is a full-time wife, mother, home educator and recovering control freak. She lives with her husband, Paul, and their two surviving children, along with two wily, wiry fox terriers in northern Illinois.

Claudia Black, Ph.D., is a renowned author and trainer recognized for her pioneering work with addictive family systems. Her book, *It Will Never Happen To Me,* is a primer for understanding children of addiction. She has authored twelve books, produced twenty videos and guested on nationally syndicated television shows. Contact Claudia at *www.claudiablack.com.*

Carol Bonomo is the author of books on Benedictine spirituality for the rest of us. She is also an ardent ukulele enthusiast and lives with her husband, Felix, and cockatiel, Sonny (who has speaking parts in her books), in Lake San Marcos, California. She can be reached at *carol@carolbonomo.net* and *www.carolbonomo.net.*

Cynthia Borris is the author of *No More Bobs,* a lighthearted romantic comedy, numerous short stories and her specialty, slice-of-life humor pieces. She resides in Northern California and can be reached at *http://www.cynthiaborris.com.*

John Bradshaw is author of five *New York Times* bestsellers. John has been selected by numerous psychologists and the readers of *Common Boundary* as one of the most influential writers on emotional health in the 20th century. A counselor, theologian, management consultant and public speaker, John is one of the primary figures in the contemporary self-help movement.

Stuart Brantley has written poetry since he was thirteen years old and is now working on a book that will help other survivors of sexual abuse find hope to live, and bring more male survivors forward to talk about their own journey towards healing and wholeness.

Rachel Caplin is founder of *CurvOlution*™, a Size Acceptance Movement empowering girls and women to stop obsessively struggling to change their bodies and learn to love and accept the ones they have. *CurvOlution* ™ informs and educates through the contagious energy of music and dance and captivating outreach programs. Contact: *www.curvolution.com* or *rachel@curvolution.com*.

Jenna Cassell is a freelance writer, independent consultant, media producer, educator, interpreter, counselor and founder of an American Sign Language media company. She's received over twenty media production awards and is included in multiple *Who's Who*. Jenna can be reached by e-mail: *jencass@san.rr.com*.

Ruth Coe Chambers, author of *The Chinaberry Album*, likened to *To Kill a Mockingbird*, has published short stories and articles. A second novel is under consideration and a third in progress. A member of the Kalliope Editorial Readers' Board, she's also a member of the First Coast Writers' Festival planning committee.

Debrah Constance founded A Place Called Home in 1993. APCH now offers its youth members many programs including an all-day school in collaboration with the L.A. Unified School District. APCH serves over 4,000 children in its present location, a 10,000 square-foot facility. For more information on APCH, visit *http://www.apch.org*.

Barbara Croce was born and raised in Belgium, Europe. She came to live in the United States in 1982 where she raised three great kids with her husband and best friend, Rich. She fills her days with day trading, being an aerobics instructor and writing.

Joseph Cruse, M.D., is one of the foremost addictionologists in the world. An original member of AMSA (American Medical Society on Alcoholism), Dr. Cruse was the founding medical director of the Betty Ford Center and with wife, Sharon Wegscheider, was the former co-director of Onsite CoDependency Program. An author and lecturer, Joe is now a world traveler in retirement.

John Crusey took advantage of the opportunity to write and learn a lot about himself after being diagnosed with Parkinson's disease. He lives in Piqua, Ohio, with a wonderful wife and stepson. Three other children are married and have given them four beautiful grandsons. You can contact John at *jcrusey@woh.rr.com*.

Linda Day lives in Burbank, California, with her fiancé and three cats. She enjoys reading, music, sunsets and football season. She drives a red Miata, paints her fingernails purple and doesn't believe she will ever grow old, in spite of the fact that she recently became a grandmother!

Tian Dayton, Ph.D., is the author of recovery bestsellers *Forgiving and Moving On, Trauma and Addiction* and twelve other titles featured in *The Process* documentary. Tian is the Director of The New York Psychodrama Training Institute at Caron, has a private practice in Manhattan, and is a guest expert on NBC, MSNBC, *Montel, Rikki Lake, John Walsh* and *Geraldo*. Visit *www.tiandayton.com* for further information or to receive free e-daily affirmations or e-newsletter.

Martin Dodd began recovery in 1964. Four years later, he founded and then directed Sun Street Centers, a community-based addiction recovery and prevention program in Salinas, California. He retired in 2000 and now enjoys creative writing, traveling and courses in literature. You may contact him at *gopumps@aol.com*.

Julia Jergensen Edelman is a freelance writer and the editor of *The Phoenix* newspaper, a monthly publication that embraces recovery, renewal and growth in Minneapolis, Minnesota. She also writes a monthly column focused on the joys and pitfalls of parenting titled *Slices of Motherhood*, and *Transitions*, geared toward women.

John C. Friel, Ph.D., is a licensed psychologist in St. Paul, Minneapolis, and Reno, Nevada, whose practice includes individual, couple and family therapy as well as ongoing men's and women's therapy groups with his wife, Linda. A *New York Times* bestselling author, John is recognized for his professionalism and humor and is a popular speaker. Visit *http://www.clearlife.com*.

Carol Davis Gustke holds a B.S. in individual and family relationships from Western Michigan University. Her slice-of-life stories have appeared in top selling magazines and her first book, *Sacred Harvest*, was released in 2002. She is a member of the pastoral staff at a local hospital in Battle Creek, Michigan, where she resides with her husband, Art.

Erin Hagman is the pseudonym for a writer living and ministering in south-central Pennsylvania.

Miriam Hill's writing credits include: coauthor of *Fabulous Florida*, contributor to *Chicken Soup for the Bride's Soul*, several contributions in *Reader's Digest, Grit Magazine, St. Petersburg Times* and *Poynter Institute Online*. Her work was judged First Place for Inspirational Writing at the Southeastern Writers Conference in 2002 and 2004.

Debbie Heaton is an accomplished photographer. She designates most of her time to helping her community acquire and maintain substance abuse prevention services.

Patricia Holdsworth resides in South Florida and works in the field of human resources. After earning her degree in sociology and psychology, Pat worked as a drug and alcohol counselor. Her story is dedicated to her mother, Ilene Buckalew, and her sister Lois Shornock, who like Pat, share their stories to inspire others along the journey. E-mail Pat at: *path2happiness@yahoo.com*.

Janell H. is a happy fifty-year-old woman about to celebrate her twentieth year sober! She has three adult sons, teenage boy/girl twins, four grandsons and a granddaughter. Janell works as a medical assistant at a local clinic and is a member of Alcoholics Anonymous.

Debra Jay is an addiction specialist, a professional interventionist and author. Debra and her husband, Jeff, write a monthly newspaper column and have co-authored the book, *Love First: A New Approach to Intervention for Alcoholism and Drug Addiction*. Debra and Jeff live in Grosse Pointe Farms, Michigan. Visit *http://www.love-first.net*.

Marilyn Joan loves to write short stories, children's stories and poetry. Although a lot of sad memories occasionally haunt her, Marilyn has overcome many ghosts and hopes to one day publish the children's stories and articles she loves to write.

Arianna Johnson attends high school in Southern California and enjoys writing poetry, reading mysteries and listening to her favorite band, Linkin Park. Arianna will be pursuing a career in writing in the future. She can be reached at *Bluskys4evr@aol.com*.

Deb Sellars Karpek's sobriety and quality of life are a direct result of her participation in Women for Sobriety. She is a role model for new women coming into the program and helping them is a form of giving back, which strengthens her own sobriety. Visit *http://www.womenforsobriety.org*.

Betty King is the author of two books, *It Takes Two Mountains to Make a Valley* and *But—It Was in the Valleys I Grew*. She is a freelance writer, newspaper columnist and speaker. Visit her Web site *www.bettyking.net* or e-mail her at *baking2@charter.net*.

J.I. Kleinberg is a California-based freelance writer whose clients include individuals and corporations in the travel, healthcare and design/print industries, as well as a wide range of other businesses.

Ted Klontz is the executive director and co-owner with his wife, Margie, of Onsite Workshops located in Nashville, Tennessee. He has two adult children who live in Illinois and Hawaii.

Tom Krause is the author of *Touching Hearts—Teaching Greatness* and is a ten-time contributor to the *Chicken Soup for the Soul* series. An international motivational speaker and keynote presenter at the National Speakers Association National Conference 2001, Tom lives in Nixa, Missouri, with wife, Amy, and sons, Tyler and Sam. Contact: *www.coachkrause.com*.

Lisa Kugler is a therapist currently working on her doctorate in clinical psychology. Undeterred by the "statistics" of people who come to treatment and then have continuous ongoing sobriety (reportedly one out of ten), Lisa believes that if even one life has been changed by recovery then the work that she does is worthwhile.

Earnie Larsen is a nationally known author and lecturer. He is a pioneer in the field of recovery and is known and loved for his ability to touch the hearts of hundreds of thousands of people who have accepted the challenge of creating change in their lives. For more information, visit *www.earnie.com*.

Christine Learmonth has cared for her terminally ill sister since July 2002. Her love of writing helps her cope during the difficult times. She will continue to cultivate her passion until her vision of being a published writer becomes a reality.

Benneth Lee is a nationally known trainer and consultant in the criminal justice and addictions fields. He has lectured throughout the United States, West Africa and Israel. He can be reached at 773-375-3084.

Bob Lew resides in Sarasota, Florida, and celebrated thirty-one years in AA in October 2004. After a career in business he returned to school, earning his master of theology degree and is currently the Director of Chaplains at The Unity of Sarasota Church. He is married, has two grown children and four wonderful grandchildren.

Jaye Lewis is an award-winning writer whose first book, *Entertaining Angels*, celebrates life from a unique perspective. Jaye is happily married and lives in southwestern Virginia. A domestic abuse survivor, Jaye never tires of encouraging others toward their own victories. Contact Jaye at *jlewis@smyth.net*.

Perry D. Litchfield is the founder and CEO of Bayside Marin Residential Treatment Center in San Rafael, California. He is an accomplished attorney, mediator, arbitrator, building contractor, real estate broker and chemical dependency counselor. Further information about Perry and his work is available at *www.baysidemarin.com* and *www.resolutionremedies.com*.

Steven Manchester is an accomplished speaker, and teaches the popular workshop *Publish: See Your Work in Print* for Southcoast Learning Network in Massachusetts, and the Learning Connection of Rhode Island. When not spending time with his sons, writing, teaching or promoting his published books/films, Steven speaks publicly to troubled children through the Straight Ahead Program.

Lee R. McCormick is the founder and co-owner of two progressive treatment/ healing programs, The Ranch, located in middle Tennessee, and The Canyon at Peace Park, in Southern California. His programs are based on the evolutionary process known as Spirit Recovery and he is dedicated to living and sharing the happy, joyous and free truth of recovery.

Letitia Trimmer Meeks' loss of her parent as a child was life-changing. God has given her a perspective on life and death that has enabled Letitia to help others who have lost parents as well as people who have experienced the loss of other loved ones.

Jane Middelton-Moz is a bestselling author and highly regarded clinician specializing in childhood trauma, suicide prevention and community intervention. Her latest book, *Bullies,* has been widely praised as an essential resource for schools and parents. Jane is the director of the Middelton-Moz Institute, a division of the Institute of Professional Practice. Contact: *jmoz@ippi.org.*

Jann Mitchell is the author of two books about recovery, *Organized Serenity* (1992) and *Codependent for Sure! An Original Joke Book* (1992). She divides her time between the United States, Sweden and Tanzania, where she sponsors an African preschool and AIDS orphans. Reach her at *jannmmitchell@aol.com.*

Jerry Moe is the National Director of Children's Programs at the Betty Ford Center in Rancho Mirage, California. He is internationally known as an author, lecturer and trainer on issues for children from addicted families. Jerry has been developing programs and facilitating groups since 1978.

Deirdre Morris has been a writer and a runner for twenty years. In addition to her work in organizing large sporting events, she writes fiction and poetry, and is currently working on a young adult book about a female athlete. Originally from New York City, she currently lives in Sweden with her husband, Petter, and their son, Gavin.

Patricia O'Gorman, Ph.D., is a psychologist in East Chatham, New York, and a lecturer known for her warm and funny presentations. Patricia is the author of *Dancing Backwards in High Heels: How Women Master the Art of Resilience,* and co-author of *12 Steps to Self-Parenting* and *The Lowdown on Families Who Get High.* Visit *www.ogormandiaz.com.*

Julie Orlando has been sober since October 22, 2000, and credits her faith in God and her work with Women for Sobriety as constant sources of strength. In honor of her daughter, Julianna Maria, she is active in the Chromosomes Deletion Outreach program. Learn more about this and other genetic abnormalities by visiting *http://www.chromodisorder.org.*

Todd Outcalt is the author of ten books, including *The Best Things in Life Are Free* (Health Communications). He is a United Methodist pastor and has written widely about cancer-related issues.

Terry P. is a grateful, recovering alcoholic, wife, mother of six, grandmother of seventeen and guardian of a Westie. With family and a spiritual journey, her life has included teaching, advertising, writing, volunteering, gardening, bicycling and piloting a single-engine plane.

Kay Conner Pliszka has won numerous school and community awards for her work with at-risk students. Now retired from teaching, she is a freelance writer and an inspirational and motivational speaker. Kay also helps educators plan and facilitate self-esteem workshops and retreats. Contact Kay via e-mail: *K.Pliszka@prodigy.net* or write to 1283 Weaton Ct., The Villages, FL 32162.

Jennifer Reinsch has a master's degree in counseling and has worked with children and families in social services for over fourteen years. Her husband and daughter can usually find her buried in a novel. She enjoys writing poetry and short stories and this is her first national publication.

Carla Riehl is an author and speaker touring nationally on *Calm, Confident, and Assertive: How to Speak Up, Say No, and Still Love Others.* She was awarded three Clios (advertising's Oscar) and an Emmy for singing TV/radio commercials. Her new book is: *52 Miracles—A Year of Truly Miraculous Stories of Ordinary People.*

Sallie Rodman is married to her high school sweetheart, has three children and two grandchildren. With a certificate in professional writing from California State University, Long Beach, she has written stories for *Chicken Soup for the Mother-Daughter Soul, Chocolate for a Woman's Courage, The Orange County Register,* and various magazines. Contact her at: *sa.rodman@verizon.net.*

George Roth is an award-winning speaker and author. His imaginative and dynamic keynote presentations emphasize the power of acquiring new perspectives and inspire gratitude for the simple blessings of daily living. He is a member of the Screen Actors Guild and AFTRA. George can be contacted at: *gmr@georgeroth.com.*

Thom Rutledge, a psychotherapist in Nashville, Tennessee, is the author of *Embracing Fear: Finding the Courage to Live Your Life* and co-author of *Life Without Ed.* As a speaker Thom has been called "the most entertaining tour guide along the road less traveled." For more information, see *www.thomrutledge.com.*

Mark Sanders is an international speaker whose workshops have reached thousands throughout the United States, Europe, Canada and the Caribbean Islands. Topics include Team Building, Motivating Employees to Excel, Strategic Planning, Stress Management, and The Therapeutic Benefits of Humor in the Workplace. He can be reached at *onthemark25@aol.com.*

Jenni Schaefer is a singer/songwriter, speaker and author of *Life Without Ed: How One Woman Declared Independence from Her Eating Disorder and How You Can Too,* based on her work with psychotherapist Thom Rutledge. Jenni is devoted to sharing her recovery story with others. Visit *www.jennischaefer.com* for more information.

Lisa J. Schlitt lives in Kitchener, Ontario, with her husband and four children. She enjoys writing poetry in her spare time and finds true beauty in all of God's creations. She strives to teach her children that although one soul differs greatly from the next we are all deserving of love and respect. Contact her at *pschlitt@golden.net.*

Emily Schroder is a teenager who is actively pursuing her dream of writing. In addition to being published in *Chicken Soup for the Recovering Soul,* she has won an honorable mention award for another piece of writing and captured second place in a county-wide speech contest. Emily is also dedicated to enjoying a rewarding, full life with diabetes. For more information on Juvenile Diabetes visit *http://www.jdf.org.*

Shannon is living a life of grateful recovery, maintaining a 40–45 pound weight loss and enjoying her life as a wife, mother, teacher and writer.

Elva Stoelers is an award-winning Canadian writer. Her work has been broadcast on *CBC Radio Canada* and published internationally in a variety of small press parenting magazines. She currently teaches Creative Writing for Surrey Continuing Education while adventuring into the marketing process with her first novel.

Raquel Strand works as a wedding photographer, writer and mother. Every Christmas she still listens for reindeer and believes in the gift of hope. As a wise person once said, "Work like you don't need money, love like you've never been hurt, and dance like no one is watching."

Abraham Twerski, M.D., is the founder and director emeritus of the Gateway Rehabilitation Center and Associate Professor of Psychiatry, University of Pittsburgh School of Medicine. Dr. Twerski is also an ordained rabbi, son of the noted Hasidic rebbe Jacob Israel Twerski, served as a pulpit rabbi before becoming a psychiatrist and authored over 20 books on spirituality and health.

Andrea W., aka Sala Dayo Nowelile, is a native child of Detroit, Michigan. She is a yet unpublished, but "trusting and believing" first-time writer with an upcoming book, *Me and Baby G*. She also sings gospel, jazz and blues, as another expression of her gratitude!

Elizabeth Walton is currently completing her master's in education while working as a high school teacher and private music instructor. An aspiring writer, she is presently completing her first novel. She hopes that her writing will reach young adults and have a positive impact on their lives as they deal with the confusing and troubling issues of adolescence.

Sharon Wegscheiseder-Cruse is a nationally known consultant, educator and author. She was the founding chairperson of the National Association for Children of Alcoholics. She is a family therapist who has conducted workshops worldwide and has consulted with the military, schools and treatment centers. She is a past winner of the Marty Mann award as a top communicator. She makes her home in Las Vegas with her soulmate Dr. Joseph Cruse. She has three adult children and seven grandchildren.

David Wilkins lives in San Jose, California, with his wife of twenty-nine years. This is his third contribution to a *Chicken Soup for the Soul* book, and he is currently finishing his first novel. Until he is "discovered," he is a Director of Manufacturing and Materials at a small medical device start-up company.

Peter Wright describes himself as a "low-bottom, stand-up drunk." The bleakest days of his life were spent in the company of San Francisco's homeless under the freeways. Sober now for twenty-one years, he has written two autobiographical works, *All Things Betray Thee* and *A Drop of the Hard Stuff*. Contact him at *www.liverpoolsailor.com*.

Permissions *(continued from page iv)*

Touched by a Higher Power. Reprinted by permission of Godwin H. Barton. ©2001 Godwin H. Barton.

Silent Rage. Reprinted by permission of Kay Conner Pliszka. ©2000 Kay Conner Pliszka.

Summer Treasures. Reprinted by permission of Jane Middelton-Moz. ©2004 Jane Middelton-Moz.

The Skeleton in My Closet. Reprinted by permission of Elva Stoelers. ©2000 Elva Stoelers.

How Dry I Am. Reprinted by permission of Julia Jergensen Edelman. ©2003 Julia Jergensen Edelman.

A Little Band of Gold. Reprinted by permission from "Humble Pie: St. Benedict's Ladder of Humility" by Carol J. Bonomo, published by Morehouse Publishing. ©2004 Carol J. Bonomo.

How Long Will It Last This Time? Reprinted by permission of Janell H. ©2004 Janell H.

The Codependent Diet. Reprinted by permission of Linda S. Day. ©2004 Linda S. Day.

A 4C Woman. Reprinted by permission of Deb Sellars Karpek. ©2003 Deb Sellars Karpek.

The Letter. Reprinted by permission of Tracey W. Lee-Coen. ©2004 Tracey W. Lee-Coen.

How Am I Going to Pay for All This? Reprinted by permission of Earnie Larsen. ©1992 Earnie Larsen.

Friends of Bill W., Please Come . . . Reprinted by permission of Jim C., Jr. ©2003 Jim C., Jr.

Around the Room. Reprinted by permission of Earnie Larsen. ©2003 Earnie Larsen.

A Miracle in the Making. Reprinted by permission of Jann Mitchell. ©1982 Jann Mitchell.

The 202 Club. Reprinted by permission of Lee R. McCormick. ©2004 Lee R. McCormick.

The Seat. Reprinted by permission of Andrea W. ©2004 Andrea W.

Serendipity or Higher Power. Reprinted by permission of John Bradshaw. ©2004 John Bradshaw.

The Enabling of the Disabled. Reprinted by permission of Jayne Thurber-Smith. ©2001 Jayne Thurber-Smith.

A Promise of Spit and Dirt. Reprinted by permission of Cherie Ward. ©2003 Cherie Ward.

A Glimpse of Sanity. Reprinted by permission of Peter Wright. ©2004 Peter Wright.

With a Little Help from My Friends. Reprinted by permission of Rev. Bob Lew. ©2004 Rev. Bob Lew.

Dancing with the Elephant. Reprinted by permission of Patricia Holdsworth. ©2003 Patricia Holdsworth.

Charlie. Reprinted by permission of John C. Friel, Ph.D. ©2003 John C. Friel, Ph.D.

My Little Son Showed Me the Way. Reprinted by permission of Earnie Larsen. ©2002 Earnie Larsen.

The Little Yellow Room My Higher Power Built. Reprinted by permission of Shannon. ©2003 Shannon.

Hope. Reprinted by permission of Lisa J. Schlitt. ©2003 Lisa J. Schlitt.

Healing Tears. Reprinted by permission of Loretta McCann Bjorvik. ©2002 Loretta McCann Bjorvik.

Free Flight. Reprinted by permission of David Mead. ©1996 David Mead.

Whispers of an Angel. Reprinted by permission of Julie Orlando. ©2004 Julie Orlando.

Looking for a Sign. Reprinted by permission of Jenna Cassell. ©2000 Jenna Cassell.

Recovery: A Reason as Well as a Road. Reprinted by permission of Reverend Ed Donnally. ©2004 Reverend Ed Donnally.

The Richest Man in the World. Reprinted by permission of Earnie Larsen. ©1999 Earnie Larsen.

A Birthday to Remember. Reprinted by permission of Loretta McCann Bjorvik. ©2003 Loretta McCann Bjorvik.

Angels Dancing. Reprinted by permission of the Anonymous contributor. ©2004 All Rights Reserved.

Panning for Gold. Reprinted by permission of Ted Klontz. ©2004 Ted Klontz.

Out of the Blue. Reprinted by permission of Miriam Hill. ©2003 Miriam Hill.

Perfect Grief. Reprinted by permission of Mark Sanders. ©2004 Mark Sanders.

To Do the Work of Angels. Reprinted by permission of Brian Luke Seaward, Ph.D. ©2004 Brian Luke Seaward, Ph.D.

Memory of Two Friends. Reprinted by permission of David R. Wilkins. ©1995 David R. Wilkins.

The Grace of God Shows. Reprinted by permission of Stuart Brantley. ©2003 Stuart Brantley.

A Light at the End of the Tunnel. Reprinted by permission of Debra Jay. ©2004 Debra Jay.

Tears. Reprinted by permission of Arianna M. Johnson. ©2003 Arianna M. Johnson.

Christmas Hope. Reprinted by permission of Raquel M. Strand. ©2003 Raquel M. Strand.

Amanda Stays Safe. Reprinted by permission of Jerry Moe. ©2004 Jerry Moe.

We Can Still Sing. Reprinted by permission of Jennifer M. Reinsch. ©2004 Jennifer M. Reinsch.

Could You Be the One? Reprinted by permission of Mark Sanders. ©2004 Mark Sanders.

Choices. Reprinted by permission of Tom Krause. ©2000 Tom Krause.

I Am the Story I Tell Myself. Reprinted by permission of Mary Barr. ©2003 Mary Barr.

Take Care of Yourself. Reprinted by permission of Ann Best. ©2004 Ann Best.

You Become What You Want to Be. Reprinted by permission of Marilyn Joan. ©2004 Marilyn Joan.

Carry On. Reprinted by permission of Tom Krause. ©2000 Tom Krause.

My Mom's a Party Girl. Reprinted by permission of Carla Riehl. ©2004 Carla Riehl.

Twenty-Four Hours to Live. Reprinted by permission of Ted Klontz. ©2004 Ted Klontz.

Vita. Reprinted by permission of Elizabeth Batt. ©2004 Elizabeth Batt.

My Best Friend, Jack. Reprinted by permission of George M. Roth. ©2002 George M. Roth.

As My Life Turned. Reprinted by permission of Betty King. ©2004 Betty King.

He Sat Alone. Reprinted by permission of Steven Manchester. ©2002 Steven Manchester.

Stress Management 101. Reprinted by permission of Abraham J. Twerski, M.D. ©2003 Abraham J. Twerski, M.D.

Build It and They Will Come. Reprinted by permission of Perry D. Litchfield. ©2004 Perry D. Litchfield.

Black Is a Primary Color. Reprinted by permission of Christine Learmonth. ©2003 Christine Learmonth.

And the Wisdom to Know the Difference. Reprinted by permission of Carol Davis Gustke. ©2004 Carol Davis Gustke.

Not a "Piece of Cake" for Me. Reprinted by permission of Emily L. Schroder. ©2003 Emily L. Schroder.

The Indestructible Dignity of Humankind. Reprinted by permission of Abraham J. Twerski, M.D. ©2004 Abraham J. Twerski, M.D.

Gratitude. Reprinted by permission of Lisa Kugler. ©2004 Lisa Kugler.

By the Dawn's Early Light. Reprinted by permission of Terry P. ©2004 Terry P.

Wise Beyond His Years. Adapted and reprinted by permission from "Miracle of Recovery." ©1989 Sharon Wegscheider-Cruse.

Bill Saves the Bill. Reprinted by permission of Tracey W. Lee-Coen. ©2004 Tracey W. Lee-Coen.

My Father's Eyes. Reprinted by permission of Erin Hagman. ©2004 Erin Hagman.

Legacy. Reprinted by permission of Letitia Trimmer Meeks. ©2003 Letitia Trimmer Meeks.

Bare Bottoms and Dancing Toes. Reprinted by permission of Cynthia Borris. ©2001 Cynthia Borris.

"I Love My Body!" When Do You Ever Hear Women Say That? Reprinted by permission of Rachel Caplin. ©2004 Rachel Caplin.

The Dead Zone. Reprinted by permission of Debbie Heaton. ©2002 Debbie Heaton.

Late Night Movies. Reprinted by permission of Sallie A. Rodman. ©2004 Sallie A. Rodman.

Recovery's Unlikely Destination. Reprinted by permission of Patricia O'Gorman, Ph.D. ©2004 Patricia O'Gorman, Ph.D.

The Journey to Me. Reprinted by permission of Linda S. Day. ©2001 Linda S. Day.

From Victim to Victory. Reprinted by permission of Jaye Lewis. ©2000 Jaye Lewis.

Miracle at Wal-Mart. Reprinted by permission of Ruth Coe Chambers. ©2004 Ruth Coe Chambers.

The Red Peanut. Reprinted by permission of Tian Dayton. ©2004 Tian Dayton.

The Faces of Heroes. Reprinted by permission of Todd Outcalt. ©2004 Todd Outcalt.

The Dying Battery and the Recovering Codependent. Reprinted by permission of Thom Rutledge. ©2004 Thom Rutledge.

Legacies Left Behind. Reprinted by permission of Claudia Black, Ph.D. ©2004 Claudia Black, Ph.D.

A Light Touch. Reprinted by permission of Earnie Larsen. ©2003 Earnie Larsen.

Fat, Stupid, Ugly. Reprinted by permission from "Fat, Stupid, Ugly" by Debrah Constance, published by Health Communications, Inc. ©2004 Debrah Constance.

I Will Not Give Up. Reprinted by permission of Deirdre Morris. ©2001 Deirdre Morris.

Now I Am Whole. Reprinted by permission of Betty King. ©2003 Betty King.

Out of the Mouths of Babes. Reprinted by permission of Jerry Moe. ©2004 Jerry Moe.

Through the Eyes of My Heart. Reprinted by permission of Barbara A. Croce. ©2003 Barbara A. Croce.

Fully Alive. Reprinted by permission of Elizabeth Walton. ©2004 Elizabeth Walton.

Adult Children of Alcoholics World Service Organization
P.O. Box 3216, Torrance CA 90510, Phone: 310-534-1815, *www.adultchildren.org*

Created to serve the fellowship of Adult Children of Alcoholics by sharing information and experiences with one another and by applying the Twelve Steps upon which Alcoholics Anonymous is founded.

Al-Anon Family Group Headquarters, Inc.
1600 Corporate Landing Parkway, Virginia Beach, VA 23454-5617
Phone: 757-563-1600, Fax: 757-563-1655, *www.al-anon.alateen.org,* Contact: *WSO@al-anon.org*

Al-Anon's program of recovery is based on the Twelve Steps, Twelve Traditions and Twelve Concepts of Service adapted from Alcoholics Anonymous (AA). Includes Al-Anon Family and Alateen information.

Alcoholics Anonymous
P.O. Box 459, 475 Riverside Drive, New York NY 10015
Phone: 212-870-3400, Fax: 212-870-3003, *www.alcoholics-anonymous.org*

Alcoholics Anonymous is a fellowship of men and women who share their experience, strength and hope with one another that they may solve their common problem and help others to recover from alcoholism by applying the Twelve Steps, Twelve Traditions and Twelve Concepts of Service.

The Alliance Project
1954 University Avenue West, Suite 12, St. Paul, MN 55104
Phone: 651-645-1618
Fax: 651-645-1576, *www.defeataddiction.org,* Contact: *schommer@mr.net*

The Alliance Project is an effort by a broad cross-section of organizations that share common concerns about the devastating disease of alcohol and drug addiction and the dramatic lack of proper public response to this growing health crisis.

American Council for Drug Education (ACDE)
164 W. 74th Street, New York NY 10023
Phone: 800-488-DRUG, *www.acde.org,* Contact: *acde@phoenixhouse.org*

The American Council for Drug Education is a substance abuse prevention and education agency that develops programs and materials based on the most current scientific research on drug use.

Anorexia Nervosa & Associated (Eating) Disorders
Box 7, Highland Park, IL 60035
Phone: 847-831-3438, *www.anad.org*

A nonprofit corporation seeking to alleviate the problems of eating disorders, to educate the general public and professionals in the health care field, and to encourage and provide research to discover the causes of eating disorders, methods of prevention, types of treatments and effectiveness.

Center for Substance Abuse Prevention
5600 Fishers Lane, Rockwall II, Rockville, MD 20857
Phone: 301-443-0365, *www.prevention.samhsa.gov/,* Contact: *nnadal@samhsa.gov*

CSAP connects people and resources to innovative ideas and strategies, and encourages efforts to reduce and eliminate alcohol, tobacco and illicit drug problems both in the United States and internationally. CSAP fosters the development of comprehensive, culturally appropriate prevention policies and systems that are based on scientifically defensible principles.

Cocaine Anonymous World Service Organization
P.O. Box 2000, Los Angeles, CA 90049
Phone: 800-347-8998, *www.ca.org*

CA is a fellowship of men and women who share their experience, strength and hope with each other that they may solve their common problem, and help others to recover from their addiction.

Codependents Anonymous
P.O. Box 33577, Phoenix, AZ 85067
Phone: 602-277-7991, *www.codependents.org*

Codependents Anonymous is a fellowship whose common purpose is to develop healthy relationships through applying the Twelve Steps and principles of CoDA to daily life.

Community Anti-Drug Coalitions of America
901 N. Pitt Street, Suite 300, Alexandria, VA 22314
Phone: 703-706-0560, Fax: 703-706-0565, *www.cadca.org*, Contact: *webmaster@cadca.org*

CADCA's mission is to create and strengthen the capacity of new and existing coalitions to build safe, healthy and drug-free communities. The organization supports its members with technical assistance and training, public policy, media strategies and marketing programs, conferences and special events.

Debtors Anonymous
General Services Office, P.O. Box 920888, Needham, MA 02492
Phone: 781-453-2743, *www.debtorsanonymous.org*

DA's primary purpose is to stop debting one day at a time and to help other debtors to stop incurring unsecured debt.

Gamblers Anonymous
International Services Office, P.O. Box 17173, Los Angeles, CA 90017
Phone: 213-386-8789, *www.gamblersanonymous.org*

GA is a fellowship of men and women whose primary purpose is to stop gambling and to help other compulsive gamblers do the same.

Join Together
441 Stuart Street, Boston, MA 02116, Phone: 617-437-1500, Fax: 617-437-9394, *www.jointogether.org*, Contact: *info@jointogether.org*

Join Together, a project of the Boston University School of Public Health, is a national resource for communities working to reduce substance abuse.

Marijuana Anonymous World Services
P.O. Box 2912, Van Nuys, CA 91404
Phone: 800-766-6779, *www.marijuana-anonymous.org*

MA uses the basic Twelve Steps of Recovery founded by Alcoholics Anonymous to recover from marijuana addiction.

Narcotics Anonymous
World Service Office, PO Box 9999, Van Nuys, CA 91409
Phone: 818-773-9999, Fax: 818-700-0700, *www.na.org*, Contact: *info@na.org*

Narcotics Anonymous is an international, community-based association of recovering drug addicts.

National Asian Pacific American Families Against Substance Abuse (NAPAFASA)
340 East 2nd Street, Suite 409, Los Angeles, CA 90012-2818
Phone: 213-625-5795, Fax: 213-625-5796, *www.napafasa.org*, Contact: *napafasa@apanet.org*

Information and materials to assist Asian and Pacific Islander parents in protecting their children and youth against alcohol, tobacco and other addictive substances.

National Association for Children of Alcoholics
11426 Rockville Pike, Suite 100, Rockville, MD 20852
Phone: 888-554-COAS, Fax: 301-468-0987, *www.nacoa.org,* Contact: *nacoa@nacoa.org*

NACoA's mission is to advocate for all children and families (children of substance abusers, parental addiction, alcoholic parents) affected by alcoholism and other drugs.

National Association for Children of Native Americans
1402 Third Avenue, Suite 1110, Seattle, WA 98101
Phone: 800-322-5601, Fax: 205-467-7689

Facilitating positive change in individuals and communities to break the intergenerational cycle of addiction among Native Americans.

National Clearinghouse for Alcohol and Drug Information
SAMHSA's PREVLINE
P.O. Box 2345, Rockville, MD 20852
Phone: 800-729-6686, Fax: 301-468-6433, *www.health.org,* Contact: *info@health.org*

Covers the latest information on substance abuse prevention and treatment. Information for the public and health professionals. Latest research findings. Daily related news articles. Special sections online specifically for parents, teens and youth.

National Clearinghouse on Families & Youth (NCFY)
P.O. Box 13505, Silver Spring, MD 20911-3505
Phone: 301-608-8098, Fax: 301-608-8721, *www.ncfy.com,* Contact: *info@ncfy.com*

Established by the Family and Youth Services Bureau, U.S. Department of Health and Human Services, serves as a central information source on youth and family policy.

National Coalition of Hispanic Health and Human Services
1501 16th Street NW, Washington, DC 20036
Phone: 202-387-5000, Fax: 202-797-4353, Contact: *info@cossmho.org.*

Connecting communities and creating change to improve the health and well-being of Hispanics in the United States.

National Council on Alcoholism and Drug Dependence
20 Exchange Place, New York, NY 10005
Phone: 212-269-7797, 800-NCA-CALL (24-hour affiliate referral line) *www.ncadd.org*

Provides education, information, help and hope to the public. It advocates prevention, intervention and treatment through offices in New York and Washington, and a nationwide network of affiliates.

National Drug Prevention League
16 South Calvert Street, Baltimore, MD 20202
Phone: 410-385-9094, Fax: 410-385-9096, *www.ndpl.org,* Contact: *augustus@erols.com*

The NDPL is working with families, schools, communities, special populations, media, research and medicine—that working together we might prevent drug use.

National Families in Action (NFIA)
Century Plaza II, 2957 Clairmont Road, Suite 150, Atlanta, GA 30329
Phone: 404-248-9676, Fax: 404-248-1312, *www.nationalfamilies.org*
Contact: *nfia@nationalfamilies.org*

Information for families on drug effects, prevention, updates on latest scientific findings, surveys and other information.

National Foundation for Abused and Neglected Children
P.O. Box 608134, Chicago, IL 60660-8134, *www.gangfreekids.org*
Contact: *nfanc@hotmail.com*

Provides information on parenting, and prevention and treatment of child abuse and neglect.

National Hispano/Latino Community Prevention Network
P.O. Box 2215, Espanola, NM 87532
Phone: 505-747-1889, Fax: 505-747-1623, Contact: *hmontoya@aol.com*

Connects Hispanic and Latino parents with others working in communities. Focus is on the power of family.

National Inhalant Prevention Coalition
2904 Kerbey Lane, Austin, TX 78703
Phone: 800-269-4237, Fax: 512-477-3932, *www.inhalants.com*
Contact: *NIPC@io.com*

Complete information for parents on the abuse of inhalants.

National Institute on Alcohol Abuse and Alcoholism (NIAAA)
6000 Executive Boulevard - Willco Building, Bethesda, MD 20892-7003
Phone: 301-443-3860, Fax: 301-480-1726, *www.niaaa.nih.gov*
Contact: *niaaaweb-r@exchange.nih.gov*

Supports and conducts biomedical and behavioral research on the causes, consequences, treatment, and prevention of alcoholism and alcohol-related problems.

National Institute on Drug Abuse
www.drugabuse.gov

NIDA's mission is to lead the nation in bringing the power of science to bear on drug abuse and addiction.

Overeaters Anonymous World Services Office
P.O. Box 44020, Rio Rancho, NM 87174
Phone: 505-891-2664, *www.oa.org*

OA offers a program of recovery from compulsive overeating using the Twelve Steps and Twelve Traditions of A.A. OA is not just about weight loss, obesity or diets, it addresses physical, emotional and spiritual well-being.

Partnership for a Drug-Free America
405 Lexington Avenue, New York, NY 10174
Phone: 212-922-1560, Fax: 212-922-1570, *www.drugfreeamerica.org*

Tips and resources for talking with kids both before and after they've started using drugs.

Sex Addicts Anonymous
P.O. Box 70949, Houston, TX 77270
Phone: 800-477-8191, *www.sexaa.org*

A spiritual program based on the principles and traditions of Alcoholics Anonymous.

SOS National Clearinghouse
5521 Grosvenor Boulevard, Los Angeles, CA 90066
Phone: 310-821-8430, Fax: 310-821-2610, *www.secularhumanism.org/sos*
Contact: *sosla@loop.com*

SOS is an alternative recovery method for those alcoholics or drug addicts who are uncomfortable with the spiritual content of widely available Twelve-Step programs. SOS takes a reasonable, secular approach to recovery.

Substance Abuse & Mental Health Services Administration
Room 12-105 Parklawn Building, 5600 Fishers Lane, Rockville, MD 20857
Phone: 301-443-4795, Fax: 301-443-0284, *www.samhsa.gov*, Contact:*info@samhsa.gov*

The Substance Abuse and Mental Health Services Administration is the federal agency charged with improving the quality and availability of prevention, treatment and rehabilitation services in order to reduce illness, death, disability and cost to society resulting from substance abuse and mental illnesses.

U.S. Department of Education, Safe and Drug-Free Schools
400 Maryland Avenue, SW, Washington, DC 20202, Phone: 800-USA-LEARN
www.ed.gov/offices/OESE/SDFS, Contact: *customerservice@inet.ed.gov*

The federal government's primary vehicle for reducing the use of violence and alcohol, tobacco and other drugs through education and prevention in the nation's schools.

Women for Sobriety
P.O. Box 618, Quakertown, PA 18951-0618
Phone: 215-536-8026, *www.womenforsobriety.org*, Contact: *NewLife@nni.com*

A nonprofit organization dedicated to helping women overcome alcoholism and other addictions.